BOIL MY HEART FOR ME

Boil My Heart for Me

H. Baxter Liebler

Foreword by Mark Maryboy

Preface by Paul Zolbrod

Afterword by Joan Liebler

University of Utah Press
Salt Lake City

∞ Printed on acid-free paper

LIBRARY OF CONGRESS CATALOGING-IN-PUBLICATION DATA

Liebler, H. Baxter (Harold Baxter), 1889–1982.
Boil my heart for me / H. Baxter Liebler ; foreword by Mark Maryboy ; preface by Paul Zolbrod ; afterword by Joan Liebler.
p. cm.
Originally published: New York : Exposition Press, 1969.
Includes bibliographical references.
ISBN 0-87480-464-7 (alk. paper)
1. Liebler, H. Baxter (Harold Baxter), 1889–1982. 2. Navajo Indians—Missions—Utah—Bluff. 3. Missionaries—Utah—Bluff—Biography. 4. Navajo Indians—Social conditions. 5. St. Christopher's Mission (Bluff, Utah)—History. I. Title.
E99.N3L634 1994
979.2'59—dc20
[B] 94-17862

Foreword

Mark Maryboy

My father coined the phrase "boil my heart." He was one of the first students of Father Liebler at the St. Christopher Mission school in Bluff, Utah. The interpretation of that phrase was done by my uncle, David Police.

Growing up, my whole life revolved around the mission. I was born there, and I was raised across the San Juan River on the south side, on the Navajo Reservation. Father Liebler and all the people who ran the mission will live forever in my mind because the teachings at the mission had much impact on my life.

Father Liebler was the first white man I came to know. I watched him conduct services every Sunday. Reading his book now, we only see his perception of the people and the activities at the mission. I feel fortunate to have actually spent time with him, and I can speak from the perspective of the Navajos on how we saw him as a person.

Father Liebler was called "Long Hair" by my people. As we watched him in church, we heard him talk and sing in the Navajo language, which we understood clearly. He was one of the kindest men I have ever known. As a child, for the longest time, I thought he was Jesus Christ.

When you got into trouble, Father Liebler never whipped you, whereas the other church officials might do so. But Father Liebler would sit right down with you and explain what he felt was right and wrong. He always associated these teachings with scripture. He made us feel at ease. We came out from these talks with him with a long-lasting sense of understanding.

Father Liebler didn't just stay at the mission. He would go all over giving masses and services at the peoples' homes and would visit the sick and perform blessings for them. He had a lot of respect for Navajo culture and proved it by helping out at our squaw dances and other gatherings with food, clothes, and donations.

From his book one has a sense that he and the others at the mission had failed when Frank Benally was killed while serving in the military. We do not think they failed at all. Several of us from the mission school have gone on to colleges and universities and received various degrees. Others of us, who were also first-generation graduates of the mission, went on the become teachers, social workers, and nurses. I myself learned basic math and English there and continued my education to graduate from the University of Utah. I still go to church at the mission, and although I do not spend as much time there as I did when a child, the memory of those days is always with me.

From my viewpoint today, I find the tone of this book somewhat patronizing. At the time Father Liebler began working among the Navajos, we were not even citizens of the state of Utah. I guess he wrote his book as a typical white person, with a patronizing attitude toward us, his students and parishioners. What I enjoy about this book, apart from the tone, are his comments on Navajo religion, culture, language, and especially what he has to say about my relatives from long ago. For me it is a good documentation of Bluff, Utah, during those times.

As for Father Liebler, the man, I am glad I can remember him as a kind-hearted person, rather than just the man who wrote this book. That kindness and concern is what I wish to pass on to any reader of *Boil My Heart for Me.*

Mark Maryboy is presently San Juan County, Utah, Commissioner and Navajo Nation Council Delegate from Aneth, Utah.

Preface

1994

It is well that the University of Utah Press has agreed to reissue this book. It occupies an important place in the fabric of America's quilted past—a past whose unjoined segments can arouse easy misconceptions or evoke passionate misreading—especially during an era pleased to call itself multicultural and postcolonial. Its author has an arresting story to tell about one man's earnest effort to bring modern Christianity to traditional Navajos dwelling in Utah's "Navajo strip." Read carelessly it may invite dismissal as yet one more episode in this nation's long and often violent history of westward conquest. It calls for a more careful look than that, though. A tight cohesiveness binds its individual parts to form a single cloth, placing the tapestry of America's frontier history in a broadened perspective too long unrecognized. Temptation is always strong to judge former errors by current enlightenment; but doing so too glibly comes at the price of failing to see how today's conventional wisdom is often the slow outgrowth of yesterday's bold new thought or action.

1

As this new edition goes into production, little more than fifty years have passed since Baxter Liebler first rode horseback onto the northernmost edge of the Navajo reservation in Utah's remote southeast corner. With the twentieth century then nearly half over, it is hard to imagine him entering a place more resembling the old nineteenth-century West of mule-drawn wagons and mail robberies.

Somehow this curiously selfless clergyman had managed to find such a place awaiting a modernity that he himself could help bring.

Less than a hundred miles of all-weather roads served approximately seventy-five thousand Navajos scattered across an expanse roughly the size of West Virginia. Slightly more than two people per square mile occupied a vast land of high plateaus, flat mesas, inaccessible buttes and deeply eroded grasslands. A grounded, single-wire system worked only sporadically for those few who had telephones, while a lone short-wave radio transmitter located at tribal headquarters in far-off Window Rock remained virtually useless for lack of receiving sets and maintenance.

In Father Liebler's own words, ". . . there was no mission, no school, no medical or hospital facility for the Navajos" in that part of Utah. Mail arrived three days a week across forty miles of sometimes-impassable roads to Bluff's few whites. In the 1880s a small band of Mormons had tried settling the region, but gave in to wind and drought and soon asked the Church for permission to farm elsewhere. On that meager land only a few hardy descendents of those first pioneers now coexisted with "a group of American Indians who had never come in contact with the Gospel" (p. 19).

According the the 1940 census, San Juan County overall had a population of 4,712, 1,443 of them Navajos. Countywide there were 1,328 dwelling units. Of those, 460 were equipped with flush toilets, 595 with refrigerators, and 670 with radios—all north of the San Juan River which marked the upper boundary of the Navajo Reservation. To the south, where the Navajos mostly lived, a mere 39 of 349 dwellings had private baths or running water. Three hundred twelve had no indoor toilets, and 297 had neither indoor or outdoor facilities. Only 37 of those homes had any electricity.

It would seem that at the dawn of the nuclear age, Baxter Liebler and his small party were returning to the "primitive economic and political conditions of the frontier" that Fredrick Jackson Turner had called a defining factor in America half a century earlier. No doctor or dentist apparently served Bluff City in the early 1940s; the one-room schoolhouse faced the prospect of closing for lack of a teacher; people nearby had access to but a single telephone in a town that was little more than some simple dwellings clustered around a gas station and a grocery. Outside of a few agricultural staples, apparently nothing was produced in the area; land claims were evidently made based on use rather than purchase; law and order depended pretty much on the good behavior of residents.

H. Baxter Liebler's story thus raises an intriguing question. In leaving the familiar comfort of his Greenwich, Connecticut parish to bring the Gospel to the Navajos, was he evading history or helping to make it by building first a mission in Bluff, then a school, and next a hospital—drawing attention thereby to a people and a place totally overlooked? Evangelizing aside, it mattered little elsewhere in the world that these people had access to no medical facilities or schoolbooks or social services. They lived a markedly different life in their own traditional way, generally unhampered by outside influence except for the economic hardship forced upon them by mandated sheep reduction in the thirties. Functioning on the outskirts of a mainstream cash economy, they relied mainly on the horse for transportation; they dwelled in log hogans; they spoke little if any English; and they received no formal schooling. They lived pretty much as they had since returning from the forced exile of their ancestors in 1868, adhering to their traditional ceremonial ways in the "primitive" condition in which Father Liebler found them.

If at the time of Baxter Liebler's arrival the Utah Navajos existed uniquely as a premodern people in a modern world, the entire tribe remains illustrative in today's multiethnic America as well—or would if more were known about their own early encounters as newcomers themselves to an older pre-Columbian frontier. Descendants of a long Athabascan migration from the north, they probably began wandering into the Southwest as early as the twelfth century, probably through an intermontane corridor. Or so one theory maintains (Masse). According to another, they began arriving from the high plains several centuries later as buffalo-hunting Apacheans trading with Puebloans in the upper Rio Grande basin—not differentiating themselves as Navajos until they settled there and began raising sheep. Although scholars remain divided over exactly when they began arriving and which route they may have followed, it is clear that by the late sixteen or early seventeen hundreds they were trading with the Pueblos (Schaafsma). In either case, though, they made their way into a region long occupied by Puebloan descendants of the Anasazi.

In describing their entry into the upper Rio Grande region, Ruth Underhill speculates on that earlier "frontier" encounter at a human level. "If any lone-wolf huntsman from the north or any group of wandering families caught a glimpse of the Pueblo village, cornfields, and ceremonies, they must have seemed almost supernatural," she writes (p. 15). She goes on to describe a way of life different indeed from anything seen before, anticipating subsequent arrivals of waves of Europeans beginning with the Spaniards—likewise strangers to the different way of life they found. Initially these earlier newcomers settled sparsely in small canyons and dry arroyos uncoveted by the village-dwelling Puebloans. They very likely occupied first the upper Chama valley to the east of the continental divide and then moved into the easternmost reaches of the San Juan basin along Largo Canyon on the western side. Adapting in a way characteristic of new settlers anywhere, they acquired what they could, whether by hunting and gathering, by trade, or by seizure.

In this case, however, the newcomers apparently saw themselves as proselytes rather than teachers. From the Rio Grande pueblos they learned to plant corn and weave. They spliced elements of Tewa cosmology to their own worldview. And they later acquired horsemanship and herding skills from the Spaniards—constantly absorbing new ideas and methods into an identity very much their own. Fortunately for them, they settled in places desirable neither to the Spaniards who began moving into the Rio Grande Valley in the sixteenth century nor to the Anglo-Europeans who took possession following the Mexican war. In their steady growth as a people linked by a shared language and culture, they were evidently invigorated with a frontier vitality. They thrived on trade and adaptation, staging raids, making do as needed, and gradually developing a distinctive worldview. Once emplaced, their culture blossomed creatively in the early 18th century and flourished until they were rounded up and forced to move elsewhere during the Civil War. They became expert horsemen, avid sheepherders, and renowned weavers. Perfecting dry-farming techniques, they raised crops in land too arid to support others; and they developed a storytelling tradition of sacred and poetic proportions still awaiting full recognition.

Expansionist in ways that foreshadowed the Americans who would eventually encroach upon them, they gradually advanced westward along the San Juan basin, first along the river and then south into the Chaco wash and the high desert country of northern Arizona. With few exceptions they remained pretty much undisturbed, keeping to themselves except to stage small but frequent raids on Pueblo, Mexican, and eventually American settlements until the United States Army turned its attention to them during the Civil War. In 1863 they were rounded up by Kit Carson under the command of Brigidier General James H. Carleton and literally herded to Bosque Redondo in southeastern New Mexico—"away from the haunts and hills and hiding places of their country," in the words of General Carleton, where they could "acquire new habits, new ideas, new modes of life," and learn "the art of peace," and "truth of Christianity" (Thompson, p. 256, quoted in Iverson, p. 9).

After four years of hapless capivity in that bitterly inhospitable place, they were allowed to return to what they now considered their sacred homeland. While in one way a cruelly mismanaged disaster, in another their captivity solidified the Navajos as a tribal unit and strengthened still further their capacity for adaptation. Washington had abused them as a single people and they now saw themselves that way—sovereign and united in the adversity they had endured. To what they had already acquired as a result of their earlier past as hearty newcomers, they added enough new knowledge from their Anglo captors to begin trading with them successfully. Unified by their disastrous experience, they could return to territory uncoveted by anyone else. There they lived and in many cases prospered pretty much by their own standards until an energy-hungry America discovered rich deposits of oil, uranium, and coal on their land after World War II.

Although their numbers were reduced from an estimated fifteen thousand before their defeat in 1864 to little more than half that with the census of 1870, they now occupy North America's largest and most numerous reservation in the country. Indeed, their population has just about tripled since Father Liebler first settled among them. Their language is still spoken, their ceremonies are still being taught, and it can fairly be said that their culture is very much alive.

2

Regrettably, Father Liebler seems to relent to little of that here. Like others eager to introduce to them the testaments of Christianity and mainstream American life, he displays neither an awareness of the Navajo past nor a generous curiosity about the central place of their own sacred traditions. In his benign desire to package modern medicine and formal education with the Gospel he wished to introduce, he apparently presumed the Navajos to have no longstanding stories of their own, no traditions to articulate, no tenable philosophy to trade along with their jewelry and rugs. Implicitly, cultural exchange would occur in one direction only.

In reckoning the Native American presence that way, he was not alone, of course. Among the first Anglo-Americans to write on the Navajos, Army surgeon Jonathan Letherman fairly typically pronounced them "neither industrious, moral, nor civilized," and claimed, "they have no knowledge of their origin or of the history of the tribe" (p. 294). Twenty-five years later Washington Matthews—another army surgeon—argued otherwise, insisting that their "ceremonials might vie in allegory, symbolism, and . . . intricacy . . . with [those] of any people," and that the Navajos possessed "a pantheon as well stocked with gods and heroes as that of the ancient Greeks" (p. 23). Little attention was given to his findings, however; with few exceptions it has not occurred to subsequent investigators to accept the spoken record of Native Americans as viable history or full blown sacred testimony. Such as it was, Navajo culture, like that of other tribes, has remained unexplored until very recently save as ethnographic data, a resource for museum displays and the tourist trade, and hapless inspiration for Hollywood. Even when recognized as victims, they were presumed to have nothing worth hearing except for some quaint legends or superstitious myths and no civilization of their own to impart.

Indeed, a reader encountering this book in the postmodern era will quickly spot its Eurocentric insensitivity with the wisdom that enlightened hindsight generously allows. *Boil My Heart for Me* returns to press in a postcolonial age that acknowledges the cultural myopia of European dominance. In keeping with such newly revised awareness, Edward Said in *Culture and Imperialism* identifies four assumptions that prevailed as imperial Europe spread its power and influence across the globe. First, notions of superiority elevated the West in its own estimation because Europeans see theirs as an "advanced" civilization. Second, carelessly used terms like "primitive," "savage," "degenerate," and "natural" strengthen those claims of superiority. Third, on the pretense of learning about non-Europeans or improving their lot, domination of them has been reinforced by anthropologists, missionaries, and bureaucrats. And fourth, that dominion has boosted western culture at the expense of native cultures, which were all too easily dismissed (p. 108–9).

Readers now can now recognize those assumptions in Father Liebler's account easily enough, and see how subtly they can curtail the vision of the most well-meaning observer. Thus a careless reading might very well result in the glib dismissal of this book as little more than a string of entertaining episodes illustrating old-style colonialism on the eve of its demise. Sufficiently interesting to read in that light alone, though, Father Liebler's book thus assumes importance at one level as a primary-source record of cultural, political, and economic domination protracted well into the twentieth century. For readers seeking yet further proof of western wrongdoing—so easily recognized now that it has become part of today's thinking—*Boil My Heart for Me* can certainly serve that purpose. Otherwise, this book might seem to contribute little to what has been written about the Navajos and nothing to current historical scholarship save for some quaintly naive anecdotes about establishing yet another Christian enclave on a latter day frontier outpost.

3

At a deeper level, however, this twentieth-century story of a nineteenth-century-style encounter between two cultures—one allegedly advancing and the other ostensibly receding; one with a message to offer, the other destined to accept it—takes on added importance and a greater fascination. For it must be observed that Liebler's cultural insensitivity was not monolithic or all of a piece—leading, perhaps, to the possibility that neither is the history of America's frontier necessarily a monolithic narrative of unmitigated takeover by intrusive harbingers of an advancing culture where ostensibly none yet existed. Nor in its greater and as yet largely unwritten scope does that history account for every North American incursion of one people upon another.

Neither is it entirely fair to focus only on the isolated examples of Father Liebler's muted intolerance or thinly disguised paternalism. Readers can just as easily find passages where he struggles to surmount the constrictions of his orthodox theology and conventional European values. That admixture in fact adds a richly quilted texture to this book. For every instance the author gives of institutionalized racism, several more indicate some inner urge to transcend it. After he is warned by fellow whites in Bluff "not to pay a Navajo more than a dollar" for a day's labor, he offers a construction worker more than three times as much in defiance of "a rather desperate attempt to maintain a white supremacy," to cite one example (45). For another, he speaks approvingly during a 1950 visit to the Verde Valley School in Arizona of its "great ideal . . . to produce men and women on fire to eliminate racial prejudice and discrimination" (160)—a declaration he feels moved to make a good five years prior to the Montgomery bus boycott and nearly a decade before the civil rights movement was fully under way. Could it possibly follow that a growing new tolerance of America's broad ethnic base might possibly originate on a frontier where differing cultures merge even while they clash?

As Father Liebler knowingly continues to influence the Navajos they likewise influence him without his full recognition. By his own words wishing to "help them within the framework of the Navajo tradition" (p. 82), he gradually incorporates some of their traditional ceremonial methods in his ministrations. He places the Baby Jesus in a cradleboard when he duplicates a manger scene at Christmas, for example, and uses sandpainting to illustrate the crucifix. Such gestures anticipate the growing influence of Pueblo and Navajo artistry throughout the Southwest and elsewhere in America, and suggest a spreading reach of Native American influence upon American life—still neither adequately recognized nor by any means complete to this day. A reader need only look at the picture of Baxter Liebler opposite page 163 to appreciate his own receptivity to Indian style that kept company with his desire to impart doctrine. On one hand such a photograph might suggest the appropriation of an Indian manner of dress by the proverbial predatory White Man; on the other it could signify an adaptive proclivity equal to that of the earlier Athabascan newcomers who alternately raided and learned from the Pueblos when they settled on the Southwestern frontier.

Although Father Liebler shows insensitive disregard for some aspects of Navajo culture, he grows comfortable with others. He masters the complex system of Navajo kinship terms; he learns clan names; and he becomes fluent in Navajo—an extremely difficult language for English speakers to master. If he makes glib, offhanded remarks that show an abject ignorance of Navajo religion on some accounts, on others he manages to understand it well enough to incorporate some of it at the pulpit and in the daily round of his ministry. His story is so intimate, in fact, and so warmly detailed, that it invites wonder about how the Navajos might have interacted one-on-one with their Pueblo predecessors as personal contact grew between those peoples long before Columbus. Father Liebler is obviously of two minds in his regard for the Navajos and therein lies this book's hidden dimension, with its own deep and important account to recite. As the newly arrived emissary from a different world, he fits an all-too-little noticed American archetype spanning wave after wave of incursions beginning with the Navajo intrusion into Pueblo territory and continuing through the likes of Cabeza de Vaca, John Smith, Henry Rowe Schoolcraft, and Willa Cather's Father Jean Marie Latour. Perpetually begging to be told and retold, this two-tiered story tells something about history's cyclical repetitions along with relating a singular interlude occurring in its linear march. It describes a subtextual frontier more intellectual than physical where newly arrived people happen upon those already emplaced, each viewing the other curiously while mutually adapting—sometimes with nervous uncertainty—to new languages, new technologies, new ways, perhaps even new visions in an ongoing process of cultural renewal on the world's many frontiers, past and present.

Father Liebler was ultimately a man of goodwill and high intelligence who struggled sometimes knowingly and sometimes in spite of himself to overcome a deep ambivalence in serving a church itself often uncomfortably ambivalent: notice the signs of its wavering uncertainty in matters of doctrine and church government on this cultural and ecclesiastical frontier. Anticipated here as in earlier stories is a newly eclectic multicultural union that has become a defining factor in late twentieth-century America. As someone with his own modest version of a story necessarily told and retold, this New England clergyman represents the best of his kind—honest in displaying the limitations of his vision, earnest in his struggle to transcend them, and essentially peaceful in the errors he made and strove to surmount, sometimes knowingly and sometimes in spite of himself. We should not dismiss such men and women out of hand for unwitting shortcomings readily seen fifty years later with the enlightened hindsight history eventually bestows.

An Acknowledgment: My thanks to Curtis Schaafsma and Joan Liebler for their help in gathering information respectively on the early Navajo presence in the Southwest and living conditions in Bluff, Utah during the 1940s and 50s. Any errors or inaccuracies in this essay are of course my own.

PAUL G. ZOLBROD

Bibliography

Iverson, Peter. *The Navajo*. Albuquerque: University of New Mexico Press, 1981.

Letherman, Jonathan. "Sketch of the Navajo Tribe of Indians, Territory of New Mexico," *Tenth Annual Report of the Board of Regents of the Smithsonian Institution*. Washington, D.C., 1856, pp. 294–97.

Matthews, Washington (1897). *Navaho Legends*. Salt Lake City: University of Utah Press, 1993.

Said, Edward W. *Culture and Imperialism*. New York: Alfred A. Knopf, 1993.

Schaafsma, Curtis E. "Early Apachaeans in the Southwest: A Review," in Wilcox and Masse, *The Protohistoric Period in the North American Southwest: A.D. 1450–1700*. Tempe: Arizona State University. Anthropological Research Papers no. 24, 1981, pp. 291–320.

Thompson, Gerald. *The Army and the Navajo*. Tucson: University of Arizona Press, 1976.

Turner, Frederick Jackson. "The Significance of the Frontier in American History." *The Early Writings of Frederick Jackson Turner*, Everett E. Edwards, ed. Madison: University of Wisconsin Press, 1938.

Underhill, Ruth. The Navajo. Norman: University of Oklahoma Press, 1944.

Wilcox, David (1981). "The Entry of Athapascans into the American Southwest: The Problem Today," in Wilcox and Masse, *The Protohistoric Period in the North American Southwest: A.D. 1450–1700*. Tempe: Arizona State University. Anthropological Research Papers no. 24, 1981, pp. 213–56.

Wilcox, David, and W. Bruce Masse. *The Protohistoric Period in the North American Southwest: A.D. 1450–1700*. Tempe: Arizona State University. Anthropological Research Papers no. 24, 1981.

Preface

David Police, obviously as a messenger for an older relative, came bearing a request. "Dzaan Bell, he say, 'You boil my heart for me, you say dat to Faa Leeah,' he say to me."

A perfectly reasonable request, since we had the equipment necessary. I said to David, "You say to John Bill, 'You carry your heart right over here, I boil it for you,' you say that to him."

An obvious problem in adapting a primitive language to modern conditions is that of finding a vocabulary for items in general use today but unknown to the ancestors who formed the language, or even those who used it a generation ago. The process is really very simple and began in the far distant past. When the Diné (the Navajo people) first encountered corn and took it to themselves, they called it enemy food—a name which it bears to this day. When the Spanish brought horses, money, exotic fruits, etcetera, for which the Navajo had no names, they either used corruptions of the Spanish words or, more often, made up descriptive names in their own tongue. The horse became "pet" almost to the exclusion of all other livestock, money took the Spanish names, from peso to centavo, and most fruits took on descriptive names; for example, peach was "big berry" and apricot became "little big berry." The parts of the automobile followed the trend begun with the introduction of the wagon: wheel is its leg, tire is its foot, headlights are its eyes, and battery is its heart, and quite naturally the process of recharging a battery that has grown weak is called boiling. This explains David Police's request.

At the risk of preaching a little sermon right here (text: Psalm 104:15, ". . . bread to strengthen man's heart") it would seem that we have an apt symbol of what a living mission can do for a primitive people whose culture, while it was adequate to the conditions of their old life, needs constant "boiling" to fit them for life in modern times, and above all for the eternal life to which the Son of God calls them. Knowledge and power through instruction and the means of grace are the "heart boiling" which St. Christopher's Mission came to offer to the Navajo of southern Utah. End of sermon!

I cannot possibly express adequate thanks to Joan Eskell and Diane Brady for the difficult work of typing the manuscript and reading proof.

Introduction

It has often been said that the white man writes the histories. Long before I came to the Navajo country to live, an old Indian in the East asked me if I knew the difference between a frightful massacre and a glorious victory. I let him tell me: "A frightful massacre is when the Indians win; a glorious victory is when the white men win."

Everybody who has read anything about the Navajo people knows about "the Long Walk," when the United States Army, convinced that the Navajos were "like wild animals who can no more be trusted than the wolves that run through the mountains,"* rounded them up and put them into a prison camp at Fort Sumner in New Mexico. There they were kept for four long years, until they announced themselves ready to sign a treaty that would forbid them to make war against white people and would confine them to a reservation where they would earn their subsistence by farming and sheep raising.

It is a curious thing that in our culture any and all folk tales that deal with the brave, and even desperate, struggle to defend home, family and land tend to present such struggles as heroic and entirely laudable unless and until the defenders happen to be Indians—those perennial obstacles to progress and civilization who "cannot be trusted." Ruth Underhill, a leader in the modern school of historians who find something to be said for the Indians' side, keenly notes that in the struggle for the possession of New Mexico neither side could be trusted to hand the country over to the other side.

I got my first lesson about the Long Walk when I was making out an application for a lady who wanted old-age assistance. She gave her age as eighty and her birthplace as Alkali

---

* Ruth Underhill, *The Navajos*, p. 111.

Creek. An elderly man known as Eddie Mexican Clansman was in the room, and as he spoke fairly good English, I turned to him and said, "Eddie, this lady says she was born at Alkali Creek in 1865; according to what I read, all the Navajos were gathered down there at Bosque Redondo in that year. How could she have been born at Alkali Creek?"

Eddie cocked his head to one side, and with a wry smile said, "You tink dey got dam all?" He slowly shook his head and turned back to the picture magazine that had held his attention when I interrupted him.

It seems quite clear that Kit Carson didn't get them all. No man could assemble statistics at this late date, but the unwritten history of the Navajo people makes it clear that a great many did not go on the Long Walk at all. But they felt the pinch nevertheless. Kit Carson, commanding a regiment of less than peace strength, largely volunteers and untrained for any sort of fighting, could have done little, but he was aided by the ready zeal of the Navajos' traditional enemies among the Pueblos and Utes who knew the country and its hiding places and who could survive under conditions that would be fatal to whites. No doubt thousands of the Navajos got away, but they lived in hiding for many years, and they failed to get the rather generous rations of livestock, wagons, blankets and flour that were distributed to the survivors of the concentration camp when they signed the treaty and were settled on the reservation. And like their fellows who did go on the Long Walk, they lost their crops and most of their livestock, for Carson fought with fire and a scorched earth policy rather than with firearms.

While hunting for our straying cows or horses, we have from time to time picked up a number of stone axheads and other artifacts, which we assumed were left by the ancient peoples who inhabited this country seven centuries ago. One day an old Navajo man visiting us picked up such an axhead and held it, weighing it in his hand. "Who made this?" he asked.

"Ana'sazi, I guess," I said.

He smiled knowingly. "No," he said, "maybe my father. When I was a boy, before the Mormons came here, we used these to lop off the branches of trees. We burned the trees down—it was easier than chopping—but for the branches we used these axes, stone-made." (The Navajo word for ax, even a steel one, has the root *stone* in it.) "And our knives were flint." This last was hard to say, for the word for knife is also the word for flint.

Some years later I was going out to feed the livestock and heard a resounding explosion far away. We subsequently learned that this was the first atomic blast, set off in New Mexico. Slowly it came to me that I was living and working with a people who in one generation were passing from the Stone Age, which characterized my own ancestors of twenty centuries ago, to the Atomic Age, of which I know very little even now. And I felt a bit impatient with my own impatience at the slow progress of our Navajo people.

It is this people and their response to the eternal Gospel that this book is about. If they are sometimes amusing, sometimes exasperating, they never fail to charm and fascinate me, and they ever deepen the love for them that led me to cast my lot with them.

1

The sound of a horse's hooves aroused me from my reading. A rider had come to within a hundred feet of where I lay under the juniper tree; he sat looking rather amusedly at the spectacle of a white man all in black, surrounded by saddlebags, cooking utensils, canned goods and other gear. In an instant I was on my feet and at his stirrup leather.

The customary Navajo greeting: "Yá'át'é"* ("Good").

Hopefully I asked, "Speak English?"

He shook his head. Painfully I extracted from my meager vocabulary the Navajo words for "Horse—sorrel—burro—gone—two days."

I might have saved myself the trouble: he knew all about it. Pointing with pouting lips in an easterly direction, and with gestures indicating canyons, hills and other natural features, he ended with what were unmistakable English words, "Maybe two miles." Then, like a Boy Scout who had done his good deed for the day, he gathered the reins and kicked his mount in the flanks as if to take off.

Frantically I made signs for "I follow" and "bridle," dashed back to my camp, picked up a bridle and was with him. It wasn't easy. Every time I caught up with him he trotted ahead for a few hundred feet. A man can outwalk a horse, but I was in no condition to keep up with a trotter. Suddenly, near a clump of junipers he opened out his lariat, threw it and waited for me to reach him. Behold, a sorrel horse! But alas, it was larger and thinner than mine. Sadly I summoned a few more Navajo words: "That not my horse."

---

* In Navajo words: The four vowels sound as in *art, end, in, no.* If they are doubled (aa, ee, ii, oo), the sound is lengthened. If they have an acute accent (á, etc.), the voice is raised to a slightly higher pitch. The apostrophe indicates a momentary holding of the breath, as in Amos and Andy's famous O-o; we would write it ó'o. Consonants sound approximately as in English.

He smiled patiently and said, pointing with his thumb at himself, "*My* horse," and signed for me to mount. This looked like luxury travel. Quickly I adjusted the headstall of the bridle and in a moment we were off at a gallop. That pony had a dorsal fin that would shame a shark! I felt as if I were being bisected from the crotch up, but I hung on and tried to convince myself that this beat walk-and-trot on foot. After what seemed an interminable journey he drew rein and pointed with pouting lips to where my pony and burro were grazing placidly in a grassy draw. Never did animals look more lovely! I thanked my guide with some coins, turned his sorrel loose and made for my mounts. The burro had lost the crude hobble I put on him, but he was easily caught. I tied him to a bush, roped the mare and released her hobble. But I guess I forgot to tell her that her forefeet were now separable, for no sooner had I mounted than she took off on one of those ten-foot leaps that hobbled horses use when they want to get places fast, and with my "incision" still tender from the Navajo horse's dorsal fin, I momentarily forgot the joy of finding the beasts.

Next, to find the way back to where my gear was stored. I had hoisted a white flag above the juniper tree to distinguish it at a distance from a million or so completely identical specimens—but how to get in sight of the flag? Well, even a tenderfoot parish priest from the eastern seaboard has to use his mind sometimes, and call upon the stored-up lore learned in his youth as a "Woodcrafter." The wind had obscured my tracks, so they weren't the answer. The sun had been almost directly behind me all the time I was following my guide, so now the obvious thing was to aim at the point on the horizon where the sun had recently set.

Simple as that. But five or ten minutes on that course brought me to the rim of a canyon a hundred or more feet deep lying directly across my path. They can't do this to me, I thought: this wasn't here an hour ago. Now, Reverend Father, don't panic. Sure, you're far from home and you don't know where you are and night is coming on, but that has happened before and in all probability will happen many times again.

This canyon is a watershed and must flow towards the San Juan River—that is, northward. So if you follow this rim to your left, southward, you may find the head of the canyon, get around it, and even find your flag before dark. And if not, you've got your beasts and can keep warm.

Nothing to it. It turned out to be a box canyon which my guide had skirted without my even noticing it and in another half hour the moonlight revealed the white flag. I fed the animals the corn I had bought at Mexican Water Trading Post and picketed them securely (you may be sure of that!) for the night.

There was no coffee the next morning. The scant half-pint of water that remained could not be shared with coffee grounds.

My destination was Mexican Hat, the only point at which the San Juan River was bridged between Shiprock, some sixty miles upstream, and Marble Canyon, two hundred miles downstream. The trader at Mexican Water had assured me there could be no danger—by maintaining a course a few degrees west of north I should strike either the river or a dirt road which led to the bridge. In the former case just follow the river downstream; in the latter case just follow the road to the right, or northeasterly. It seemed very simple. I learned a lot of things from this trader.

I had been surprised to see so few Navajos on the way, and said as much.

"No," he said, "you don't see them. But *they* see *you*. I knowed you was comin' for three days!"

The sun was high in the heavens and poured merciless heat upon the desert when I got my first view of Monument Valley. The trail went through a gap between two buttes, and I came upon the sight suddenly. It was indescribable, as anyone who has seen it will tell you, and it took me some time to come back to earth and select some landmark to the north which should be my cynosure. The vista lay straight ahead, the alley to my left. I spurred my pony, pinked the burro and started.

One rider only came into view. He knew a bit of English but followed the Navajo pattern of first-meeting conversation. It stays in my mind because of its bearing on the opinion so often held by Americans that Indians have no sense of humor. After the customary "Yá'át'é" he said. "Way you goan?"

"Mexican Hat," I answered.

"Way you come fum?"

"Three days ago from Shiprock, five days from Farmington, twenty days from ocean, far away."

"On*nat* hoss? Twenny days fum ocean?"

"No. Train–bus–horse from Carson's Post. How far here to Mexican Hat?"

"Bout ten mile. On your hoss, mebbe fitteen mile! Well, I *see* you." And he was off.

Darkness was coming on—the canteen had long been empty before those "fitteen mile" were covered—but a clear, cool pool of running water, the smell of which spurred pony and burro to a final dash, made it far from a dry camp. Before the animals stirred the pool's muddy bottom, I managed to fill canteens and coffeepot; then I let them drink to their bellies' content. There was a taste to that water—not unpleasant—strange, yet hauntingly familiar. It brought an image of a marble counter like that of a soda fountain. But I slaked my thirst and went to sleep.

Shortly after dawn certain abdominal sensations, plus some very definite noises from the animals, solved the riddle of the water. I am certain that I had bought the very same thing at a Grand Central Station soda fountain under the trade name of Pluto Water. It was undoubtedly an error to make coffee—but then, it wasn't the first mistake of my life, nor the last. I had missed the study of chemistry in both high school and college, but I did have a sort of feeling that alkali destroys acid and that hydrochloric acid is essential to normal digestion. Digestion ceased entirely, and if I had had sense enough to stop eating, all might have been well. But I didn't have sense. I had a good breakfast, saddled up and headed for Mexican Hat. It couldn't be far, and I hadn't the heart to press my animals, as I knew all too well how they were feeling, so they sauntered leisurely on. At about noon the murky waters of the river came into view—the river whose name in a few years was to give me the sobriquet of "Padre of the San Juan."

Back in New Mexico, not far from Shiprock, I had talked with the driver of a vanadium truck, Joe Hunt, who told me that his brother ran the trading post at "the Hat" and would certainly welcome a visitor from the far-off East. But at the bridge spanning the river, although I could see the trading post, I could see no sign of life. Ah, well, it's only a step, I'll ride across; there must be somebody there.

But the burro had other ideas. I could not drive him, so I tried pulling him. He preferred to be choked to death, and I stopped that just in time. I used the pointed stick that the trader at Tees-nas-bas had told me about. "You want a stick, Father, not a whip, but a stiff stick with a sharp point, and if he lags behind, let him have the point right near the tail." Seeing my shocked expression, he added regretfully, "I'm sorry, Father, but there ain't no *nice* way to drive a burro!"

But at this bridge no nice or un-nice way would stir him. Too weak to fight, I tied him to a bush and rode across on the mare. At the trading post a tall, long-faced Navajo was pushing a wheelbarrow laden with partially squared stones, or "rocks," as I learned to call them, but he set it down and responded to my greeting, making it clear that he knew no English. Less clear was the information that the trader had gone to Flagstaff because his wife had a toothache, and would not be back until the next day. I lay down exhausted in the narrow strip of shade on the north side of the building and was soon asleep.

The din that woke me could be nothing short of the collapse of the bridge, I thought, but it turned out to be the approach of the State Road Maintenance man, dragging behind his yellow truck a homemade drag built of railroad rails and assorted bits of hardware. The man, however, was the important item: wiry, of medium height, with a smile that should melt the hardest heart. We were friends within minutes, "nature's nobility" shining through his picturesque language. Nothing could have made me feel his innate kindness as did his simple praise: "Ya done goddam good to make it across this country, you bein' a stranger from the East. Somathem trails is reely sumbitches!" Dan offered me his tent for as long as I wanted to stay, and he said, "When you come to Bluff, don't stay no place but at my house. It'll be just like your house to come and go as you like."

Later, Dan's partner, Claude Powell, came along, and with the truck to pull and shovels to goad, they got the burro across the bridge.

The trader returned next day, and as his brother Joe had predicted, he was the soul of hospitality. His wife, Grace, had been an Episcopalian in Arizona, attended a convent school, and was probably the only person in the southern part of San Juan ever to have seen a clerical collar. Ray was a Mormon priest, he told me.

"Gee, I didn't know that. Why didn't you ever tell me?" Grace exclaimed.

"You never asked me," returned Ray. "Oh, I'm not a good Mormon—I smoke and I've drank a lot and don't go by the rules, but I'm still on the books." He told me a lot about the Mormon church, which I was glad to hear, inasmuch as I was hoping to spend the rest of my life in this area. He also told about his father's narrow escape from scalping. Ray was, and is, in my opinion, one of the best Navajo speakers among the traders, and he gave me some tips on the language. He also told me of the Mormon attitude toward the Navajo, and his information was later confirmed by those I spoke to in Bluff. "We believe in being kind to them, teaching them higher standards of living, especially cleanliness, but we don't evangelize them, because the dark skin is a sign of the curse of God."

2

It took several days for the waters of Gypsum Creek to get out of my system. Ray and Grace dropped in frequently to see that I lacked nothing, and the Navajo, known as Harvey Bik'is, was an occasional visitor at Dan's tent, where I lay most of the time. He was less communicative than most Navajos I had met, but at least he gave me my first Indian name, which was Priest-With-Sore-Gut. Navajos give a name according to the natural feature that first strikes them. Very Tall, Very Fat, Has-Lots-of-Mules, Curly Hair, Big Nose, No-Teeth, Blind Man, Woman-Runs-Around, Mustache, are common names, if not all complimentary, and I knew I wasn't getting off so badly. It was hot in the tent but Grace thought that we should know whether I had fever and if so, how much, and produced her clinical thermometer. It registered 108 degrees, which was the room temperature, so we had to let it go at that.

During those restful days there was time for me to look backward at the circumstances that had brought me to this land in search of a location for a proposed mission to the Navajo Indians. For years, whenever an extended vacation from my work as rector of St. Saviour's Church in Old Greenwich, Connecticut, made it possible, I had gone into the Southwest, convinced that somewhere I would find a tribe or group of American Indians who had never come in contact with the Gospel. On former trips by car, I had taken others along, usually young people from the parish. They didn't know the object of my search but were happy to see spectacular country and picturesque Indians. But at every place I went I found one or more missions already established. A year previously Father Davis of Farmington, New Mexico, had said, "Why don't you look into southern Utah? I've heard that the Navajos there are as primitive as any Indians on the continent. And I've never heard of a mission there." So here I was, two thousand miles from home, in a borrowed tent, and so sick I couldn't walk! I reminisced further and thought of the many forces that had been at work from boyhood on to bring me to this place.

As a boy I had read not only *Hiawatha* and *Leatherstocking Tales* but Ernest Thompson Seton's animal and Indian stories, especially *Two Little Savages,* which came out in serial form in the *Ladies' Home Journal* and inspired me with an interest in Indians that never completely died out. At the age of eleven I became what I considered a horseman: my father bought a combination mare, and on days when my elders did not need her and the carriage I saddled her up and learned to ride. I even bought a McClellan saddle at Bannerman's—great-grandfather of the thousands of Army stores—and learned not only how to stay on but how to mount and dismount at a gallop, to hold the stirrup leathers in my hands and raise my feet far above my head. Later, when the mare was moved into a straight stall so that the cob Nellie might have the box stall, I learned to gallop around with one foot on each.

Then I thought of meeting the great writer himself: he had bought a large wooded tract in Cos Cob. I pondered how I could possibly crash the gate and get to see him. Here my mother came to the rescue. "You have all his books, and authors always love to autograph their books. Let's drive up there tomorrow afternoon and hope we find him home." We did, and he was delighted to autograph the books. When he heard that some other boys and I had organized a small "tribe" of Woodcraft Indians, he invited us to come to an encampment on his estate with six other tribes. Often in the years to come I camped there with other Woodcrafters from many parts of the nation, and even met some real live Indians.

Seton never tired of telling, nor we of listening to, stories of his life with the Sioux, Chippeway and others. I read Catlin, Schoolcraft and many other serious writers and visited the Museum of Natural History in New York City (by this time I was attending Horace Mann School, then located at 120th Street and Broadway, spending summers only in Connecticut). I even adopted, so far as I could, what I fancied was the Indian religion. Christianity I had definitely rejected at the age of four, when with the help of my big brother I saw for myself that it wasn't Santa Claus but my parents who put the presents under the Christmas tree, then lied about them. With one voice they taught Santa Claus and the baby Jesus. Both were obviously one and the same device—a labor-saving device to make children good! If you're not good, Santa won't bring you anything: if you're not good, Jesus won't take you to heaven. A plague on both fakes!

College is where country boys lose their faith. College is where we learn that the earth was not made in six days, that man is descended from the ape and that God is not a nice old gentleman sitting on a cloud and waiting to welcome those who sing His praises while on earth. Before I had finished my freshman year at Columbia, I had things straightened out in my own mind. If God is even decent, He has had to reveal Himself to man at least clearly enough so that man can find as much of divine truth as he needs. The Bible could not be the answer, because there were hundreds of denominations warring one with another, not only on minutiae but on fundamentals, such as What is God? Who is Jesus Christ? How is man justified? What is the ministry? and all basing their arguments on the Bible. The Bible, then, could not be the answer.

I can hardly imagine anyone who could have been more bitterly prejudiced against Catholicism. It was "servant girls' religion," and we were of the Best People. Only with great misgivings and under severe limitations was I allowed to play with a neighbor boy who was a Catholic. I even believed a boy who warned me against letting the Catholic upstairs maid ever see me undressed, because Catholics believe, he said, that if she could see my private parts daily for forty days she would surely go to heaven and I would be her slave there! Of course, by the time I got to college I had put such ideas aside, but the prejudice remained. High-school history courses had taught me much about the secular power and corruption of the church, but there was also much, indirectly learned, about the beauty of parish life and monastic life, of the zeal and devotion of Catholic missions. And even though I rejected the Bible as a blind leader of the blind, I could not but see that it witnessed to the historic church. In apostolic times Christians did not go to church to hear the Bible read, to listen to sermons, to give money, pray and go home—they went to Mass, just like Catholics. The first day of the week meant not Sunday comics and Sunday school, but Mass. And apostles forgave sins in the name of Christ, just like Catholics. And those who disagreed with them went out from them, just like Protestants. It was a bitter pill for me. But the conclusion was crystal clear: if God is, He has spoken, and His voice is the Catholic church.

I wandered into St. Paul's Chapel on the campus of Columbia University for the fifteen-minute midday devotions conducted by Dr. Oldham, later bishop of Albany. His sincerity was unquestionable, but he had nothing for me. I never met him, even to clasp his hand, as I had done with others the half dozen times I had attended church before. But one day a junior took me by the arm in the chapel porch. I shall never forget him—the first man who ever spoke to me seriously about religion. He invited me to his Bible class at Earl Hall. I learned not much, but he persuaded me to seek out my parish church, St. Paul's in Riverside. I objected that no one except old Mrs. Lockwood ever went to church. He laughed and said, "Well, now there will be two of you going!" Charles Kennedy later became a priest, served a brief ministry in the Bronx, came to an untimely death. I preached a Lenten sermon to his congregation once, in about 1919. God rest his soul!

At St. Paul's in Riverside came the revelation that the Episcopal church, the church of my baptism, claimed to be not a Reformation sect but the historic continuation of the English church—the church that had sent Boniface to my ancestors in Germany, the church of St. Thomas à Becket, of Richard the Lion Heart. This was no easy thing to accept. I dug up my old high-school textbooks, in which (I was sure) I had read of the founding of a new church by Henry VIII. I read again about the divorce, the Acts of Royal Supremacy, the Acts of Uniformity, but to my amazement found no vindication of my deeply ingrained idea. Now, if the Catholic religion were true and the Catholic religion were the religion of the Episcopal church, I didn't need to make a change—I needed only to use the means of grace that were available. (Incidentally, I found that Mrs. Lockwood was not the only attendant at church. She was driven in her fine carriage past our house every Sunday morning, while we read the funnies, and we used to think that nobody else went. I still have the Bible she gave me when I went to the seminary.) Confession, Confirmation, First Holy Communion, followed in what seems in retrospect rapid succession. By the beginning of my sophomore year I was conscious of a vocation to the priesthood.

How these two strains came to fuse into one could be a long story. As I lay in Dan's tent I recalled one evening at the seminary, Nashotah House, when Canon Douglas addressed the student body, not on music, for which he was then internationally famous, but on missions to the American Indian. He knew the Indian cultures well and respected them; he deplored the efforts of missionaries to destroy all that remained of the beauty of Indian life and thought instead of sanctifying it and enriching it with the truth and grace of the Gospel. I could not recall a single sentence of his talk, but the basic idea sank deep into my soul. Now, thirty years later, I might be facing a new life in which Canon Douglas's theory might be put into practice.

A few days before I got to Mexican Hat, as I was lying on the ground, head on saddle, looking up into the cotton clouds flitting across the deep-blue sky, I saw numerous figures take form and dissolve. Gradually a particular one took shape and stood out in stark clarity. Pure white against the blue, arms spread in blessing over Navajoland, the unmistakable form of the Saviour, vested in alb, showed itself for some minutes before breaking up. From that instant there was never a doubt in my mind that all that had ever happened to me was a preparation for that which lay ahead.

St. James's Day came, and I felt strong enough to offer Mass in the tent. St. James's Day is also St. Christopher's Day, and it was good to make Eucharist—Thanksgiving—for protection and guidance on that journey and to register the vow that if God would allow me to set up a mission in this area, it would be dedicated to St. Christopher, who carried Christ across the water and became the heavenly patron of earthly travelers. I feel certain that this was the first Mass ever offered in that vast area.*

---

* Father Escalante, with a small band, explored much territory around the Colorado River in 1776, but it is unlikely that he was able, for want of sacramental matter, to celebrate Mass by the time he got to the "Crossing of the Fathers," some eighty miles from Mexican Hat.

3

Bluff City, Utah, in 1942 presented a very different picture from that which greets the passing tourist today. Now there are motels, a hotel, at least two cafes and three general stores. The main street is lighted at night, nearly every house has electricity, and more than half have telephones. The main artery of travel is black-top paved, and there is a jail and a resident full-time deputy sheriff.

When I first drew rein there, the town boasted one general store, and the post office was a portion of a front porch partitioned off. About eighteen or twenty houses were occupied; there were two bathtubs and one telephone, and nearly every house had an outdoor privy of the most-approved government-specification type erected by the CCC during the depression years. Most of the houses were of squared stone ("rock" is the western word—we even had the ceremonial "laying of a corner rock" two years later) and some were two stories high, one actually having a "down-and-under"—meaning a cellar. These houses had been erected in the boom days, when Bluff City was the cattle center of southern Utah and when skilled labor was still cheap. But they were built without footings or adequate foundations, and most, if not all, had walls serried with cracks where the weight of the building proved too much for the lower courses of masonry. The church house (a term the Mormons wisely use to distinguish the building from the organization) had been condemned as unsafe and torn down some years before, but the reduced population found the Relief Society building adequate for the weekly Sunday school. There being only a handful of Mormon priests in the village, there was no "church" on Sundays, just Sunday School.

Aunt Jennie was the first inhabitant I called on. I had been told that she was a cosmopolitan character, the soul of Bluff's cultural life and a very important person; nor was I disappointed. She welcomed me as if I were an old friend and had a cup of steaming coffee at my side within minutes. She asked politely what church I represented, and when I said, "Episcopal church," I added (knowing that our church's nearest parish or mission was three hundred miles to the north), "Have you ever heard of that?"

"Have I ever *heard* of it?" she exclaimed, "Vy, I practically *belong* to it. I am a Lutheran!"

In dogmatic theology at the seminary I had somehow passed an examination that included the question "Name at least twenty of the condemned heresies of Martin Luther," but here in this oasis, surrounded by Mormonism, I was inclined to take Aunt Jennie into my arms as a sister in the faith! Aunt Jennie was born in Sweden, had been reared in Denmark, lived in Massachusetts when a girl, married a Mormon and lived in Salt Lake City ("but I never could svallow Joe Smith!") and later in Verdure and finally in Bluff. Her husband was now dead, but many of his children by a previous marriage lived in the county and she was seldom without company, although she lived alone, with her shaggy dog as protector. Her hair was white, her hands and head trembled with a mild palsy, but her mind was always alert. Her "worst thing" was provincialism, and she never tired of expressing pity for her neighbors who "don't know anyt'ing because dey never been any place but right here in Bluff, or maybe fifty miles avay." But she loved those she pitied, and they loved her.

My sorrel mare was footsore after the long trip, and I borrowed a pony from Dan to explore the region east of Bluff. I encountered many Navajos on their way to or from the trading post at Bluff. I found out where they forded the San Juan River, and viewed their cornfields, on the river-bottom lands on the Reservation side of the river. A map told me that I stood not far from a central spot—Montezuma Creek and Aneth to the east; Mexican Hat, Oljeto and Navajo Mountain to the west, and all in Utah, where, as far as I could find out, there was no mission, no school, no medical or hospital facility, for the Navajo. I echoed the words of the great Mormon leader Brigham Young: "This is the place!"

That night I talked long with Dan and his wife, Pauline. "I have been talking with a lot of these here Navvies," he said. "They all want you to settle here. They been told about it, some way. They won't tell me much about it, but maybe Randolph will tell you when you get to know him even better'n I do.

"If you wanted that land out east they call Hyrum's field, where you seen that cornfield and the walls of that rock house, where I was goin' to put a tradin' post up, only Pauline wouldn't live so far from this here culture center of Bluff—well, I say, if you wanted that land, I believe me and John, my brother-in-law, could fix it so you'd have as good a title to it as anybody's got in Bluff.

"And we shore would he'p you, any way possible. I been friends with these Navvies a long time. They talk to me. They shore need someone to teach them. My sister Eva (he pronounced it Evva), she's the best member of my family, a real sweet character, she likes 'em and treats 'em good. So does the widow of the last Mormon bishop: she kinda nurses 'em with herb medicines. But they can't do what you can do. I got another sister in Arizona is Cath'lic, and I know a little somethin' about it. I ain't nothin' myself in the way of religion, and I respect 'em all, but I can see differences. So—you make up your mind. . . ."

Back in Connecticut less than a week later, I wrote to the Bishop of Utah, Dr. Arthur Moulton, and laid before him a proposition which, as he told me later, was like nothing he had ever seen or heard of. His answer was most kind, but, he said, "Navajos live in Arizona and New Mexico; you want one of those bishops—not me."

I had a road map of Utah. With water colors I tinted the area between the Arizona line and the San Juan River, which was clearly marked on the map as NAVAJO INDIAN RESERVATION, and sent it to him, politely calling his attention to the fact that according to the *Living Church Annual,* he had jurisdiction over the entire state, and this area was distinctly within the same.

Stupid, unsophisticated me! I figured out later that he was stalling for time, checking with my own bishop as to what sort of nut this was who planned to set up a mission in an uninhabited area, asking for no money or other help, only his permission, his blessing, and "if God grants us a convert, will you come down and confirm him?" At all events, by the time he had studied my map he was ready to welcome us with open arms.

4

St. Saviour's Church, in Old Greenwich, Connecticut, was in a peculiar sense my baby. In 1918 a moribund Presbyterian group had decided that their only hope of survival was to submit to "prelacy" and "turn Episcopal"—since it was well known that "Episcopals are all rich." They asked me to help, and although in the early days some might have felt that they had made a rash choice, twenty-five years of steady plodding, patient teaching and constant forward-moving produced a beautiful church building, a devoted congregation enjoying all Catholic privileges, and an enviable reputation as a spearhead of the movement in Anglicanism for the recovery of all that had been lost in the Reformation. The time had come for me to yield to a younger and more vigorous priest, while I devoted what vigor remained in me to the pioneer work of the West, to bring this precious gift to the Navajo people. I resigned the rectorship in January, 1943, to take effect at the end of June, thus allowing what I considered ample time to find a well-qualified priest to pick up the mantle I was about to drop. It was a most heartbreaking decision, for much of me remained not only in the hearts of the people but in the very fabric of the building whose architecture reflected my love for the Southwest. Fortunately I was in a position to present the reasons for my resignation in terms of a wonderful vocation to a new work, so that there was little, if any, feeling that they were being forsaken.

Two problems remained to be worked out in that all-too-short six months: to recruit a handful of volunteer workers and to set up machinery for raising the money we would need to keep us alive.

I sent a circular letter to all the religious communities of our church, asking their prayers for this venture of faith and requesting the names of any of their recent postulants or novices who might have failed in a vocation to the strict religious life but who might be suitable for such an active project as I had in mind. Father Joseph, O.S.F., invited me to speak to the Franciscan Friars, and told them that if any wished to volunteer for this work their request would "receive serious consideration." This brought me Brother Michael, and later on Brother Juniper. One of the convents suggested Esther Bacon. Among the early volunteers from other sources was Helen Sturges, who had been caseworker and executive secretary for the Church Mission of Help in Connecticut, where I had been a member of the board; more recently she had been parish visitor at All Saints', Henry Street, St. Clement's and the Church of the Crucifixion in New York City. I felt that her experience with many races might fit her for work with the Navajos. She also introduced me to Dr. Gladys Reichard, Professor of Anthropology at Barnard College, who had written a Navajo grammar and claimed to have mastered the Navajo language. Gladys, out of the goodness of her heart, agreed to give me lessons in the language, and I came down from Old Greenwich to Barnard for about ten two-hour sessions. I shall hold her in grateful remembrance always, for although I was disappointed not to get a great many words and paradigms, she did insist upon proper pronunciation of the difficult sounds in the Navajo language—sounds which few white men make any effort to master—and this insistence served me in good stead.

The story of the departure from Old Greenwich would be incomplete without a reference to the dinner served by the parish on my last Sunday there. It was the Sunday in the Octave of Corpus Christi Day and we held the traditional procession with the Blessed Sacrament at the morning service. Many friends, by no means all of whom were communicants of the parish, were there both for the service and for the dinner. At the dinner, perhaps the most memorable speech for me was the one delivered by Father Ganley, pastor of St. Catherine's Roman Catholic Church, in which he said, "Father Liebler is going out among the Indians to do God's work, and it is the duty of every one of us to pray for God's blessing upon him and for the success of his work."

The following day we were off. Helen drove her own car, a Plymouth convertible, heavily laden, with Brother Michael beside her. I drove the Ford pickup, bought for the project for three hundred dollars, and more than heavily laden, with Frances Liebler and Catherine Lucas as passengers. We had arranged to meet Esther Bacon at the public campgrounds north of Cambridge, Ohio, as she was driving her own car from West Virginia; I knew of the place from having camped there on previous trips into the Southwest. When we got there, a few hours after the projected meeting time, we found numerous campers, all of whom greeted us with mock reproaches, as: "Where you guys been? Is a lady here lookin' for you, says you're late." "Are you the people that were to meet a nurse from West Virginia? She's been here, and got tired of waiting, but she'll be back." I felt that I already knew our Esther and why it was that she had already tried her vocation in nearly every religious community of the Episcopal church without finding one that suited her. But when she appeared, beaming with joy and enthusiasm, I felt ashamed for having made a snap judgment.

Traveling by car, with rationed gasoline and rationed tires, was not simple in those days. The thirty-five-mile speed limit was in force everywhere, and each time a tire blew it meant an interview with the local ration board to secure another miserable retread. The members of the boards were uniformly kind and generous, but the delays were insufferable. Finding camp sites, pitching tents and taking them down, cooking meals—all this slowed us down even more, so that it took nearly two full weeks to complete the trip.

One approaches Bluff from the north by a road—then just dirt—which drops rather suddenly into Cow Canyon. I brought the pickup to a stop, in order to give instructions to all drivers. Brother Michael leaped out of the Plymouth, ran to me in great excitement.

"My God in heaven, Father, why didn't you *tell* us! This is *beautiful!* I never *saw* such country! How did you let us imagine we were going into a deadly Sahara Desert? My *God,* it's beautiful!"

It was in the heat of the day, by far the least favorable hour for bringing out the gorgeous colors in the landscape. Cow Canyon has a few cottonwood trees, and their rich green sets off the reds and yellows, the eroded whites and the corroded browns of the canyon walls. We all stopped and let it sink in. I had to admit that a concern for the people who lived there had temporarily blinded me to the beauty of the land. There came to me a verse of a psalm: "The lot is fallen unto me in a fair ground; yea, I have a goodly heritage."

Less than an hour later we were at Hyrum's field. Pauline Hays showed us the irrigation system, took us up one of the canyons where there was a spring of good water and bade us make ourselves at home. If we liked the site, Dan and his partner, John Johnson, would talk it over with us. We pitched our tents near a lateral ditch—too near, the mosquitoes told us, so we moved the following day. But here come the Navajos. . . .

I had been asking questions about recovering my sorrel mare, or some other horse, so that we could go across the river and try to explain our purpose to the Navajos. But that was not necessary: they came to us. The first group dismounted, came with hand extended and the usual Navajo greeting on their lips: "Yá'át'é."

I responded properly, and the next question was of course, "Where do you come from?" Gladys had prepared me for this. It would have been ridiculous to mention Old Greenwich, or even Connecticut, places quite beyond their ken or imagination, but they knew that Washington was far away to the east, near the sea, and the source of all troubles, and so she had taught me to say: "From beyond Washington."

The next question, too, came according to the book: "Where are you going?" and my prefabricated answer was: "I am not going. I sit here." All this had been drilled into me by Gladys until she was satisfied, and Gladys was a teacher not easily satisfied.

The result was dismaying. They started to jabber, obviously delighted to meet a white man who knew their language so well. They met many traders and others who made no real effort to master the difficult and strange sounds, the high and low tones, the nasalized vowels, the modes and aspects of the verbs, and this obviously was an experience. But of course it turned into something really mysterious, for although my pronunciations and intonations were correct my vocabulary was as yet extremely limited and I could neither understand the Navajos nor converse with them to any extent. Dan told me afterward that they came to him quite puzzled and asked, "What sort of white man is this that talks like a Navajo but only says a few words, and then won't say anything more!"

The day after our arrival we got John Johnson to plough up a small garden area, possibly a half acre. He brought his team of horses from Bluff for the purpose. It didn't seem decent to ask him to bring a harrow the next day, so we raked the ground ourselves and he taught us how to make furrows for irrigation. Also, wisely he taught us how to plant. All the neighbors were just *too* polite; they knew we were "educated" and so assumed we knew at least the simple ordinary things. Fortunately, however, I took the trouble to ask. As a boy I had done a lot of gardening, and one rule I remember was to plant seeds to a depth equal to four times the diameter of the seed. Here we plant corn six to eight inches deep to give it a stable basis as it grows; otherwise, if a wind were to come up while we were irrigating, the whole stand would be found lying in the mud.

This garden was a good idea. Aside from providing some

fresh vegetables, it was a symbol of at least two things: our desire to support ourselves insofar as we could, and what was even more important to our purposes, our determination to stay where we were. The question "Where are you going?" continued to be posed. Perhaps our answer, "We sit here," was a little more convincing when they saw us plant.

Esther's dog, Shawnee, provided divertisement. Apparently he challenged a skunk and came off second best. We came off worst.

Every morning the Angelus aroused us at the first sign of daylight. That the bell was a large frying pan struck by a hammer handle only served to remind us that it was a call to work and to eat, as well as to pray. Our little portable altar was set up, and Mass began as soon as it was light enough for me to see the pages of the missal.

The very first Sunday was memorable. We slept later, planning to start Mass at about nine. While there had been a lot of singing in the course of our trek from the East, it hadn't really occurred to me that here was a group of six people who not only had decent voices—at least four of us, Brother Michael, Esther, Helen and Catherine, had outstanding voices and the ability to sight-read. Furthermore, all were familiar with the better-known plain-chant masses—De Angelis, Marialis, Dominicalis—and I don't hesitate to say that those Sunday services, with no congregation, were better done, technically, than one would find in many a good-sized parish. As I was taking off my vestments I happened to look at the canyon wall to the north and saw a burro standing, two small Navajo children astride him. Brother Michael had seen them. "They sat and watched the whole service from up there, with never a move," he said. Well, was there a congregation, or not?

The next Sunday, during Mass, I was distracted by sounds of whispering behind me. My group is too well brought up for that, I thought—perhaps some sort of emergency? Mass being finished, I realized that we had at least an embryo congregation: a whole family had been hiding behind the sagebrush, watching and listening. They came out, Sadie with baby in cradleboard, Randolph, her husband, and Jennie, Dan, Frank, Claude and Pauline. They joined us in the "coffee hour" without which no Episcopal church service is complete and were assured that hiding was not necessary. The following Sunday they were present at the Mass, and from that day to this we have never had a Sunday Mass without Navajos in attendance.

5

Our delight over irrigation farming as seemingly a great improvement upon the eastern system of hoping or praying for rain (Helen expressed it characteristically: "How nice to be able to control the weather with a few shovelfuls of earth") was due for some moderation when we found out that every storm washed a considerable amount of sand or dirt into the main ditch, often enough of it so that the head gate had to be closed and time allowed for the drying of the ditch bed before it could be cleaned out.

Every spring a ditch boss was elected from the surrounding area served by the ditch, and a rate of pay was decided upon. This was purely on paper and by barter. A man with a team of horses might get twelve dollars a day, a man on foot with nothing but a shovel might get eight dollars—on paper. The footman, or single man as he was called (irrespective of matrimonial status), usually had the hardest job. He would be either in the bottom of the ditch, ready to seize the arms of the slip, fill it and send it up, then ready for the next one—and we generally had three teams to each filler—or he would be on the bank, ready to dump each slip as it came up.

When the ditch was clean and water let in through the head gate, the ditch boss figured up the status of each man. His credits for hours of work were balanced against the acreage he had under cultivation, including hayfields. Those who were ahead collected produce, usually hay or corn, from those who were farther down the ditch. It was a basically just and equitable system, and it worked well.

Foolishly I tried to inject into the meeting some elements of parliamentary procedure: motions, secondings and the like, especially the reduction, if not the elimination, of the custom of having two or three members talking at once. However, I soon found that their system was best after all; I mentally resigned as self-appointed reformer when Dick Nielson, the ditch boss, hammered for silence and said, "I'm gonna make a motion—I know as chairman I ain't supposed to make a motion, but I'm gonna anyway, an' I move that whatever the majority votes, that's what we'll do."

This precedent-shattering proposal might have been met with silence, but no, Bob Wise had a better idea. "Well, that's all right, if the majority is *right,* but if it *ain't,* and only *one* says what's right, *that's* what we ought to do."

Toward the end of August, John Johnson, Brother Michael and I were near the head gate, cleaning out accumulated sand from the ditch, when a sudden storm of rain and wind arose. We sought shelter under an overhanging ledge of rock and watched. The wind whipped the waves in the river into a fury, and finally carried tons of sand right into the ditch, filling it to the level. John shook his head, laughed a mirthless laugh, and commented, "Vel, dot's de end of de ditch for dis year!" We walked back to our camp through a slightly abated downpour; more than half of the ditch was filled with sand, our tents had blown down, and much of our corn lay prostrate in the field. We began to understand what had brought Bluff so close to becoming a ghost town. Since 1880 the Mormon farmers had fought this river for a living. In 1885 a petition was sent to church headquarters in Salt Lake City asking that they be allowed to move to a less rigorous area to the north, where higher elevation brought more moisture and dry, that is, non-irrigated, farming would be possible. The petition was granted, although a double blessing was promised to those who remained. The result was the establishment of two new towns,

Blanding and Monticello, the latter now the county seat and both far larger than Bluff. But to this day the older inhabitants of both towns maintain an affectionately nostalgic feeling for Bluff, and seem never to tire of saying that their parents were born there.

6

Randolph lay in the shade of a cottonwood, hands behind his head, right ankle resting on left knee, the picture of relaxed comfort. It was a Sunday afternoon. We purposely suspended work on our buildings on Sundays, and tried to use the time for catching up on correspondence, making financial reports to the treasurer and similar work that did not look like work to the Navajo.

Randolph, with his facile command of English, was a really good neighbor. He taught me many words of Navajo, although with no conception of grammar he couldn't do much with verbs or other fine points. His exposition of the singular, dual and plural showed both his limitations and his ability to overcome them.

"Wite man tokkin Navajo wantsa say 'eat' he say 'chinny-ah-go,' is no good. Navajo is tokkin Navajo he wanna say one man eat, he say 'ee-yan'; two man, he say 'o-san'; maybe tree man four man lotsa man eat, he say 'da-o-san.' " I doubt whether the idea of singular, dual and plural could have been better expressed.

Looking up at the blue sky that Sunday afternoon, he burst into a subject that he probably had been pondering for some time.

"Faa Leeah, you gun meg skoo for chiyun?"

"School for children?" I countered. "Do you people want a school here for your children?"

"Yeah, we reely wannit. Lotsa tine we tokkin boudit. Wan tine I make ledda to Washeendoan. Wite man in tradin post he write it for me. I say, 'Washeendoan you meg skoo for chiyun rah here,' I say. We sho needid skoo. Washeendoan he doan nev ansa me back. I dno smadda. Maybe Washeendoan she doan know readin write. Nev ansa me back."

I spent a moment wondering into which file Randolph's letter had found its way in Washeendoan, but I don't know how they name the waste baskets and so got back in the groove.

"Well, Randolph, if we make a school for your children, how many right around here would go to it? I mean, that we could count on regularly, day after day?"

He was silent. I thought at first he didn't understand me and repeated the question in simpler language, but noticed that he was counting on his fingers.

"Bout sixty."

"Randolph, if you can get forty, even, we will make school."

"At be good. Me I went skoo Shi'rock. Din learn nu'n. All tine fightin, and sit in jail. No good. I wan my kits learn good. You make skoo, Faa Leeah, at be good skoo."

So was conceived St. Christopher's School. I explained to him that for the present we had to get a roof over our heads, some place to use as a church building when the weather got too cold for out-of-doors Mass, but I promised him that by September of the following year there would be a school for the Navajo children.

At this time it was estimated by such competent judges as the New Mexico Indian Association that if all the government and mission schools on the Reservation were filled to capacity, not more than one-fifth of the school-age children would be able to attend. Randolph was among the minority desiring school for the children. The typical attitude was expressed by an old Navajo in the Oljeto area. He spoke no English, nor did he care to. His comments, freely translated, were to this effect: "They want us to send our children to school. We need our children to herd the sheep, to carry water and firewood. They don't teach anything useful in school. They don't teach how to herd sheep, how to weave, how to track animals. They teach them to talk American and to read and write. That is no good. Nobody understands American except only the traders and the teachers. The traders can talk Navajo, so we don't need to learn American to talk with them, and the teachers we can get along without. And nobody can read, so what is the use of writing?"

As long as the Reservation was the whole world to these people, the philosophy was unanswerable. As long as the population remained static and the range did not deteriorate, the sort of idyllic existence that they loved might continue unchanged indefinitely. But alas, the nearer one is to such problems the harder it is to see or to cope with them. John Collier, when he was Commissioner of Indian Affairs, had taken action towards the preservation of the range. He saw that forage was growing less each year and at an accelerated rate because erosion and overgrazing were allies, each helping the other in the war of destruction. He enforced stock reduction as the first step in defense of the range land. But he had not the means of explaining the reasons for stock reduction to the Navajo. The result was a very natural resentment over the government's interference with the rights of the people and its very obvious effort to reduce prosperity, which in their minds was measured by the number of sheep a family owned.

Randolph came home one day exuberant from a meeting at Mexican Water. "Washeendoan he rah ova dere hisself. He said it, evsing gun be awright. Evvy family gun have two hunned sheep. No more John Colly."

It was a foolish thing that I did. I tried to explain the government project. Already we had been suspected of being government agents in disguise. Several government employees, hearing of our work, had dropped by to welcome us into the field, and the shield on the side of a car or pickup was evidence enough to bring suspicion against us. But I did it anyway.

"Randolph, listen. You think they're going to let you have two hundred sheep?"

"Yeah. Two hunned."

"And your married daughter, Jennie—she will have two hundred sheep, too?"

"Yeah, evbody two hunned." So I went through the family: Dan, Frank, Pauline, leaving out only those who were not yet nubile. To each an affirmative, but towards the fifth I thought I detected a shadow of uneasiness. But I brought out the obvious, pitilessly.

"Do you know how many sheep that is, Randolph? Five families with two hundred sheep each? That means a thousand head. *What are they going to eat?* Your little bunch of sheep has cleared the ground here around your hogan so that it is a desert. What would a thousand sheep do to the countryside?"

He was silent for a while. "Yeah. I din sink about at. Not nuf feed. Atsa trouble." But within an hour I heard him telling another Navajo that everything was going to be all right: he had Washington's personal assurance that every family was to be allowed two hundred sheep.

We were to have many other illustrations of the way Navajos think, and this obviously is one of the prime considerations in any sort of mission work.

7

The decision as to building site could not be put off forever. Available water settled it. The canyon rim, from whose top the children on their burro had witnessed the first Sunday Mass, had a massive upper formation of Morrison sandstone; below this were sedentary deposits of red shale. Between the two we could detect moisture, and it was evidently enough to sustain a heavy growth of brush down to the talus. With a water bag in hand I scaled the wall and found a delightful area where water dripped from overhanging ledges several yards in either direction. It wasn't hard to assemble enough to catch a bagful. It tasted good to me, but I didn't trust my own taste, nor did I want to take the responsibility of a decision. All agreed that it was good water.

Everybody knows that water is essential to life, and that bad water is definitely bad. But many to whom we have told our story do not realize what this meant to us. There usually was water in the irrigation ditch, but it was muddy as cocoa and full of what is politely called organic matter, fine for irrigation but dangerous to drink, and possibly even to handle, unless boiled. For our culinary water we had to go to Bluff with jars, bottles, cans or whatever containers we could find.

Now it appeared that we had a source of pure, clear water within two hundred feet, but it was a vertical, or very nearly vertical, two hundred feet. And it just dripped. To fill that desert water bag had taken me three minutes by the watch. And nobody could climb down that precipice with more than one full water bag.

Again Dan to the rescue.

"Man name of Lee has ranch house near the Hat. Lots of one-inch pipe lying around. I've a mind he'd be glad to sell some of it. Don't need priority ration to get *that*."

Lee was ready to sell not some but all of it. Shrewd bargainer—the supply had been picked over until the best sections had been taken, leaving for us the bent, the broken, the bits with "buggered" threading, at eight cents a foot. We accepted, and the little old Ford pickup leaped over the road like a mountain goat. But we found that loading twenty-foot pipe into the eight-foot bed of a pickup was not simple, especially as we would have to take it over dips and washes with profiles like the letter V. But there was ample bailing wire around (Mormon twine, or Mormon buckskin, it is called locally), and we managed somehow. Fortunately there were enough couplings.

The next day we devised what I have always considered a masterpiece of engineering. Assembling the dripping water into a clay tank just below the source, setting the pipe in such wise that water, and not clay, mud or sand, would go through it, hardly did more than start the project. The pipe had to be tied with Mormon twine to shrubbery or rocks along the steep declivity, and then came the really artistic touch. We got two of those fifty-five-gallon oil drums; one, with the top open, stood upright on ground level; the other was set horizontally over it, a faucet attached to the smaller hole, while the water pipe, by means of a Rube Goldberg system of twists and joints, was inserted into the larger hole. Thus we could at all times get pure water into our containers simply by turning on the tap; the overflow would run into the open-top barrel and provide ample water for the livestock. If a large family of Navajos came by on horseback and all their animals wanted to drink, emptying the lower barrel, it was only necessary to turn on the spigot for a few minutes. It is impossible to describe the satisfaction we derived from this simple device, and in later years, when we actually piped water into the house, we felt rather ashamed of living in such luxury!

The procuring of water settled the question of location completely. Dan and John conveyed to us by a bill of sale all their right, title and possession, in consideration of three hundred dollars duly paid and delivered, receipt of which is acknowledged, and so forth; and the bill of sale was duly recorded in the county clerk's records. So we turned our attention to building.

8

On August 1, 1943, Helen wrote to her family in Connecticut:

> Our garden is up—corn about 6 inches, beans doing well, also endive, turnips, melons and squash. A Bluff neighbor who just called says that we can raise apricots, peaches, English walnuts, figs, grapes, peanuts, sweet potatoes.
>
> Men told us that we could dig a well anywhere and get water. This appealed to us, for we were hauling our drinking water and

culinary water from Bluff in jugs, bottles or anything we could find. So we started to dig. Passing neighbor kindly told us, "Shore ya kin dig a well any place in the river bottom, but you shore have to make forms out of lumber, and drive them down as you dig; if ya don't them quicksands will just suck you down and the sides of your well will cave in." So, we abandoned that project. Lumber would have to be hauled 30 miles down a winding dirt road, and we had no money for that sort of luxury.

We've done a lot of thinking about location. We have bought the land—not really getting any title, but just a bill of sale covering the improvements—fencing, irrigation system, and the four walls of a stone house about 30′ by 20′. It covers maybe a hundred acres. We rather liked the idea of putting the Mission buildings and church towards the south, with an approach from the south, but again a neighbor asked us to think what might happen if a gopher bored a hole in the irrigation ditch. We might wake up to find ourselves afloat in a sea of mud. However, to get up to the northern part of the land meant building a bridge. It also means that visiting Navajos would have to come through the fence, and they seem incapable of closing a gate. An open gate would expose our garden to all livestock grazing about.

So, we experimented with adobe. It was rather fun, playing mud pies. We borrowed wooden forms from a specialist in Bluff, an adobe man—seems every man in Bluff is a specialist; one is a powder man (dynamite, to you), one a car mechanic, one a riprap man, and so on. Anyway, we turned out about a hundred adobe bricks, but before they were a day old it was obvious that they had too much sand—they crumbled. The next hundred cracked—too much clay. Third try was good, we thought. We asked the adobe man's criticism. He looked our factory over. "No horse? Ya gotta have a horse, and a big paddle and a center pole, see? And as your horse goes 'round and 'round he works this paddle in the mud. . . ." The Padre looked meditatively at the canyon wall. "Centuries ago, God made mud into rock for us and tons of it lie there waiting for us to use."

Olin Oliver, helpful soul, lent us a work horse—a mare with following colt. We made a ladder-bridge and walked from our camp to the site daily; with a stone boat (here they call it a "rock-sled") we began to assemble piles of rock at the site. Again John Johnson's wisdom saved us from the consequences of our ignorance: "Dem red rocks is purty, but the first rain will melt them like so much salt. White rock is much harder."

Day after day we gathered the rock. It would do your heart good to see Frances, astride a 17-hand work horse, ferrying the stone boat (I mean rock-sled) back and forth, the Navajo boys whom we hired at a dollar a day loading the sled, one of us at the site unloading it. She, whom you could more easily picture gracing a formal tea, enjoyed this phase of the work more than any, I think. Her aunt, Anna Marks, was a noted breeder of horses and dogs in Connecticut, and Frances is thoroughly at home with every kind of horse, from a chunk to a thoroughbred. It was through their love for horses that she and the Padre got to know each other back in their high-school days.

Olin has promised us a milch-cow and calf. Modestly, he says he is short of pasture, and will be grateful to us if we will let them graze on our land, and we can have the milk, all but a few quarts for the calf. . . .

If Helen only knew it, Olin had other ideas. The Mormon church has forbidden polygamy, but the idea is far from being eradicated from the minds of the faithful. Catherine and Helen would make him a fine couple of wives, if only it could be arranged, but since it couldn't, he would have to make up his mind which to woo. He confided as much to me, and I didn't feel it was my place to advise him one way or the other. I doubt whether his heart really broke when he found that neither of them entertained sentiments more emotional than honest gratitude.

It was during this rock-assembling project that I got a good lesson in the logic of Navajo language. Tom Jones, about sixteen years old, who spoke a little English, came to me at the end of a day's work.

"You gimme money, Fodda, me go hone."

"You want to go home, Tom? When will you come back?"

"No come back."

"Aren't you coming back?"

"Yes."

"*When* are you coming back?"

"No come back."

"Don't you want to work here any more?"

"Yes."

It seems impossible that I was so stupid, and he must have thought me quite obtuse. He was perfectly logical all the way through, and I was following the customary English conversational idiom which regards a double negative as a negative. Eventually the light dawned, and from that time on I have tried to be careful always to ask a positive question, as, "*Do* you want to come back?" It is particularly exasperating now with children who have had some schooling, because some of them react in the American idiom, and others, still thinking in Navajo while they speak English, stick to the logical Navajo system. The only way to be sure is to confine one's questions to clearly positive ones.

9

In addition to the availability of water and of the four walls of the projected trading post, there was one very important consideration—and no doubt it had influenced Dan's choice of a site for the trading post: this was the fact that the Navajos who lived on the south side of the San Juan River had a traditional fording place less than a mile upstream, and the trail to the store in Bluff would bring them within easy reach of our place.

The twenty-by-thirty-foot building would of course be completely inadequate for a mission, but it was a beginning; all it needed was some doors and windows, a roof, the extermination of ants that had built themselves a neat hill inside, and some arrangement for getting a heating plant with smoke vent. We had some democratic consultations about plans—this was before "group dynamics" had become popular in the church, but the basic idea that a handful of ignoramuses can get into a huddle and produce wisdom was familiar. I was the only one of the group who had had any practical experience with building, and I thought I had some pretty good ideas about the sort of buildings we should and could produce, but at the end of the conference I knew that what was to be would be far better than what I could have planned. They all had some idea of what would "be nice to have," but were patient and respectful when I brought up such matters as footings and the thrust of a roof. We all agreed that it was necessary to get this one building closed in, before cold weather if possible, but in any case soon! Then we would start on a wing abutting the west and another the east side, as time, strength and money allowed.

It was soon evident that cold weather was going to win the race unless we did something to speed up construction. To the rescue came our first Navajo punster.

He was of a stocky build, middle-aged, with a profile that indicated strong opinions and a smile that would win friends anywhere.

He held out his hand in the usual Navajo dead-fish manner, but I could feel the palm well hardened with toil.

"You éé'niishoodi"—pointing to me—"me just Shoodi."

As Will Rogers used to say, "It don't take any time to tell a joke—it's explaining it that takes the time." But I must take the time. The first missionaries to the Navajo were the Franciscan Fathers, in the southern part of the Reservation. They of course wore the ankle-length habit of their order. Navajos called them "the one who drags his garment." *éé* means "clothing," *nishood* means "he drags," and the final *i* signifies one who, or that which, does or has something. Later the term was applied to any religious teacher or minister, and to distinguish, if necessary, the Catholic from the Protestant, the qualifying phrase was added, "the one who drags his garment his-garment-is-long" or "the one who drags his garment his-garment-is-short." Now, our visitor because of his diminutive stature, had been nicknamed Shorty by the whites, and he accepted this as his name, but being, like most Navajos, unable or unwilling to pronounce the sound of the letter *r* or to allow the *t* sound directly before a vowel, it came out Shoodi.

But our punster was not making a merely social call. Picking up a hoe with which I had been mixing cement for the fireplace and chimney, he indicated his own qualification as either an entered apprentice or a master mason and signified his willingness to devote his talents, for a consideration, to the task of speeding up our building project. We discussed both the project and the consideration at some length, his command of English being approximately on the level of my command of Navajo. I had been warned by the whites in Bluff not to pay a Navajo more than a dollar a day for any kind of work. Although I respected very highly their advice in matters in which I had had no experience, I couldn't help seeing in this "warning" a rather desperate attempt to maintain a white supremacy and to leave unmolested a source of cheap labor. I consulted the Mission's pathetic bank balance and roughly estimated the probable influx of contributions, and Shoodi was hired at three dollars and fifty cents a day, with the warning that he might be laid off without notice if the money were not available.

Shoodi started off next day on the east wing, while I continued with the fireplace, chimney and gable ends of the former store, which we were already beginning to call the Mission House, the rest of the staff being kept busy sledding the building materials from the talus of the canyon wall.

By the time Shoodi had completed the second course above the footing he realized that he would need a helper, so that two could work simultaneously, one on either side of a wall, and avoid the loss of time and the fatigue involved in continually crossing from one side to the other. I had had enough experience in masonry to see the good sense and the economy to the mission in Shoodi's request, but the money wasn't coming in that fast. However, I hadn't counted on the Navajo's casual attitude towards any job. No sooner had Tom Mustache been added to the crew than the two announced that they would be away for a few days, to undertake some professional work. It seemed that Shoodi was a medicine man and Tom a singer, so they took four days off to sing and three more to sleep it off, and this sort of thing repeatedly interrupted the building project, at least to the point where the offerings from our small group of benefactors kept us in the black.

Both Shoodi and Tom had set up tents on our land, and their families kept house for them. At one time I began to hear an unusual amount of Navajo vocal music at night. It appeared that Shoodi's little girl, Bessie, then about eight years old, was very sick, and he, in his professional capacity, was singing over her nights, while continuing his work as a mason during the day. Our clinical thermometer indicated that the condition was really serious. Our offer to take the child to a doctor in Blanding was respectfully declined: Shoodi had no money for such foolishness, but appreciated our obvious concern. After several days, when there seemed to be no improvement, I asked Shoodi if he were going to continue to sing. He said, "No sing. Tomorrow—" and he turned his extended right hand over, palm down. Shoodi's gestures were always graphic: it was clear that he had given up hope of the child's living. Still he was not interested in a white man doctor. Just on the chance of doing something that might help, I said, "Do you want me to try what I can do for Bessie?" His face lit up instantly. "Yes, you can maybe save her," he said in Navajo.

The sulfas had only recently been made available. A doctor in the East had given me a supply of the less toxic type, with careful instructions. I still had the local authorities to consider, however, and wasn't the least bit eager to take unnecessary chances. The telephone in Bluff happened to be working. I called Dr. Bayles, described the symptoms and told him I had sulfadiazine. He told me what to do. In those days the sulfas were administered quantitatively in proportion to the weight of the patient and strictly at three-hour intervals. Helen, always ready to spare me unnecessary fatigue, insisted upon taking the midnight and 3 A.M. administrations. By noon the next day Bessie's temperature was normal. Our insistence that she remain in bed was overruled, and she was packing (carrying) water before sundown, with the other children. Shoodi's contempt for white man's medicine remained unrelieved, however, and the cedit was given to the power of the priest's God. Who was I to contradict this?

The following day I went over to the Shoodi camp to check on Bessie's condition, which I found satisfactory. Under a blanket was a lump which moved and soon gave out a wail, the unmistakable cry of a newborn baby. My startled inquiry was smilingly met with the information that Shoodi's eldest daughter, Jessie Lilly (probably so named because when she was born she was "jes a lilly girl") had delivered a daughter during the night. Usually a Navajo child doesn't get named for some time after birth; however, with the introduction of vital statistics, pressure is often put upon parents. In this case the grandfather anticipated my question as to the naming of the child by asking me, "That tall woman that brought the medicine for Bessie in the nighttime, what is she called?" And when I said, "Helen," he added without hesitation, pointing to the lump under the blanket, "This one, Helen. Helen Shoodi."

It seemed that the father of Helen and of her sister Bessie had by this time gone off to Montezuma Creek to start a new family with Helen Littlewagon, so that the baby was for some time called Helen Shoodi, but by the time she went off to school the name of Yellowman was taken by both Helen and Bessie, and it was used until their marriages. With my perhaps conservative background I'm afraid I started off with a poor opinion of Mr. Yellowman, but later I learned that most of Shoodi's sons-in-law found life difficult and tended to wander off seeking more pacific environs. Especially after the state began to provide, through its Welfare Department, Aid for Dependent Children, Shoodi was among the first to figure out that life in a welfare state could be rather simple if one saw to it that each of one's daughters had a few dependent children. Let no one doubt the sagacity of the "primitive savage." I have always loved Seton's story about the Indians who ploughed in their hay and planted locoweed when they found that Uncle Sam was paying more for it than for hay; and about those who started coyote ranches because the bounty was so attractive!

Cold weather, as I have noted, was closing in. My previous knowledge of this country had been only that gained in the summer—and for some reason one thinks of the desert as always hot. If I had the foresight to chop some wood, the teepee in which I slept could be quickly heated by a fire in the sheet-metal stove; even getting up in the dark of the morning was less of an ordeal, since I moved my cot to a point from which I could start a fire without crawling out of the blankets. In a few minutes the place was comfortable, except near the ground, and the only socks I possessed were of cotton. I bethought me of some friends in the East who had promised to knit anything needed, and sent picture postcards with a plea for wool socks to at least six of them. One expects to be forgotten by some old friends but not in half-dozen lots; not one of them responded. It was only in the following spring that we learned of a mail robbery at Thompson, Utah, in which all the letters written that week end, not to mention a silver and turquoise bracelet that Brother Michael intended for his sister's birthday present, were stolen. Of course, when our eastern friends learned about the robbery, they either thought we had been seeing too many Westerns, or else, if they did believe it, imagined the scene as it invariably appears on the screen—masked bandits surrounding the mail coach, "Throw down that box . . ." and the rest of it. Rather a letdown to have to admit that a man saw the unattended mail sack at the railroad depot and just tossed it into his pickup and drove off! Those who saw him assumed that he was an employee and thought nothing of it. He took the sack to a remote canyon, opened everything, took what he wanted and left the rest. Snow buried all the evidence until the spring thaws.

Our altar was still out of doors, and I continued to say Mass at 7 A.M. to allow Helen time to have breakfast and drive to Bluff where she was teaching. Once the water in the cruet froze; after that Brother held it in his pocket until needed. Although

I have ordinarily been rather careful not to invent or devise rites or ceremonies, I found great comfort in having a vivid red hot-water bottle on the altar—discreetly covered with a fair linen cloth, of course—with which to warm hands and fingers that otherwise would be too rigid to perform their sacred functions.

10

I haven't told how Helen got to be a schoolteacher. Soon after our arrival the white citizens of Bluff began telling us of their difficulty in getting a teacher for the school. It was thought that the county authorities were just itching for a good reason to close the Bluff school. It had only eight pupils, and the law regarded that as a minimum average daily attendance to justify maintaining a school. The teacher who had resigned the previous spring had in the opinion of the parents been less than satisfactory. "A right sawry teacher, if you ask me," was the estimate commonly heard, even if you didn't ask. The county board let it be known that no teacher had been signed up, nor had they any idea where one could be secured. The influx of a group of six educated people, all with diplomas, and at least half of them with more than one degree, naturally put ideas into the minds of the citizenry in relation to their problem. We were formally "waited on." It was heartbreaking to refuse. We felt we had a job to do, and we needed all our time to get at it. Stories of schoolboys exploding rifle shells in the school stove, chasing the "right sawry" teacher with hunting knives until she barricaded herself behind the piano, of one girl child (known as Puss) biting the teacher's arm until the blood ran—all these didn't make the job very attractive.

Helen went to Bluff for mail and water one day while we were considering the problem. Puss came up to her.

"If you'll be our teacher, I won't bite you. I *like* you. If you'll be our teacher, I'll give you one of my melons."

"Do you raise your own melons?" Helen asked.

"Shore, got to, t' git money for school clothes and shoes. Paw lets me have a piece of garden. I hitch up th' ole bitch 'n' plough—"

"You hitch up *what?*"

"Th' ole bitch. Hell of a name for a mule, but that's what we call her. Melons'll be ripe pretty soon. I'll give you *two!*"

That night nearly all the parents called on us and appealed for help. It was irresistible: I yielded, provided that efforts would be made to get a teacher to relieve Helen as soon as possible.

Next morning Helen saw Puss again. Thinking this a good time to lay down some conditions, she started off, "If I *should* take the job, would you children really behave and try to learn?"

Puss was scornful. "If you *should* take it! Hell, you done *took* it. But I promise I won't bite you nor act up. An' I'll still give you two of my melons."

The schoolhouse had been built of "rock" in the days of Bluff's prosperity. Although the walls were cracked and most of the windows broken, one room had been kept in reasonable repair and boasted a wood- or coal-burning stove, and a large kerosene lamp for dark days.

A book could be filled with tales of Helen's career as teacher of the Bluff school, but as I am mostly concerned with the work and life of the Mission and the Navajo, one or two samples must suffice. The textbook used in second grade had a title that suggested that its contents were selected for their relevance to the everyday life of the child. The book told about the milkman delivering milk in bottles—but these children got their milk from the cows' streamers; the book showed electric-light bulbs, evoking the comment, "You cain't make me believe a man kin touch a button on the wall 'n' make a light go on"; the book showed the mailman delivering at the door—but these children walked to the front-porch post office three days a week for their own and their neighbors' mail; it showed school buses, street lamps, railroads—Ah! there was something! had any of the children seen a train? No answer. After a long pause a third-grader scornfully reproached a classmate, "Why, Mr. Butt! You a-settin' there a-chawin' off your nails 'n' sayin' nothin' 'n' a-lettin' Miss Sturges think there ain't a one of us ever seen a train, when you know perf'ly well you seen one when you went to visit yore uncle in Grand Junction. Shame!" Mr. Butt gathered up his courage and admitted that this was so. Mr. Butt, incidentally, is now postmaster at Blanding.

This teaching experience, in addition to providing stimulating dinner talk, gave Helen a good insight into one-room-school techniques and a familiarity with the currently approved textbooks and pedagogical theories, and in general made the opening of St. Christopher's School the great success that it was destined to be.

11

Came Brother Juniper! It was the twenty-first of October, 1943, and a really dark night. I cannot do better than to let him tell it as he wrote it to a friend in the East—

> The first idea I had of the Mission—I pictured the location as something out of a movie. A few large cottonwood trees, a lazy, flowing stream, easily splashed across on horseback, towering cliffs, a near-by trading post. How wrong I was! It was night when I arrived, having travelled by train to Grand Junction, Colorado, and by mail truck to Blanding, Utah, where Father picked me up in the Mission truck. It was loaded with lumber that stuck up all over the cab, so that at every crossroad in the town we had to lift the telephone wires to get through without breaking them.
>
> About two miles out of town a bumping noise announced a flat tire. There was with us a young man from Bluff, Olin by name, who had come along to help Father; he immediately got

out, gathered a pile of brush and had a fire going in minutes—both for light and for warmth, for it was late October and at an elevation well over six thousand feet. With the tire changed we were off again, and about forty-five minutes, or twenty miles, later we dropped down into a narrow canyon road; we delivered Olin to his house, and turned out eastward toward the Mission camp. As the noise of our approaching truck bounced off the high cliffs to our left, there was a sudden burst of fire ahead of us. Those at the camp had heard us coming, and built up the fire and had hot chocolate ready when we arrived.

The flames disclosed an army squad tent, an umbrella tent and a couple of other small tents and a Plains-type Indian teepee. Far back in the shadows I could see the outlines of a building without a roof. No cottonwood trees, no lazy river—I could hear a roar in the distance which I later learned was the river tossing its gigantic sand-waves into the night air—no trading post within miles. Little did I think that the year I had planned to spend here would turn out to be two decades or more!

The next morning I was awakened by a weird sound, and as I sat up, Brother Michael said, "Oh, that's just Randolph, welcoming the dawn. Think nothing of it." Not long after this, the Angelus was rung on what I later learned was an old Pennsylvania Railroad engine bell, now hung on a tripod in the midst of the camp. After Mass and breakfast, I was given my first job: Olin had an old outhouse, which he had been using as a pig-pen since the CCC had erected his fancy new privy, and he gave it to us for its original purpose. I had the job of digging the hole and setting the thing up and putting a door on it. This last bit of refinement was a mystery to some of the neighbors, who thought that a pleasant view was preferable, but they conceded that in real cold weather . . . well, anyway, this crude outhouse was a considerable advance over the sage-brush device that had served hitherto, and it became one of our first teaching aids. Navajos saw at once the advantage of this step toward better sanitation, and several of them followed suit.

Brother Juniper's arrival brought the staff up to five; by this time both Frances and Esther had departed. His previous experience in building was most valuable and we got right at the job of closing in the Mission House. I had provided masonry gables to the east and west walls, leaving sockets for the ridgepole; our next problem was to get logs long enough and strong enough for the roof. There were cottonwood trees on the land (although Brother Juniper couldn't see them the night of his arrival), but they were gnarled and crooked. Dan pointed out that just across the river, on the Reservation, were some tall straight ones, and while we might not go over and cut them down, any Navajo could, and for a slight consideration might be prevailed upon to do so and float them over to the north shore. A man known as Nesbit agreed to accept the assignment. I tied a knot in his lariat to determine the length desired and gave him four dollars as a retaining fee. A month later he came back and reported that he didn't think he could handle the job, and if we would give him a good hot meal he would pay back the four dollars. It didn't seem good business practice or a good lesson in moral theology, but I squared things with my conscience by telling him he had to pay the four dollars anyway, and we would be delighted to have him as our guest at dinner.

In the meantime the citizens of Bluff, in solemn meeting, decided to give us a large crib of cottonwood logs which the CCC boys had erected as riprap but which had never been used. This generous gift provided everything needed for the rafters but left us still without a ridge. Again Dan to the rescue. "Rye Butt has a haypole I figure he never will use, and he might be disposed to sell it." Rye was so disposed, and for ten dollars it was ours. We dragged it to the camp behind our pickup, but Dan was the first to see that three tenderfoot missionaries (I think they never called us dudes) could never get it up into place. "D'ye think you'd be all ready to have that hoisted into place by Sunday afternoon? If so, I think I know of a couple or three elves who might give you three a hand." The elves turned out to be himself and two husky members of his road crew. Needless to say, the job got done, and by the end of the week the rafters were in place and the work of cutting, peeling and laying the smaller parallel poles was well in hand. By Thanksgiving Day we were ready for our first "indoor" Mass.

The quotation marks have meaning. The door was an opening

in the masonry, but we hung a blanket over it to keep some heat in. The windows were smaller openings, and we blocked them up with whatever material was at hand. The roof as yet consisted only of the log rafters and the smaller cottonwood poles laid crosswise upon them. The interstices allowed what light we had to come through; they also provided a ready exit for the heat generated in the kitchen stove and one small wood stove designed for heat. But the walls of the house served as a windbreak, and also emphasized, as all church building should, the community aspect of worship. It was a real Eucharist, a Thanksgiving, not only for the privilege of being allowed to work with the Navajos, who gathered with us to render their thanks, but also for a few luxuries to be enjoyed. In the face of this, who could complain of chilly draughts, stinging reminders that the anthill had not been completely evacuated, guttering altar candles or squalling babies?

12

I think it was shortly before Thanksgiving that a baby was brought in for our medical attention. The child was said to be nearly three years old but was far too small and all skin and bones. The parents pointed to a small hole in the child's neck in which could be seen a hardened white substance like ivory. I guessed it to be indurated pus and urged them to get the boy to a doctor without delay. This they refused, even when we offered transportation, and there seemed little more that we could do except pray.

On December 7 a young man who spoke a little English came to see me and asked me to go visit a sick baby. "Who is the baby?" I asked.

"My uncle."

I had had a few surprises in the way of mothers and daughters delivering babies at about the same time, and more than once had encountered uncles or aunts as much as eight or ten years younger than their nieces or nephews, but this one seemed a bit farfetched. The young man, Sam, was in his early twenties, and I expressed surprise at his having an uncle who was still a baby. But he explained, "My big brudder's baby." The Navajo word for one's sister's child differs very slightly from that for a paternal uncle. This investigation was of course carried out while moving—a sick call cannot be delayed while one tries to solve the mysteries of Navajo relationship terms. Sam had also conveyed the message that the father of the child had asked me to bring some water. This seemed a strange request, when the hogan was not far from a small spring. As we went along I wondered if the request might imply a desire for baptism; anyway, I picked up a half-gallon jug.

As we approached the hogan there were the unmistakable sounds of a medicine man at work—song and rattle. As we entered, the medicine man stopped his song. Whether it was just the end of the song or an interruption I couldn't tell, but it had the descending slide of nearly a full octave that characterizes the conclusion of many Navajo chants. A glance at the patient showed that this was my three-year-old with the ivory inlay, but oh, what a skeleton! There was hardly a bit of flesh left on the poor little wasted body. The medicine man looked up at me with a welcoming smile, summoning his best English.

"Me mellicin man. Me make prayer good. You make Jesus-talk. Jesus-talk he good." Holding up two fingers closely joined together, he added, "Two good make strong good."

I asked the parents if the request for the water had been prompted by a desire for baptism for the baby. Five months of association with the Navajos had not yet taught me that "Yes" is the answer one will almost always get to any question. Anyway, I got it this time.

Then, as best I could (the baby's mother had attended school in her younger days), I explained what baptism means—the regeneration of the soul, the pouring in of sanctifying grace, incorportion into the Mystical Body of Christ. "Yes, yes"—but I could see they were grasping at any straw. So I told the medicine man that I would make Jesus-talk which would make the baby's soul holy and ready to meet our Creator. If God willed to restore health despite the neglect the child had suffered, we should be thankful; if in His wisdom this little one's soul should be the first of the northern Navajos to enter into the very presence of God and to offer his continuous prayers for the redemption of the Navajo people, that would be reason for even deeper gratitude.

All the traditional ceremonies were used—salt, oils, white cloth, candle—in addition, of course, to the essential water and form of words. The flickering light of the fire was reflected in the silver coins and buttons on the mother's velveteen blouse and in the eyes of the other children, the medicine man and the parents. It was a sight never to be forgotten—the first baptism. And the mode seemed prophetic of our whole approach to this people: the cooperating medicine man, the simplicity of surroundings, together with a scrupulous observance of traditional details of ceremonial.

At dawn the next morning Randolph was at the door of my teepee. "Snoopy's baby die. He say to me, 'Ask Faa Leeda bury him.'" I learned later that such messages are usually conveyed by an envoy, much as a European ruler might use an ambassador. We had never been asked to officiate at a burial—for I naturally assumed that that was what was meant by "bury him." I made some inquiries about hour, burial site and the like, much to Randolph's surprise. The family was not, it seemed, the least bit concerned about such details: they were busy with their own ritual, which would occupy them for four days. All that was necessary, from their point of view, was that we should know where to find the body. From there on it was our concern. A request to bury, I realized then, meant not to read something out of a book: it meant get a shovel and go to work. But wait! there was one further matter. We were to make a box. How the Navajo learned about the white man's veneration for a box I have never found out, but it is hard to talk them out of it. We had a few boards, and I nailed them together in box form. Unfortunately I didn't measure the body and made the box too short. There were no more boards, so it was necessary to open one end and let the feet, wrapped in cotton blankets, stick out.

Randolph suggested a site at the opening of a small box canyon. We all took turns at the digging until we reached solid rock and decided that this was deep enough. We mopped our brows, donned vestments, and held the office for the Burial of a Child. None of the family came in sight, and Randolph beat a safe retreat as soon as he was sure that we understood his direction about the site, so we did all the rest ourselves. It was a sad thing, as death always brings sadness, especially the death of a child; but it was a joyous thing that this little boy was spared the sufferings that would undoubtedly have been his had he lived longer under such fearful neglect. And in a real sense he was a martyr—though unconsciously—for the shock of this tragedy seemed to open the eyes of the parents to the evils of malnutrition, and other children of theirs have been among our roliest and poliest.

13

The first Christmas will always be remembered. To our surprise the Navajos knew the day was coming. Before the first of December every passing visitor would ask, "How many days Keshmesh?" But when we asked if they knew what Christmas was for, they grinned knowingly, perhaps patting or rubbing their stomachs, and said, "Mucho* chinny-ago" or "Lotsa eat."

Further inquiry disclosed that Christmas was observed in a

* A few Spanish words have crept into the Navajo language, mostly words for things they hadn't known of before, as money, cattle, butter, jail. But curiously, a few expressions for which there are perfectly good Navajo equivalents are in fairly common use, e.g., *mucho biejo, no bueno* and *muchacho*—this last invariably preceded by the Navajo possessive and retained in the masculine form whether it applies to a boy or a girl.

definite manner. The trader was induced to supply flour, salt, baking powder and a few other goodies; then the Navajos would go from house to house in Bluff crying, "Keshmeshay!" much as white children demand trick or treat at Allhallows' Eve. When the whites had been drained of all that could be hoped for, the Navajos withdrew to an open area, built fires and had a feast.

It was something of a blow to me. Here I had searched for years to find an aborigine untouched by Christian tradition, and what did I find but one who had adopted the worst side effects of Christianity and *liked* them! I had thought at least I would not have to "unteach" them, but no.

It wasn't easy, although easier than I expected. We began with Randolph and the few others who could understand some English. We pointed out the degrading nature of begging, that the Navajo are supposed to be a noble and proud people, equal in everything to the whites except wealth and formal education. Christmas is a holy day, celebrating the birth of the Saviour, the founder of the Catholic church.* The festivities should center in the church. We would have Mass, as on Sundays, but after Mass was over, all who came would be our honored guests at our Christmas dinner.

The idea appealed to them; a few days after we had announced it to the few, we were led to understand that all understood and would be there. The next question was, How shall we feed them? But we took a leaf from their own book: they would do the cooking, we would supply the food. We bought a sheep carcass and butchered it; we bought as much flour as we thought would be needed.

For six weeks I had been working in every spare moment on the sermon. This was to be my first sermon in Navajo. I had done a good deal of instruction to non-English-speaking Navajos, through the invaluable *Catechism and Guide* issued by the Franciscan Fathers at St. Michael's, Arizona. By taking the

* The Mormon church considers that Christ was born in the spring of the year, and individual Mormons celebrate the traditional Christmas with family reunions and exchange of gifts and greetings but not as the Feast of the Nativity of Our Lord.

answers of the catechism and weaving them into narrative form, I composed what I thought to be a rather creditable presentation of the subject. Certainly no intelligent Navajo, I thought, could hear this and go away thinking that Christmas was just a day of "mucho chinny-ago." It took six weeks to prepare the sermon (the longest preparation of my entire ministry) and just about six minutes to deliver. In my vanity I expected them to be enthusiastic over this milestone, but apparently they took it in their stride—which, come to think of it, might have been an even greater compliment.

Meat was given out, fires blazed up in many places around the Mission House, and family groups gathered around. The women boiled or broiled the meat, made dough and patted it into flat circles which they baked on grills over the embers or fried in skillets. It was a most colorful picture. Horses, saddled, stood around; there were many wagons; even small children in bright skirts and blouses, or shirts and denim slacks, with wide-brimmed hats or cloth headbands, adorned the scene. An archery contest had been announced. On the side of a carton I made a rabbit target and explained the manner of scoring, and the men went at it. A few had brought their own bows and arrows, others used mine. We started with the target at a distance of about seventy-five or eighty feet, but everyone complained that that was too far, and we moved up to about fifty feet. Some very fine shooting resulted. It was the older men only who took part; the young men and older boys looked on, fascinated but every suggestion that they try was met with silly giggles and mutters of "Hola"—"I don't know."

I mention this because of its bearing on later changes in the Navajo outlook on life. It was in 1959, I think, that a young man not only participated but won the prize, and since then not only young men but older boys as well have participated—not always without shy giggles, but at least they have been willing to try.

It was at this Christmas festivity that I first met Jessie West Thumb. Jessie was, and is, a fine specimen of Navajo womanhood—tall, lean and erect, friendly, but never lacking in dignity. She spoke adequate English, having gone for several years to some far-off government school. Her first petition was for prayers for her son, who was in the Air Force. The significance of this request did not come home to me for a long time afterward; in fact, it seemed like a perfectly logical and natural thing.

It is worth while to digress for a moment to deal with a subject that frequently comes up with visitors at the Mission. It may take slightly different forms, but essentially it says: "It is wonderful that you missionaries are concerned for these people, teaching them cleanliness and sanitation, educating them to take their places in the world in which they have to live, but why not just let them keep their religion? Ours is good enough for us, but why do we have to cram it down their throats when their own may be just as helpful to them as ours is to us?"

Admitting that there is still much of Navajo religion that I don't know or understand, of this much I am convinced, that in its primitive form, which remains only slightly changed, it had no provision for prayer on behalf of anybody else. Jessie's request revealed an understanding of a religion beyond that of the Navajo. If a Navajo feels the need of intense prayer, or a ceremonial, as it is sometimes inaccurately called, he sends for a medicine man. He may first consult a diagnostician, known as a hand trembler, who has his own way of determining which of the many rites is indicated under the circumstances. If he prescribes a Flint Way, or some other, the patient seeks a practitioner skilled in that particular rite, arranges time, place, fee. Now, if anybody else is to derive fringe benefits, it is up to that one to make his bargain with the practitioner; it is no concern of the original patient.

Not only is intercessory prayer no part of Navajo religion, there is actually no moral code, either for the patient or for the doctor. It is not considered inept if the doctor arrives roaring drunk so long as he sobers enough to begin the rite at the appointed time—a time that of course is indicated by the position of the sun or of certain constellations. He might arrive on a stolen horse, knowing that the owner would not interrupt the rite by making a scene. He might steal from his patient if he thought he could not get the object of his desires by simply asking for it; this asking is the simpler method and usually successful, for one of the thoroughly understood principles of Navajo medicine is that the practitioner must be completely satisfied. If he were to depart after the rite in a disgruntled mood, the efficacy of the prayer would be greatly lessened or perhaps even destroyed, so he usually gets what he wants, but obviously he must have a keen sense of values and know exactly what the traffic will bear, lest business fall off. In a word, there is no sense of sin. There are codes of behavior, but these are binding only in the external forum, and getting caught and consequently getting laughed at constitute the punishment. The gods are displeased, not at deeds of violence or bloodshed, deceit or theft, but at violations of tabus; they can be propitiated by the proper rites and so the balance of beauty, harmony and peace is restored. Furthermore, the ritual is bound up with legends that despite much beauty and imagination, involve beliefs in a cosmology that cannot be harmonized with what children learn in school, and for this reason most of the children who now progress beyond secondary grades can no longer accept the old ways. It is the counterpart of the fundamentalist problem of a generation or two ago. But unless the Navajo is at least exposed to a religion that is dynamic, in that it not only holds up a code of behavior but also dispenses means of grace whereby the code can be adhered to, we may find that thousands are being graduated with book learning, a trade and nothing to anchor them to reality.

But this digression has taken me somewhat ahead of my story. We were at a point where almost none of our children could get to a school. Incidentally, Jessie's son, for whom she asked prayers, was one of six from our area who served in the armed forces in World War II. The draft board turned down hundreds without sending them up for physical examination, simply because they knew no English.

I shall undoubtedly have much more to say about Navajo religion, and especially our policy of using it as a point of departure but not something to be thrown out or trodden underfoot. But we were talking about that first Christmas.

Bear in mind that at this time we had but one building. We slept in our tents, but used the building as church, social room, refectory and kitchen. A large packing box covered with a striped blanket served to hold the altar stone, and with candles and crucifix presented a right churchly appearance. But at Christmas we had something else, quite special and unique. It was a crib group of figurines, made of clay by one of my gifted former parishioners in the East, depicting Blessed Mary and Joseph, the shepherds (we had learned by this time to call them sheepherders) and the Wise Men From the East who were, logically, Pawnees in full war bonnets. Martha, in her laudable humility, dared not try to depict the infant Saviour, so, as fools rush in where angels fear to tread, I did my best with a bit of clay from Spring Canyon. The Babe was in a Navajo cradleboard and the parents were in traditional Navajo dress. I think that this graphic presentation did more than any one thing to bring home the basic idea of Christmas. Again and again people came in throughout the day to see the group, the news having gone around, and more than once we saw them pointing to the crèche and then to the crucifix, and from the little we could understand of their words they were calling attention to the fact that here was the Saviour as a baby and here He was offering His sacrifice.

As the sun hung low in the sky the people started for their homes, individual riders on their horses, groups in wagons. All waved a joyous "Gabah! Sanchewary mawch!" The Navajos do not usually express thanks, and this was obviously a spontaneous reaction.

14

It was "on the Feast of Stephen" that Olin rode into our camp leading a beautiful black mare. He had heard that I felt the need of a saddle horse, and the underground had told him that there was some money from friends of mine for this specific purpose.

I fell in love with the mare at first sight, and called her Shioni, which, according to some book that I had read, meant "my darling," or the like. The fact that Olin, whose conversational Navajo was pretty good, had never heard the term was a surprise to me, but later on I couldn't find a Navajo who admitted having heard or used it! But it seemed a good name, and I got out a lump of sugar for her, just as I used to do for my red sorrel, Rubric, in Connecticut. But Shioni would have none of this. Helen suggested that she had probably been warned about men like me. Olin admitted, "She ain't broke yet. Don't know what sugar is." Well, we put her in the corral we had built for the work horse and fed her, and I determined to show the world that you didn't have to break a horse; all that was needed was to gentle her by getting her used to having people around, then gradually put a saddle pad on, then a saddle, then a hackamore, then lead her around with other horses being ridden so that eventually she would see that it didn't hurt, then mount, maybe ride out a few bucks, and there's your trusty mount!

Sugar wasn't the only thing Shioni would have none of. Olin finally did get a saddle on her, snubbed her muzzle close to his knee as he sat on his own gentle pony, and told me to mount. I did. Shioni didn't like it, but being unable to get her head down, she couldn't buck, and so Olin and I rode "around the block," that is, to Bluff, up Cow Canyon, across the Bench and down another canyon three or four miles to the east. We had them walking, trotting and galloping, but Olin insisted on keeping the mare's head tightly bound to his own saddle horn. Aside from a bit of chafing due to close quarters with Olin's leather, I was all right, and felt much encouraged. A few more evening exercises like this, and all would be well.

But not so, thought Shioni. She went into a panic if I so much as stepped into the corral, and finally one day, as I was trying to lead her to water, having roped her in the corral, she took off at full gallop. She must have dragged me a hundred yards or more before I decided that it would be better to burn my hands on the rope than get torn and bruised all over, and I let go. So ended the romance of Shioni and me, and I swapped her for a very uninteresting roan with a long and very thin tail, which got the name of Mogi—the Navajo corruption of our word monkey. In the meantime we had acquired a silver-blue pony, which of course would have to be called Beshlagai—Silver—since the radio was then telling the kiddies about Hi-Ho Silver. Olin also sold us a cow with calf, and we were grateful for the milk and cream. The cow was said to be Jersey-Guernsey and Hereford. She looked like a full-blooded whiteface, but gave milk like a true Channel Islander. Pasteurizing was not easy, but we got a dairy thermometer and did our very best, heating the milk over our wood-burning range to the proper point—seems to me it was about 180 degrees—then cooling it by pouring it into as many vessels, one after another, as we could (we had, of course, no ice or other refrigerant), then setting it in our "refrigerator," which was a crate covered with half-inch mesh wire and wet burlap or bits of blanket. The natives, white and Navajo, thought this was a strange waste of time and mildly amusing; they also thought it amusing that several of the townspeople had cows unable to bring a calf to birth. Utah has as fine a health department as any other state, I feel sure, but in those days our corner of the state got little attention. Rumor had it that when the inspectors came to look into the restaurants in Blanding and Monticello, they packed their own lunches. A slightly less credible legend told of a refusal to analyze the Blanding water supply on the ground that no germ could live in *that* water. But I do know that when we stopped in at what was then the only restaurant in Monticello, Helen ordered milk but asked if it were pasteurized, to which the lady who ran the place replied, "What's that mean? I never heard of that." Helen changed to black coffee. It is hard to realize how recently these conditions prevailed, when today Bluff has immaculate restaurants operated under approved conditions and one of the finest and most modern dairy farms in our county.

The principle of evaporation applied to refrigeration is well known in dry climates. Tourists are usually introduced to it through the type of water sack sold in filling stations and many shops in the Southwest. The sack is woven with just the right balance of tightness and slack, so that it holds water but allows a tiny leakage like sweat; this wets the exterior of the sack and evaporates, quickly cooling the contents. The Pueblo Indians who had lived in our area before the Navajo came probably knew and used the principle, as many rural Mexicans still do in their ollas, or ceramic waterpots; we used it in the refrigerator I have mentioned. The main problem there was to keep the blanket or gunny-sack covering wet. Some of the traders, after they got electric-light plants, made themselves air conditioners by the simple device of aiming the current from a small electric fan through a box or barrel covered with wet cloth.

I'll be getting back to the Navajos in a minute, but I can't leave this sketchy account of conditions in San Juan County without an admiring word about the cooperation and genuine human kindness shown by the Anglo* natives. As population grows the necessity for regulations grows. We had ordered some day-old chickens. They arrived in Blanding on a Tuesday morning. At that time Blanding had mail service daily, Bluff only three days a week—Monday, Wednesday and Friday. The postmaster knew that the chicks could hardly live until Wednesday afternoon, and he apparently quizzed everybody who came into the post office, "You going to Bluff today?" until he found one who was, and who most graciously delivered our chicks for us. Similarly the telephone-exchange girl at Blanding, a sister of the Hunts whom I have mentioned, went far out of her way to be helpful. There was only one telephone in Bluff, but it was on the porch of Olin's mother's house, and Olin could be counted on to bring us messages. If we broke down on the highway, it was only necessary to flag down the next car and ask the driver to tell "Myrtle" the story.

Shoodi and Tom were really getting ahead with the stone-masonry of the west wing. The hardest part was the forming of the cloister arches. Straight-coursed masonry presented no prob-

---

* The term *Anglo* is widely used in the Southwest for non-Indian citizens, whether of English or other background.

lem, but this was something else again. We made two wooden forms—there were four arches, but I planned on their completing the first before a form would be needed for the third, and so on. Well, it was a simple thing to set the forms on the imposts; then I explained, with a carefully-drawn diagram and such words of Navajo as I could command, about the need for stones properly shaped for the springers. I had to be gone for a few days, but Shoodi nodded emphatically and kept repeating, "I know, I know," and it seemed he had caught on. When I got back, he did have some beautifully shaped springers but had set them into the wall in reverse, and he was struggling with the voussoirs, which just didn't seem to want to go into place. Poor man, he was trying so hard; it was heartbreaking to tell him this would all have to come down. I pleased him a little, I think, by praising his shaping of the "rocks," and here, incidentally, I saw another great advantage of setting the masonry in mud instead of cement. It was like having a rubber at the end of your pencil. Once we got the springers and voussoirs properly aligned the work went forward rapidly; the intrados presented no difficulty until we got to the top of the arch—if the angles of the intrados were too obtuse, the keystone would not lock into place. But before the end of the day the first arch and a good part of the second had been completed, and next morning we were ready to take down the forms. I showed Shoodi how to undo a few screws so that the framework could be readily withdrawn, and left him. A half hour later he was going ahead with the second arch but hadn't touched the form. I asked what was wrong, and he said in no uncertain terms that he hadn't done all that work just to have the arch come tumbling down on his head! He thought that the form was holding the masonry up! To save time, I called Brother Juniper from his work, and in a few minutes we had the form out, and to prove the strength of the arch, Brother climbed on top of it and performed an impromptu war dance. The Navajos had withdrawn to a safe distance but were now convinced, and came back grinning, and muttering remarks that might have been interpreted, "I told you so! I knew it all the time!"

15

As the season of Lent approached I began to think more specifically about how we were to present to this people the meaning of Good Friday. Gladys Reichard had warned me that in her experience Christian missionaries cooked their goose when they told about the death of their God. She herself must have held a Nestorian idea about Our Lord, because she suggested that I might teach that Jesus, who became God, might have ceased to be God before dying. Of course, I maintained that this was impossible: Jesus didn't "become God," but God became man at the Annunciation, and only the death of God on the Cross could redeem the world from sin and death. "Well, it's your problem," she said, "but you'll find that they don't like to talk or think about death in any way." How right she was! Again and again, in trying to get complete family records, we would ask a man, "What is your father's name?" And he would just shake his head, or say "Ádin"—"he is not." If we put a little pressure, gentle pressure, on him by saying, "But he must have had a name when he was alive," the usual response would be a faraway look and a vague, "What, maybe, was his name, perhaps?" or "Forget." Now here were two basic points of Christianity which could not be changed to suit the temperament or prejudices of any race or nation—that a death can bring good, and that One was willing to make a sacrifice, even of His life, for us, and without expecting a reward. They could not be changed, but perhaps they could be effectively presented in a way that would not repel.

I mulled this thought over for a long time. The answer was not perfect, but the best of many that suggested themselves—a sand painting. Sand paintings are a recognized part of many of the standard Navajo ceremonials. They are made upon the ground, in a medium of varicolored sands, applied by letting them trickle between the forefinger and the thumb. Medicine men pride themselves on the collecting of these various sands, some of which have to be ground from bits of soft stone, and often the procuring of them involves much travel. I didn't have the time for this sort of thing, but I found a synthetic substitute could be made by mixing any fine sand with free-expression paints. Perhaps this wasn't exactly cricket, but under the circumstances it seemed justifiable.

The roof on the west wing had been completed, but we were still sleeping in our tents, so that it was a simple matter to decorate one of the cells for use as a chapel of repose for the Maundy Thursday rite. Cliff flowers were already in blossom, and sage grew in abundance all around the mission, so that a strikingly beautiful effect was achieved. Few as we were, we carried out the traditional rites with precision and care, and our people attended with obvious reverence. On Good Friday, after the solemn rites were concluded at the altar in the Mission House, Brother Juniper brought in a bucket of light-colored sand and dumped it on the ground in front of the altar; with a bit of board I smoothed it out to cover about a square yard. From the Franciscan Fathers' *Catechism* I read short selections of the story of the Crucifixion, and between the readings drew the picture with the colored sands, while Brother Michael and Helen sang suitable hymns. First I drew the Cross, in black sand, then the figure of the Crucified in beige-colored sand; the arms were flexed at the elbows, as in most, if not all, sand-painting figures, and the torso greatly elongated. Then the figures of St. Mary and St. John, one on either side of the Cross, arms similarly flexed. The sun was represented by a disk of yellow sand above the Cross. When I read of the darkness spreading over the land, I obliterated the sun with black sand.

The grapevine carried the news far and wide—a white man had made a sand painting! All day long groups or individuals came in to see it; in modulated tones they discussed it and silently filed out.

The Holy Saturday rites were carried out as fully as conditions warranted. At that time, it must be remembered, the "unrestored" usage still prevailed, with Mass in the forenoon. Towards afternoon clouds appeared in the sky, which had displayed an unbroken blue for many weeks past, and darkness came on, unrelieved by the light of the paschal moon.

I was awakened at dawn by the sound of shovels grating in gravel, and the voices of Brother Juniper and Brother Michael in the patio; rain was beating down on the roof of my tent and leaking through in various places. By the time I was dressed the Brothers had made ditches that would prevent the Mission House's being flooded. The mud-covered roof, however, was holding off only a part of the precipitation, and we had to stretch a tarpaulin over the altar and then replace the linens before we could start the Easter Mass. The congregation was not large—but we could hardly blame the people who probably were struggling with the elements as vigorously as we ourselves were.

One young sheepherder brought a day-old lamb with him to church. An occasional bleat—especially while we were singing "Agnus Dei"—was not out of place or distracting, but towards the end of the service the lamb broke its tether and made for the sagebrush that adorned the base of the paschal candle. Brother Michael, never at a loss, simply swooped the little beast up with his left forearm, and holding his hymnal in his right hand, continued the stentorian tones through the last Alleluia.

That Easter Day was also the occasion of my second sermon in the Navajo language. It might have been a little longer than the one of the previous Christmas, but there was much to work on. Christmas they knew about—as a day of feasting and merry-making. I had to open their eyes to a new thought—the observance of the birth of Jesus the Christ. But birth, at least, was a familiar phenomenon. Not so resurrection after death. I avoided the hackneyed and, to my mind, confusing comparison with the rebirth of nature after winter's sleep, for in this there had been only a sleep and no real death—and every Navajo knew that he could tell a dead tree in winter from a merely deciduous tree by snapping a twig. It was, and still is, a difficult theme, but it is central to the Christian religion and cannot be sidetracked.

From this Sunday onward I made it a practice to read the appointed Gospel in Navajo after chanting it in the course of the rite. By early spring I had accumulated a modest "barrel" of stock sermons covering the main doctrines of the church and the events commemorated throughout the liturgical year—Advent, Christmas, Epiphany, Lent, Passiontide, Easter, Ascension and Pentecost. There were probably about twenty-five or thirty of these, and I would read one each Sunday, selecting the most appropriate and adding a new one here and there as time and opportunity allowed. I mention this barrel of Navajo sermons here because I shall have occasion to refer again to it in connection with one of those fantastic legends that arose after the destructive fire of 1950.

Toward noon the rain subsided. Having in mind some errand which I have quite forgotten, I slithered into Bluff in the pickup, and as I passed Dan's house he flagged me down. "Gee, Father, that musta been a helluva good sand painting you made!" I asked what he meant—I hadn't even known that he had heard about the sand painting.

"Makin' all this rain," he said. "I don't know how many Navvies been in to tell me about it. Seems they've been spendin' their money on medicine men for weeks to bring rain, but all you have to do is make a sun in sand and blot it out with clouds of sand and use the powerful prayers, and look what *you* bring in!"

The next morning Randolph came in while we were still at breakfast. "Faa Leeah, is medicine man living up the river bout sem mile, he got boy is sick year an a half. He want you go up there and make him well. Tried all kinds Navajo prayers, don't do no good."

"Well, Randolph, I don't know that I can do him any good, but I'll go to see him and do what I can."

"Oh, you can do it all right. All Navajos know now you got strong medicine. They try lawn tine make rain, can't make any. You make big rain. Rain over Cortez, rain Tees Nasbas, rain Mexican Water, rain Mexican Hat, rain Landi [Blanding]—rain all roun. You can make at boy well."

He gave me directions and I set out. At sundown I returned,

having found not a single human being. I got more accurate directions and set out again the following day.

John was sitting by the fire in the hogan. He was perhaps eighteen years old; had been handsome but was now wasted away, hollow-eyed, pale, not much more than skin and bones. I was almost certain of tuberculosis and had taken the precaution of bringing a wide-mouthed bottle along. Getting a sputum specimen was not easy. Despite the confidence that the sand painting had inspired, there remained the knowledge that a powerful medicine man could do much if he got possession of anything—hair, fingernails, excreta—belonging to anyone. With my still greatly limited command of the Navajo tongue it wasn't easy, but I simply had to say that I couldn't do a thing for the boy unless I got this specimen. I got it. I cautioned him against spitting on the ground, told him and his mother of the necessity of boiling all dishes and spoons that he used. Then some prayers and a blessing, and I took off. At that time there was a faint horse trail along the north bank of the river, and Beshlagai apparently knew it well enough. Next day the specimen went off to Fort Defiance with a letter, and in a few days the answer came: "Bring the boy in here without delay." Another salesman's job—to try to explain what a hospital is, and how people are cared for in one, how they must do what they are told to do and how it might take many months to effect a cure—and even to suggest that it might be too late. Believe me, much prayer ascended on high as I spurred Beshlagai over that trail once more; to my surprise both the patient and the parents consented. I told them to be at the Mission soon after sunup the following day but cautioned against riding fast. Perhaps I should have recommended using a wagon in which John could have lain, but Navajos ride so easily that I thought there would be less wrenching of the lesions if he rode than if he lay in the springless wagon, bumping over a quite unimproved road.

At the hospital at Fort Defiance Dr. Sedlack gave John immediate attention. X-rays confirmed the diagnosis and John was put to bed. John's father had come with us, and his X-ray showed healed scars in abundance. Only a powerful physique could have pulled him through. Dr. Sedlack was so impressed by the answers I gave about our work that he virtually closed his office for the day and took me on a tour of the hospital, from the operating rooms under the skylights to the morgue in the basement. He introduced me to the heads of the departments with unrestrained enthusiasm as "the man who chose the most God-forsaken part of the Reservation in which to settle and work," and in response to the invariable counterquestion, "Where is that?" he would say, "Well, *you* probably never heard of it, but it's up here . . ."—spreading his hands over the Utah strip as shown on the maps which adorned the walls. In nearly every case he was right: they never *had*. Many, despite having looked at the maps innumerable times, said they didn't realize that the reservation extended into Utah. Then he would wind up with, "Well, you're *going* to hear of it, because we're going to do things for those people if I have to go up there myself."

It is years since Dr. Sedlack left Fort Defiance, but he is still "helping those people"—if it's only by reading X-rays.

16

Lengthening days reminded us that spring could not be far behind, and we had to think about getting the east wing started. When the Easter response to our mimeographed newsletter put a few hundred dollars in the bank, I sent out a call for Shoodi and Tom to come and confer. I didn't for a minute think I knew all about Navajos, but I had learned a thing or two about hiring men by the day in the autumn, when the days grew short but the payroll remained the same. Convinced that much of the trouble between Indians and whites was due to a failure in communication, I arranged for Dan to be present as both witness and interpreter.

I laid it on the line simply.

"Listen. You two built that west wing. I am ready to hire you to build the east wing. They will be alike, except for facing in opposite directions, and the west wall, inside the cloisters, will not be of rock but of boards which we will put in; also the windows will be larger, making less mason work."

Dan interpreted, and they seemed to understand.

"Now," I continued, "that other job you did for day's wages. It was not fair. You didn't work a full day after the first week. When the sun went down earlier you quit earlier, and when the sun rose later you started work later. But you always took off time for lunch and a rest after lunch. So I paid you much more than you earned.

"This job will be done on contract. You will get paid in four payments: the first when the masonry work is up to the level of the bottoms of the windows, the second when it is up to the tops of the windows, the third when it is ready for the rafters, and the last when you have brought it up to the level of the tops of the rafters."

Again Dan interpreted. Their only question was, "How much money?"

"You must tell me. You know how long you worked on the west wing. You know how much *more* that required than this one will. So figure it out, and if your figure is reasonable you've made a contract."

When this was explained to them, they went into a huddle. I didn't suppose they really knew how much money they had received; hardly ever had the amount of the payroll been the same in any two weeks, owing to the irregularity of their working. To my amazement they came up with a figure that was within a few dollars of their total pay for the west wing with its five walls, plus the work done on the gables of the Mission House—something over seven hundred dollars.

I started to roll up the plans, thanked Dan for his help and made as if the interview were over. If they could put on an act, I could perhaps play opposite and we might see where all this would lead. They wanted to know what was wrong with the figure.

"Listen," I said, "I paid too much for the first job. This job is much less than the first job, yet you want the same money. I'll find some Navajos who really want to work."

Screened through Dan, this produced a plea for some further parley. They started shaving off fifty dollars at a time. I just shook my head. After an exceptionally long and painful refiguring Dan began to laugh. I asked to be let in on it.

"Ya gotta hand it to 'em, Father. They got reason. See, they say when you're workin' on day's wages, you take it kinda easy-like: you select a rock and shape it a bit and try it in place, and light a cigarette, and study it a while, then take the rock down and shape it some more, and try it in place, and when it fits you take it down again, lay your mud, set the rock back, point up the joints, throw away your cigarette and start looking for another rock. But when you work on *contract,* boy, you rush to get things done and you wear out your clothes and you wear out your shoes, and you don't get time to rest and you *gotta* have more money!"

Irresistible as this logic seemed, I ground the men down to a four-hundred-dollar figure, and told them they would have to have the footings in and the walls three courses high by the seventh of June, the day before Corpus Christi Day, as Bishop Moulton was coming to lay the cornerstone. We had the batter boards set up, and a good pile of building stone. The men could start when ready.

The project "Summer Workers," which later became so important an item in our life and work, had not at this time been thought of, but circumstances united to give us a start. A young geologist in the employ of Vanadium Corporation (at this time uranium was still what my old dictionary calls "a useless mineral"), whose duties often brought him into our area, had a problem. His ten-year-old son was completing his first year in a convent school in New Mexico and there was no place for him to go for the summer. The geologist was on the road all the time—no life for a young boy. How about our taking him in, for a consideration, helping him a bit to keep up his studies and having him help with such chores as fitted his strength? I saw no harm in it, we could use the "consideration," and on the last day of May I brought the boy in from the nearest bus stop.

Terry proved a real asset. He was eager to work and to learn, well-mannered and obedient. He could handle a pony and bring in the cows at milking time, feed chickens and pigs, hoe weeds and even do a bit of irrigating. Brother Michael was jubilant. "We can have a thurifer for Corpus Christi Day! Oh, that is, if we had vestments for him." He and Helen went into one of those conspiracies, and before long an old black dress of Aunt Lu's had become a cassock and a cotton petticoat a surplice. Terry was getting instructions in the handling of a censer and things really looked up for the liturgical revival.

Toward the end of the week I began to get a bit concerned about our contractor. Corpus Christi Day would be the following Thursday. The batter boards looked rather dreary and forgotten at the site of the east wing, and what if there were no place to lay the cornerstone? If I was lacking in the intensity of my concern, Brother Michael made up for it. "What are we going to *do*?" was his cry.

We had the cornerstone. Dick Nielson, who has been mentioned in his capacity as ditch boss in the Bluff Irrigation Company, had lost a building by fire some years before. It had been one of those impressive turn-of-the-century houses built in the days of Bluff's greatest prosperity, several specimens of which still stand. All that was left of Dick's house was a pile of squared building stone. "Take any one of them rawks you like," he said. We did. With a hammer and thirty-penny spike it was easy to cut the date and the St. Christopher brand. The sepulcher for papers and what-not we decided to forego.

Trinity Sunday came. Still no contractors. But as the sun hung low in the sky we heard the creak of wagons. Shoodi and Tom, with their tents and gear, were not going to fail us. Their tents were pitched and fires started before dark. Early in the morning they were at work; before sundown the trenches were dug and the footings in place. We had the door frames ready for them, and by Tuesday evening two courses of masonry were completed. By Wednesday noon they decided to knock off and wait for the bishop.

We had been using the indoor altar since Thanksgiving Day, but for the special ceremonies of Corpus Christi we planned to use again the outdoor altar which had been our first masonry project. The brush windbreak and shade had of course withered and dried during the winter, and on this Wednesday morning I went out and gathered as much brush and cottonwood branches as the pickup would allow, and using the back of the pickup for a ladder, started setting the branches overhead, to protect the congregation from the already severe rays of the sun. I was barely conscious of two cars arriving—they drew up at the back door of the Mission House. My costume at the moment consisted of a pair of khaki shorts and sandals. A voice behind me said, in the kindest tones imaginable, "I asked Brother Juniper if that were one of your Indians up there, but he said it was Father Liebler." I dropped to earth and greeted the bishop in proper style, but he was not satisfied with that. My sweating torso and arms were in his embrace. "My boy, my boy! A year you've been here and only today we meet! I'm so happy to be here! This is one of the proudest days of my life! Wonderful! Wonderful! But I must mind my manners. Father, this is Archdeacon Bulkley—Dean Gardiner of our catheral—Remmister Argyle, rector of Good Shepherd, Ogden—and Mr. Frank Gregory of Emory House on the University of Utah campus."

17

Corpus Christi Day dawned into a clear sky. The bishop offered an early Mass in the Mission House, and after breakfast we began to prepare for the special ceremonies for the day. Of course, at that time we had no converts and could ask no help in sacred things from the Navajos; however, the advent of the clergy and of Mr. Gregory solved the problem of carriers of the canopy. Terry, of course, had learned his job well, Brother Juniper was master of ceremonies, and Brother Michael led the singing. Navajos had begun to arrive soon after sunrise, and a considerable number of Bluffites attended—mostly out of friendship, not unmixed with curiosity.

The clergy sang the propers of the Mass, including the stupendous "Pange Lingua" of St. Thomas Aquinas, and their ceremonial conformity would certainly not have revealed to any but the most skilled observer that this was their first opportunity of participating in such a service. The Mission House was our only building, so of course we made the procession around that, small girls sprinkling flowers and Melvin, barefoot, sounding the hand bell. All the people present joined in the "parade," and if they had little idea of the significance of the ceremony, at least they made it clear that their hearts were full of good will. Mass, Procession and Benediction over, I made my second sand painting. Its theme was the love of the Saviour represented by His pierced Heart flowing into the chalice, as was so often portrayed on banners of the Five Wounds which rallied the resistance to Erastian Reformation in England.

The ladies from Bluff helped with the refreshments that followed—in fact, many of them brought food with them—and we were able to serve all who came. Meanwhile the stonemasons were sitting patiently by the cornerstone, having mixed the mud mortar and holding their trowels in readiness.

Bishop Moulton made a sermon that is still remembered by many who were there. In a sense he was introducing us to the people. I know this sounds strange: he had never been within three hundred miles of Bluff before, and when I first wrote to him he had seemed quite uninformed of the fact that there were Navajos within his state. But Bishop Moulton was a widely known personality throughout Utah and a close friend of the Mormon hierarchy, and his picture had appeared with regularity in the Salt Lake City newspapers, as he was prominent in all civic causes and improvement measures. We at the Mission were quite unknown except to the few who had from the first befriended us, and not a little suspicion remained in the minds of the community of Bluff. German spies, Communist fifth-columnists, Jesuits disguised as Episcopalian missionaries, fugitives from justice—there might have been no end of the possible explanations of our presence. But the genial, soul-warming personality of Bishop Moulton effectively laid these ghosts.

The "corner rock" also was well and truly laid. The sun was nearing the western horizon before all the guests departed.

Shoodi and Tom took the rest of the day off, but by early morning they began to vindicate their opinion and mine of contract labor. The days were long now, and they took advantage of every minute. Before the end of the week they had the walls up to the level of the bottom of the windows, and the first payment was duly made. We were busy keeping them supplied with building materials. It took me a long time to realize what a lot of stone was needed even for a foot-thick masonry job: a pile one would estimate to be adequate for a skyscraper seemed to disappear in no time. The Ford pickup was kept on the go. The next two payments were earned and paid in as many weeks, the last in a day and a half! I think the masons themselves were convinced of the value of contract over day's work. Anyway, they were pleased, and we were pleased if exhausted.

Not the least of our worries toward the end of this project was getting the pine logs from the mountains for rafters. As soon as we began to realize how rapidly the masonry job was nearing completion under the contract arrangement (our previous estimate of speed had been based upon the day's-wages arrangement—something quite different), we knew we'd have to get them soon. It was a day's work to cut them, under the usual arrangement with the Forestry Department, and drag them to a central spot.

Woody was the answer. How many times in the years to come would Woody turn out to be the answer! I think I made a hit with him at our first meeting by guessing his age after finding out that Woody stood for Woodrow. I had pulled the same trick in my earlier days—if I met a boy named Dewey I would bet him he was born in 1898. Woody had come to Bluff with a family of three boys and a girl. He had many gifts, could overhaul a car engine, repair a tractor, level and prepare a field for planting, build a house or drill a well—but he couldn't work under a boss. The independent spirit!

"Why, I could bring them logs down for you in my flat-bottom truck in no time," Woody claimed. I told him how long they were. "Just need a red rag, I don't care how far they stick out in back." But he found out that he *did* care. "I don't know yet how I done it. Them windin' roads down from that little ol' mountain—thirty miles of 'em and I swear my front wheels never touched the ground once!"

About this time there arose a rumor that the governor of Utah was to visit Bluff. There was considerable excitement. No state governor within the memory of man had been in these parts. Brother Michael thought we should dust off our best attire and go into Bluff to pay our respects. I opposed this: we had work to do, and I was sure the governor wouldn't care whether we went in or not. Olin came galloping up. "Governor Maw and three carloads of big shots from state and county are on their way. He says the main reason he come to Bluff is to see the mission!"

There was no time to dust off our best attire, hardly enough to dust off those we were wearing. The cars were approaching. The county commissioners and their families, the sheriff and a few lesser officers made up the caravan with the governor and his bodyguard, secretary and of course Mrs. Maw. He was most gracious. If the big shots had never heard of St. Christopher's Mission, they didn't let it appear—but the leading citizens of Bluff still had their mouths open in amazement that the governor should ask to come there.

He spoke the usual kind words about our "work" (we were ashamed that so much of it, up to this time, had been just getting ourselves settled) and asserted his deep interest and concern for the Indians. This, it must be remembered, was before the changed attitude of the Mormons, and it reflected much credit upon him. The Navajos could not vote, and were considered at best a nuisance to the stockmen of the area, who *could* vote.

Uranium and oil had not yet been discovered on the Reservation. He asked about our needs. I always grow limp in the presence of such a question, but Helen was more than equal to it. She had stories of fording the river to take medication to sick Navajos at times when the spring thaws raised huge sand waves; of the danger of quicksands—a Navajo had recently been drowned despite the fact that the Navajos were generally considered to know the river bed and its perils—in a word, what was needed was a bridge across the San Juan at Bluff. The governor was all ears. He patted Helen's hand with paternal assurance. "I'll see to it personally. You will have a bridge."

One of the outstanding events of that summer was a squaw dance in our immediate vicinity. Scores of these are held every year on the Reservation, but it is a big Reservation and the dances are widely scattered. Every letter we get from a Navajo traveling far from home in the summer asks the question "Is there any squaw dance going on over there?" Most tourists who care to see something of the life of the people manage to see at least a little part of one of these affairs. Few realize that it is not primarily a social occasion but a religious healing ceremony. Its proper name is *ndaa* (probably plural of the word for enemy) or *ndaají*, meaning war way or enemy way. The ending *jí* is usually translated side—as right side, left side, elephant side (Republican) or burro side (Democrat), but it is also added to the names of most ceremonial chants, when it is perhaps better rendered way, or path. The origin of the dance is traditionally traced to the resuscitation by their mother of the slayers of enemy gods when they had swooned after their deadly combat. The common term *squaw dance* was undoubtedly coined by whites, and places the emphasis upon the most conspicious but least important phase of the ceremony. Of course the word *squaw* is not a Navajo word: it is an Algonquin word which, like *moccasin* and to a lesser extent *papoose*, has been carried across the continent by whites. Fortunately *wigwam* and *wampum* have not penetrated the Southwest, unless it be in the tourist-trap "trading posts" of the small cities. But the term squaw dance has been tacitly accepted by English-speaking Navajos, and it isn't worth a crusade to try to stop it. *Squaw* is another matter. It was used in a derogatory way, along with *buck,* to distinguish Indian women and men from whites. We have fought it by the simple expedient of using the term *lady,* specifying race only when necessary for clarity. After all, it's their country.

The squaw dance is a three-night affair; it involves three different locations, usually five to twenty miles apart. The removal of the sacred prayer stick, ornamented with tufts of grass, feathers and wool, from one location to another by a girl on horseback, accompanied by outriders, is an essential part of the rite. The stick, called *agaltsin,* has been most carefully prepared with suitable prayers and anointing with animal grease and ashes. Incisions are made with the fingernail representing a bow and a hair pack. (There are said to be schools of churchmanship, one favoring the opening of these incisions from the top, the other from the bottom, of the stick; however, these schools have learned comprehensiveness and coexistence, it seems, and either type of incision is considered sufficiently effective.) Sacred buckskin is the only kind that may be used—this is taken from a deer slain without wounding—and the dewclaws of the deer, with the tail feather of a turkey, complete the preparations. All participants are of course dressed in their best and most colorful clothes and jewelry. The patient, the cooks, the drummer and singers may be moved from one squaw-dance location to another by automobile, and nowadays this is almost invariably done, but at the time of this first one there were very few if any cars. A few white families from Bluff drove out, and at least one enterprising young farmer brought a pickup-load of melons and did a thriving business. Several Ute families came down from their homes on White Mesa, some fifteen miles to the north.

Randolph was a sort of master of ceremonies, and he had invited us to be present at any parts of the rites we wanted to see. I asked him to explain that missionaries were not dancers, and that if we came the girls would have to respect us accordingly and not expect us either to dance or to pay them off. He made the announcement, and for the most part it seemed to be accepted, except that Brother Michael's masculine charms proved a little too much for some of the ardent damsels; however, by appealing to the master of ceremonies for his intercession, virtue was triumphant.

The chief importance of this squaw dance in our eyes was its value as a publicity medium, to make known to the Navajos of the outlying area that our Mission was here and what it aimed to do. Brother Juniper reported a conversation with a Navajo from the Oljeto area whose name was Hugh Black on the official records but who was known to his own people as Olta Nez ("Tall School") because in his youth he had attended a school that was two stories high, down at Tuba City. Hugh had heard that we were planning a school.

"We don't like it, school. Washington make school for Navajo kids, piddy soon cut off their hair, cut girls hair piddy short, too. Kids forget how to herd sheep, girls forget how to weave. Wat you gonna make school for?"

Brother asked if Hugh were glad he had learned to speak and understand English and to read and write.

"Yeah, all right talk English, read and write. Good. But I just went lil bit to school, and I didn't forget herdin sheep and raisin corn. And jus as soon I quit school I never cut my hair again, and in two years I could tie up my hair pack all same my fodda."

"Well, did you see Father Liebler with his long hair? Does he look like one who is going to make the children cut off their hair?"

Hugh's face burst into a grin. "Yeah, I's thinkin bout that. Maybe your school be different. Not like Washington school. At be good."

Hugh was a man of importance in his community, and word soon went abroad that these missionaries were not enemies of the Navajo way but were going to try to help them within the framework of the Navajo tradition. Many Navajos from the country to the east of us came also, and carried back to Montezuma Creek and to the Aneth area a similar message. This was to bear fruit later.

18

Marie Jones rode her horse with the dignity of a queen. A brightly colored parasol shielded her from the direct rays of the sun. This was back in the early days of our building project, when we were setting up the outdoor altar. She dismounted, walked up to me with hand extended, then shook hands with those working with me. Obviously she knew no English; conversation was not going to be easy. The Angelus rang, and we all recited the Bible verses and prayers, after which I tried to explain that the bell had been a call to prayer and this was our response. She smiled, and said very simply in Navajo, "Prayer is good." Put into English, it sounds banal, but there was a deep beauty in it. Marie was under average height, slender and of delicate features. I can't recall now whether it was on the occasion of this first visit or later that I noticed a swelling in her neck, but as time went on it became more pronounced and although her eyes looked quite normal, I suspected an exophthalmic goiter. I gently led up to the possibility of getting her to the medical center at Fort Defiance for treatment. I finally reached Dr. Sedlack by telephone, and he agreed to admit her at once if we could get her there.

I saddled Mogi and rode out to the camp near the mouth of Recapture Wash. To my surprise both she and her husband agreed, and promised to be at the Mission by sunrise next day. We had an early Mass and took off, Helen, Brother Juniper and I. Helen and Brother Juniper hadn't had a day off for a year, and I made up my mind that there was just one place I wanted them and myself to be on St. Dominic's Day, and that was the Pueblo Santo Domingo, if we could possibly arrange it. This errand of mercy for Marie gave the occasion. We delivered her to Dr. Sedlack, who renewed his vow either to get to us or send one of his doctors for a clinic just as soon as possible. Then we took off for Gallup and Albuquerque—it was rather good to be back on a paved highway after a year of gravel and dirt—and thence northward to the Pueblo. We got there the afternoon of August 3: Monica Silva greeted us as old friends and gave us the key to the city—only cautioning us, in case we had forgotten, that cameras were not favorably regarded. On previous visits I had heard stories of tourists who were compelled to remove the films from their cameras or, if they were obstinate, had had their cameras forcibly taken from them and sometimes destroyed. Final preparations for the dance were being taken care of in a leisurely but efficient manner. In the great plaza between the two kivas the booth of evergreen branches had been erected to receive the statue of the patron saint; the whole plaza was being swept and cleaned. I was less than pleased to note that concessions had been let to carousel and dance pavilions and to pop and popcorn vendors, but we were to find that these did not interfere with the proper celebration of the feast.

Santo Domingo Pueblo had been under an interdict for several years—there was no Mass, no baptism or marriage had been performed—but now all matters of dispute between the Pueblo and Holy Church had been settled, and the Archbishop of Santa Fe himself celebrated the Mass. It was fairly well attended, although it must be admitted that had the whole Pueblo been there, the church could not have accommodated them, let alone the visitors. After the Mass the great gilded statue of the patron, St. Dominic, was placed on a litter carried by four Very Important People, a canopy carried by four more being held over it; in this style the statue was solemly conducted to the booth prepared for it, while hundreds of pious people chanted interminably a curiously lilting tune to the "Ave Maria" in Spanish.

Soon after the statue had been put in place, surrounded by innumerable lighted candles, the first dance team came out of one of the kivas, said proper devotions before the patron, and began the dance to the accompaniment of a huge drum and a chorus of twenty or thirty singers, led by a pole bearer carrying the symbol of the clan. In contrast to the Navajos, who have several dozen clans, the Pueblos have only two clans in each community. Each has its kiva—one stands at each end of the plaza—and its dance team. Seemingly independent of the dancers were the *koshare,* commonly spoken of as clowns but very obviously an integral part of the religious ceremony. Their characteristic action seemed to be the drawing of rain from the clouds to the earth below. After perhaps a half hour the other clan's team appeared and took over, while the first team retired to the kiva for rest and relaxation.

The old Spanish missionaries have been accused of converting the Indians without changing their religion further than substituting a multitude of Christian saints for a multitude of heathen deities. I have talked with many Pueblo Indians, both at Santo Domingo and elsewhere, and while there is quite naturally a considerable number of skeptics, indifferentists or plain materialists, I think that the great majority are reasonably well instructed Catholics, equal in this respect to the general average of American second-generation Irish or German Catholics, and not only satisfied with their religion but ready to suffer for it. Whether or not the Spanish missionaries were uniformly successful—after all, who is?—I believe that they were motivated by the same principles as St. Paul when he preached the "unknown God" to the philosophers on Mars' Hill, and as the missionaries to the Teutonic people who Christianized a festival celebrating the lengthening of the days in late December and gave to Christianity the riches of Christmas.

I cannot dismiss Santo Domingo without mentioning the delightful salesmanship of our hostess, Monica. She returned to her house after the dance, still dressed in the ceremonial costume, with the wooden headdress and her beautiful long hair, only slightly tinged with gray, hanging down to her thighs. "You know, Father, I dance all day with my people, my husband's people. I can't do like these people who come from Tesuque and San Juan and Sia and the other Pueblos and bring their pottery and the tourists buy them. I wonder if you would like to see my pottery? I have one here . . ." and she brought out an exquisite bowl, beautifully decorated, and so thin that although it was probably twenty or twenty-two inches in diameter, it weighed not more than two pounds, and when tapped with the knuckles it rang like a gong. Brother Juniper bought it at once, despite the obvious difficulty of getting it home without breaking it (we did!) and Helen and I took a few smaller items. Pueblo pottery is made without the use of a wheel; it is laboriously built up from the bottom by laying coils of clay that has been rolled into a rope and squeezing this to the desired thickness by hand.

Marie was returned home after a successful operation on her thyroid gland, but the routine chest X-ray revealed the presence of the number one killer of Navajos—tuberculosis. The hospital authorities had urged her to return to the sanatorium, but she refused, and this refusal she maintained for the rest of her all-too-short life. However, she wanted to know more about the faith that made people willing to take time and spend money to deliver patients to a hospital more than two hundred and fifty miles away, and with my slowly growing vocabulary of Navajo I was able to at least outline God's plan of salvation. This was for her, she decided, and she asked for baptism. By that time she was too weak to ride or to walk, and I carried the Blessed Sacrament to her—twenty-five miles in our pickup—and a few days later her son, Tom, came to tell us that she had died. The body was already buried when the news came, but Tom showed me where the grave was and I performed the burial rites, and we later had a Requiem Mass for her.

19

Considering the time and expense of erecting a new building, it didn't seem right to delay the opening of a school. Acting on Dan's suggestion, we got in touch with the proper authorities and arranged for the "permanent loan" of a CCC shack dating from depression days, one of a group of such buildings standing on the outskirts of Blanding. We had to go a hundred miles north to Moab to find a flat-bed truck large enough to move it, but we did, and it arrived at the Mission while we were in Santo Domingo. Brother Michael had selected a spot where it could slide to earth and where it has stood ever since. Of course, we had desks and blackboard, but not the traditional type. The square ends of orange crates on the laps of the children had to serve as desks, and pieces of wallboard coated with slating compound made admirable blackboards. Early in September we declared school to be in session. Randolph was our publicity agent, and he assured us that everything was going fine.

At nine o'clock we were ready for them. Helen was to be the head teacher, Brother Michael was to teach music, Brother Juniper handicrafts, and I think (don't laugh) that I was to help out with arithmetic. But not a child showed up.

We couldn't just laugh *this* off. We had gone to a lot of trouble and some expense, and certainly it shouldn't be our policy to let the Navajos think that we were a one-way street, we offering everything and they taking what they liked and offering nothing, not even their time. Randolph assured us that they had no such ideas. They appreciated all we were doing and trying to do, but this was the time of year when the Navajos culled out the lambs they were going to sell in order to keep their herds down to the number specified in their grazing permits, and the children had to help. Just be patient; they will come.

The next day came one of those storms—torrents of rain—and activity was limited to building up dikes to keep our buildings from being washed away.

But the third day of the school term began to show us what we were up against. Babies in cradleboards, grandmothers and grandfathers, and just about every age in between—all clamored for education! Young men with jangling spurs, some old men in the traditional split pants of the past generation and the hair pack (still all but universal among mature men), and children of all ages filled the little shack to overflowing. Some decision seemed necessary. Nobody, not even our Helen, could teach such a motley group, not one of whom understood more than a few words of English. Perhaps unwisely I decided to muddle through—let them see for themselves whether they really wanted education enough to work hard for it. It was rough on Helen, I must say, for despite the help that the rest of us were scheduled to give, it soon became apparent that she had the real burden. But as the days went by the muddling process began to tell. The spur janglers found that they were not going to learn to read and write in a few days; most of the older men and women were reconciled to ending their days without a formal education. The last problem was one typical among a people accustomed to seeing every opportunity and taking advantage of it. Here was their solution of the baby-sitting problem! We made a strict rule of taking no children under six. No official vital statistics were then available, and what could we do when a mother solemnly assured us that these toddlers were fully six years old! We ended up by barring those in cradleboards and letting the other tiny tots "audition" the classes in the hope that they would absorb something and not take too much of the older children's time when they had to "go out."

But during the first two or three weeks it seemed we had only auditioners. Not a syllable could we get out of any pupil. They sat stolidly with their colorful Pendleton blankets pulled up to a level just below the eyes; they watched everything that went on and heard everything that was spoken. Classroom work became a lecture, producing no visible reaction. But the passage of time justified the heroic effort. After a few weeks the strings of their tongues were loosened, and to our surprise we found that they had absorbed a good deal of what had been told them during their days of silence. From that time onward we felt that the school effort had justified itself. To be sure, attendance was less than perfect; what seemed to us a very slight excuse would keep a child out for days on end. But I am sure now that this feeling on our part was due to a failure to appreciate the importance of the home in Navajo culture. The sheep had to be herded out to pasture every morning, and this was traditionally the task of children, adults taking over only at lambing time, shearing, dipping and the autumnal culling. A healing ceremony performed over any member of the family, or even over a relative who might live several miles away, was ample reason for not attending school.

20

One of the staff at Fort Defiance Hospital to whom Dr. Sedlack had introduced me was Dr. Logan. Imagine my surprise when there came from him a rapidly scribbled note to the effect that he would have to be in Kayenta (seventy-five miles southwest of us) early in November and that he would try to get to us for a clinic a few days after that. No definite date; expect him when we saw him—no indication of how long he could stay. But we started the publicity circulating: a doctor was actually coming to treat any Navajos who were sick, and we would spread the word as soon as he arrived. We brought in both our ponies from the open range, fed them precious hay and kept them saddled. As soon as we had greeted the arriving doctor, we set out to spread the word. He had hardly had time to wash up and unpack his various kits when the patients began to come. Almost every imaginable ailment, and various imaginary ailments, were treated. Vaccinations were given, and the doctor was especially impressed by the confidence of both children and adults. He spoke of the difficulty of reaching the people in many parts of the Reservation, and he had heard stories of the "wild mans" in the Utah strip, but he was pleased over his reception here. Simply because there had been no ophthalmologist at Fort Defiance, he had been made the "eye man" there, but his specialty had in no way impaired his skill in the diagnosis and treatment of other ills. He even examined the Navajos' teeth, and although he declared that he had never seen such perfect specimens in both children and adults—many in their twenties and thirties had not a single cavity—he did find enough to elicit the promise that next time he would bring a dentist, if they could somewhere dig up a treadle-style drill.

The news that there was a doctor at the Mission quickly drifted to the white population in Bluff, and there were timid inquiries as to whether his services might, under the circumstances, be available to them. He kindly explained that as an employee of the United States Indian Service he had to limit his ministrations to Indians; but the term Indian might be broadly applied to persons who had "any considerable strain of Indian blood." A curious ethnological phenomenon suddenly appeared: Indian ancestors became more numerous. Dr. Logan, with a twinkle in his eye, and perhaps tongue in cheek, did what he could for these people. When he took off the next morning, we knew that a real friend of humanity had been among us.

Early in December a Navajo rode in from near the mouth of Recapture Wash to report that Jim Hatathley's year-old boy was seriously ill. His big brother, John, was at that time still in the sanatorium at Fort Defiance, and occasional letters from him seemed to indicate improvement; this gave Jim the encouragement to look to us for help. I rode out to his camp and was shocked to find the child in frightful condition—far too weak, I thought, to stand a trip to the hospital. With the father's permission I baptized him Joseph, but I had no medication that I thought could possibly do any good. Toward the end of the week Brother Juniper and I rode out to see how he might be progressing and found that the burial had already taken place. We barely avoided stepping over the ashen trail that marked the route on which a body had been carried from hogan to grave. The parents were in the midst of the four-day retirement, or retreat, that always follows a death in the family, so we didn't disturb them but had some prayers at the grave and returned home.

21

By the beginning of Lent, 1945, I knew that we shouldn't put off the job we had been sent out here to do: preaching the Gospel and preparing for the sacraments. I had not yet acquired any ease in conversational Navajo, much less the ability to preach or instruct extemporaneously. We were nearing the end of our second year, however, and we felt that we had gained the confidence of the people, although they continued for several years to ask when we planned to leave. Upon being assured that we had no such plan, they would ask *why* we had come—what was it we were after? What did we want? It seemed beyond their comprehension that any white man—or any man at all, for that matter—would come and live among them unless he expected some material reward.

The answer to our language problem was at hand. The Franciscans published a catechism which covered the main points of the faith, and for the most part it was in simple enough Navajo to be understood by children. We could not of course use the catechetical method, because the people were just too shy to pipe up the responses, but by weaving the answers to the questions into a continuous narrative it was not hard to present a very interesting story. We encouraged all who lived near us to attend the evening service (we had been holding Matins and Vespers publicly every day for some months past), and at the end I would sit down and read off the instruction. When Randolph was able to come, he proved to be a great help, and I think he amplified what I had to say without unduly running off into heresy. I aimed at Holy Saturday, the Vigil of Easter, as the day for public baptisms. Instruction covered Creation, the Fall of Man, Redemption, a brief summary of the earthly life of the Redeemer, His Passion, Death, Resurrection and Ascension, the formation of the church and detailed instructions on all the sacraments, not omitting a bit of eschatology. Interest waxed high, and I looked forward to at least a dozen baptisms.

Came the great day. At that time it was still customary to hold the Easter Vigil in the forenoon, and we had good attendance. To my astonishment, when the font had been blessed and I turned and invited those who wished baptism to come forward, not one moved. I couldn't believe it! They had seemed so eager, and it never occurred to me that there would be any obstacle. Randolph had gone off to work on a railroad (at that time this was the only type of labor open to Navajos aside from sheepherding), so that I couldn't appeal to him for an explanation. Unwillingly to take no for an answer, I waited a little longer and repeated the invitation. With her elbow Sadie nudged her oldest son, Dan, and her daughter, Pauline, saying in a low voice, in Navajo, "These want it." They approached the portable font. "How about you?" I asked the others. They looked shyly at the ground and shook their heads.

So Dan and Pauline were baptized, and as far as I knew they were the first Navajos knowingly baptized in the state of Utah. It seemed a pathetically poor harvest for the weeks of preparations, but we tried to accept it thankfully.

I left the silver baptismal shell and the other paraphernalia on the little table by the door after the service had ended. I don't know why I did this, nor do I know now. It wasn't just carelessness; there must have been a subconscious motive. Early in the afternoon an old man came in, just to visit. He had not attended the instruction classes, but his daughter and her children had. His attention was caught by the silver baptismal shell. He had never seen anything like it. Navajos are fascinated by shells of any sort, and of course silver is familiar to them, but this combination struck him as strange and interesting and he started asking questions. Seldom had I so felt the poverty of my vocabulary, but I worked hard and produced all the words in Navajo that I had used in the instruction classes; I told him about the shells I had picked up as a boy along the shore of the ocean; I told of how the Indians on the East Coast had used shells (wampum) as a medium of exchange; of how when God the Son became Man, he was baptized in the river Jordan, how He died for our sins (the crucifix over the altar helped at this point) and how He sent His priests into all countries to preach and to baptize. And now here was I, a priest, preaching just to one man and ready to baptize him when he should be ready. I have no way of telling how much of this first impromptu instruction he understood, but he was definitely interested. The very next day he was at Mass, and from that day to his last illness fifteen years later he never missed a Sunday Mass. After we got to know him better, he told me his real Navajo name—a fine old war name—

but he was satisfied to be known by his somewhat similar-sounding nickname which meant a yucca fruit, date or banana: Hashk'aan. He was for many years a splendid example of the Christian life to the people of the area.

In those days one seldom saw a Navajo out after dark. At about sundown the evening meal was prepared and eaten, and then the family would sit around the fire and talk about the events of the day. Soon all would shake out their sheepskins and blankets and get into bed. But late on this Easter Eve two of Randolph's younger children came quietly into the Mission House. They just stood there. I asked what they wanted—this is not a rude question in Navajo but rather like our colloquial, "Well, friend, what's on your mind?" or "Can I help you?" as the store clerks say. Without a moment's hesitation they answered in Navajo, "Baptism!" I asked why they hadn't been there in the morning, and they explained that they had had to herd sheep. It took only a few moments to get the other staff members together, and the number of baptized Navajos in Utah was doubled!

Before we retired that night, I said to the other staff members, "Do you know what I feel like? Like a sportsman who spends half his winter getting his fishing pole, his hooks and flies, his creel and reel, all ready, then goes out for a week of fishing and comes back with a handful of minnows." But I repented before going to sleep and breathed hearty thanks to the God and Father of us all. A beginning had been made. Better a small beginning that might lead to greater things than a hysterical burst of evangelistic ardor that might soon wither and die. But the mystery remained for a while unsolved. I didn't have enough Navajo to understand any answers they might give to my question. It wasn't until Randolph returned from his work that I began to make progress toward the solution.

Although the Navajos of this area had never been evangelized, someone had warned me that it was not an unheard-of thing for hell-and-brimstone preachers to come through the country, call a meeting, present vivid verbal pictures through interpreters of heaven and hell, and then ask the people which they would prefer as a permanent environment. They would take all who elected heaven down to the river for immersion and instant salvation. In order to build up an attitude toward such a situation, when discussing baptism I had perhaps placed a disproportionate emphasis on the fact that baptism may not be repeated. Once done, it is done, and may not be redone. And one of the points I overlooked was that some of our adults had had a year or more at some distant school. The government schools in the early days not only allowed but insisted on religious and moral instruction, the children being dealt out like playing cards among the various types of missionaries who happened to be available in the area. Now, it seems that both Sadie and Stella, who attended the Lenten instruction classes, had had such experience, and although they had forgotten just about everything they learned in school, they had a vague idea that they had been baptized as small children. At least, I was pleased to note, the idea of the impossibility of repeating this sacrament had gone home. Once we had got to the root of the difficulty, I was faced with the greater one of explaining conditional baptism. But I worked on Randolph and made him repeat it back to me in his own words until I was sure that he had mastered the idea; then I had him explain it to the others. Since there was no way of finding out whether or not there had been a ceremony, and if so what matter, form or intention had been used, it seemed that conditional baptism was clearly indicated. So it came about that the two ladies, Sadie and Stella, with Randolph, Hashk'aan and a half dozen others, were eventually baptized, almost two years after our arrival.

About this time we were joined by another priest, Father Clement. He had been a missionary in the Philippines and had tried his vocation with the Franciscans. Having studied architecture before going to seminary, he would be familiar with building. We soon found that he was a creative artist in various fields, from water colors and vestments to cooking and singing. His presence was a great comfort to me, as I was beginning to feel very depressed over neglecting the vast area of the Utah strip which as yet I had not even explored, not to mention giving the people any pastoral ministrations.

It was during this spring of 1945 that we began the solemn observance of the Rogations, singing the Litanies in procession and blessing the gardens and hayfields. The idea caught the imagination of the people, and we had good attendance, beginning on St. Mark's Day and continuing on the days before Ascension. Usually there were very few at the beginning—they probably forgot about it until they heard us singing, and the procession that began with a handful would end with a considerable congregation. Not only people, but dogs also seemed caught up in the spirit of piety, and one puppy occasioned a bit of distraction when, in crossing the ladder bridge which spanned the irrigation ditch, he slipped between the rungs with all four feet. He was suspended by the belly on one rung, unable to get traction, crying pathetically for help (not always in unison or harmony with our responses of "Pray for us"). Before his yelps could effectively interrupt our devotions, Brother Michael swooped down on the poor pup, lifted him by the nape of the neck and set him down, pleased as punch, on the bank of the ditch, from which point he resumed his place in the procession.

In May, Dr. Logan came back to us, together with a dentist, Dr. Cutler. They worked manfully for the better part of three days, doing what they could with their limited equipment. (There wasn't even a proper dentist's chair; in fact, we had to borrow a common dining-room chair from Jennie Barton, and Dr. Cutler had to use an old-style treadle drill.) But history was being made; it was the first time, so far as we could ascertain, that any dental work had ever been done for the Navajos of the area.

Soon after this we began using the east wing as our chapel. It was not the best arrangement to have the altar in the common room, and by devoting the wing to nothing but church services we were able to lay the foundations for a special respect for the "House of God." We had some simple benches for pews and a piece of wrought-iron pipe fitted with a top, bottom and door for a tabernacle (it continued in use until the fire of 1964), and we began at once to have the inestimable blessing of the Reserved Sacrament. Daily offices of Vespers and Matins had been the rule since July 14 of the previous year—the anniversary of our arrival—even in the makeshift oratory in the common room.

I can't leave my account of that oratory without recalling a little accident which, unimportant in itself, seemed to be a symbol of our ideal of combining ritual propriety with complete informality. An old Navajo lady who complained of sore eyes came to me as I was working in the garden one afternoon. Helen had been given some accelerated courses by doctors on the staff of the Manhattan Eye, Ear, Nose and Throat Hospital in New York City, and I told the lady to go back to the house, and find that tall woman and tell her her troubles. Assuming that this was understood, I went on with the irrigating until the sun told me it was approaching Vespertide. Much to my surprise when I began Vespers, I saw the lady sound asleep in front of the altar. There was no reason to disturb her; and when it came time to cense the altar at the Magnificat, I stepped as gracefully as I could over the prostrate form and went about my business. Toward the end she sat up, blinked and took her place in the congregation. Medication followed in due time.

22

An opportunity to explore other parts of our area came to me in an unexpected way. Adorning the common-room walls were some water-color sketches I had made back in 1910. Norman Nevills, the intrepid San Juan River boatman, saw them and said that if I would make a water-color sketch of Rainbow Bridge, the largest of our natural arches, he would invite me as a guest on his next river trip. The trip took a week, about the middle of June. Five boats made up the fleet, and it was an experience never to be forgotten. Most of the members of the group were nationally known persons and were endowed with the charm and kindness that goes with really fine minds. I shall never cease to be touched by Randall Henderson's characterization of me in his *Desert Magazine*: "Father Liebler, the desert priest with hard hands and a soft heart." My only unpleasant memory of the trip lay in the fear that the sketch would be a disappointment to Norman, for I had done no serious sketching for thirty-five years, but he made no complaint and expressed himself as pleased with the effort. Actually I made three sketches, and he gave one of them back to me. It hangs in the common room to this day.

Monument Valley seemed the place to start holding services, now that Father Clement was here to maintain the daily Mass at the Mission and to see that all ran smoothly. Brother Michael, Dan Benally and Ted were to go with us. Dan Hayes offered to let us use a shack he had erected in the valley as a place to stay overnight when his crew worked the drag on the road in that area. I asked Dan to tell the Navajos down that way to expect us on the last Sunday in July—"Sort of tell them who we are, Dan, so they'll know what to expect," I begged.

"Hell, Father, you don't need no introduction. They know *you.* They call you the missionary that *does* some good, not just talks!"

So Dan's shack became the "Cathedral of Monument Valley" and with very little publicity beyond the native grapevine we found ourselves with a well-filled church. Harry Goulding and a photographer named Frank O'Brien who was a member of the state's Commission on Publicity and Natural Resources were the only non-Navajos there. After the Mass we stood around and chatted, although we didn't have the coffee hour which has become a tradition in the Episcopal church in recent years. An old medicine man named Little Gambler* had a good deal to say, but I didn't understand it very well, so Harry interpreted it for me. "He says that he knows about mission priests and what they

* The term *adakai* really means only a cardplayer, but since nobody would think of playing cards without stakes, the translation "gambler" is usually the accepted one. The adjective "little" may refer to diminutive size but is as likely to be equivalent to "junior."

are for. They have powerful prayers and can bring rain, even in the time of drought. We've been having drought for months now; many Navajos have taken sheep away from here to the higher ground. Soon the horses will die. Then the people will die. You should pray that we get rain."

I cannot adequately describe what happened then. I heard a voice say, "You will have rain day after tomorrow." Then I listened for more, and suddenly realized that *I* had said these words. I was really angry with myself and said (not aloud but to myself), "You idiot, what made you say that? What right have you to make such a promise? Apologize at once, or you'll be in a bad way with these trusting people." But no word of apology would come. There was a long and, to me, uncomfortable silence, and then the subject veered to other directions.

We broke a spring in the pickup and had trouble driving home, as the broken end of one leaf hit the brake drum when the wheels were turned to the right. Worrying our way through Snake Canyon, I had to back up and go forward, back and forward, to get around some of the sharp curves in the trail. There was no garage nearer than Blanding, and I took the pickup to Lyman's on Monday.

On Tuesday we could see black clouds and hear rumblings of thunder to the southwest. On Wednesday I rode to Blanding on the mail truck to bring the pickup back, and while waiting outside Lyman's a car came by, honked, backed and stopped. It was Frank O'Brien on his way back to Salt Lake City. I asked casually about yesterday's weather. "It was a wonderful rain, the best in many years and the first in many months. Yes, the ground really got well soaked yesterday." I could hardly hold back tears of gratitude. What could easily be called coincidence can never be that to me. Nor, by the same token, have I any idea of explaining it.

Dan Hayes dropped in at the Mission a few days later. "Say, Father, Old Adakai Yazhi wants to go into partnership with you. With him to collect from the Navvies and you to make the prayers, he says you and him could make a lot of money!"

Storm and sunshine study of Scotch Bluff. (Photo courtesy Caplan & Thompson)

The Mission House as we found it, July 1943

The main mission building finally completed, about 1944 (note the arch forms). (Photo courtesy George W. Thompson)

Father Liebler, snapped by a passing tourist, in the late 40's

Chapel and belfry, left; Mission House, right

Brother Juniper, clipboard in hand, under that famous first arch. (Photo courtesy Clifford Gedekoh)

eral view of Mission nds, about 1956

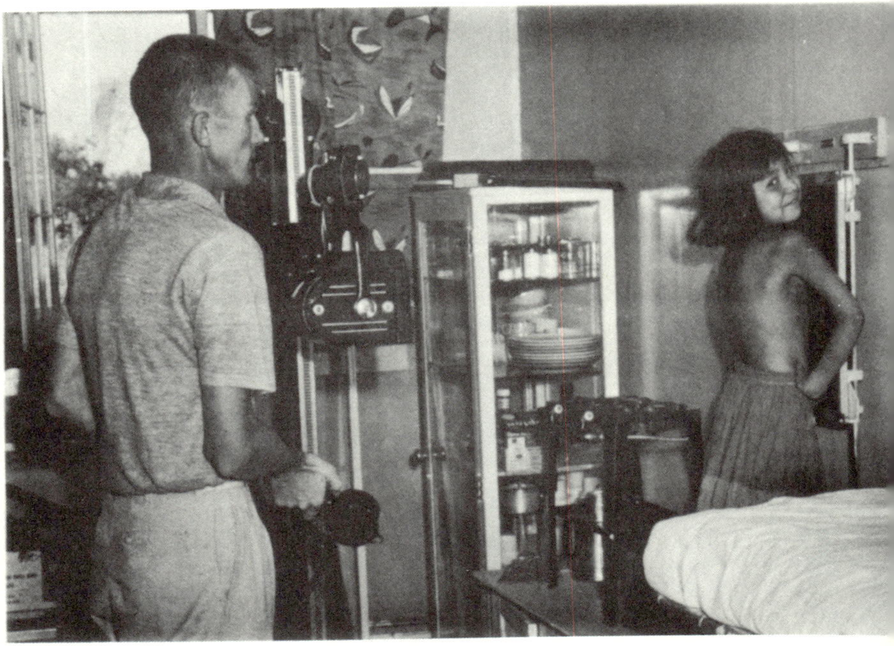

X-ray technician and machine provided by the State of Utah

Catherine, in gala attire, looks on as Government field nurse takes over

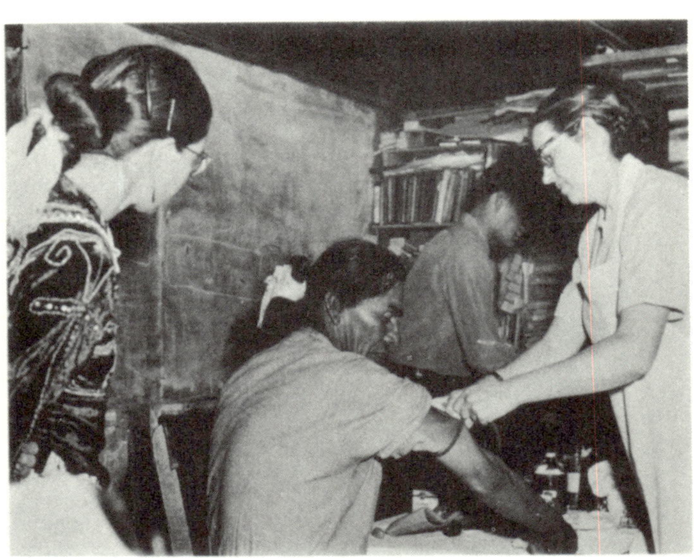

Dr. David Findley in front of "nosocome"

n the one-room "clinic" which erved from 1950 to 1954, a onvalescent patient undergoes ccupational therapy (quilt-naking). (Photo courtesy Cap-an & Thompson)

Rustic belfry and retired Penn. RR bell replace the frying pan and hammer handle that called us to prayer in the beginning

A group from first school. (Photo courtesy Clifford Gedekoh)

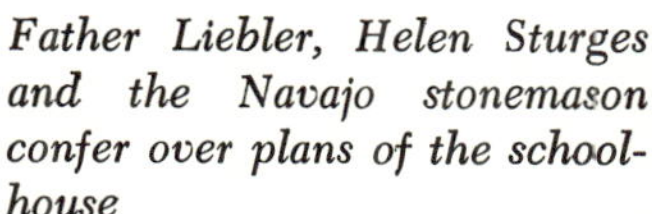

Father Liebler, Helen Sturges and the Navajo stonemason confer over plans of the schoolhouse

Soon after school got under way in the old CCC hut. (Photo courtesy George W. Thompson)

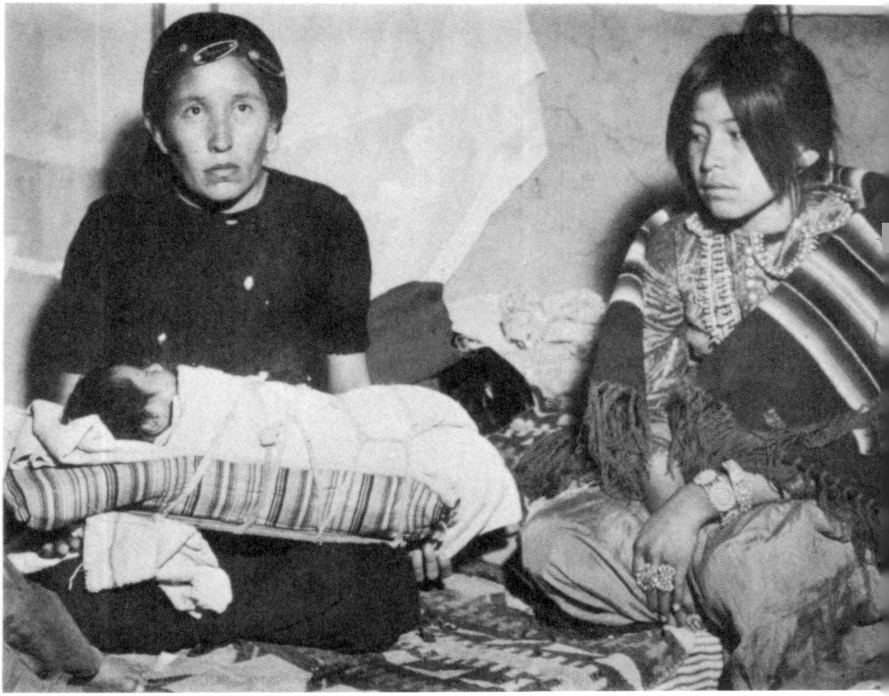

Hashk'aan, one of our earliest converts. (Photo courtesy Caplan & Thompson)

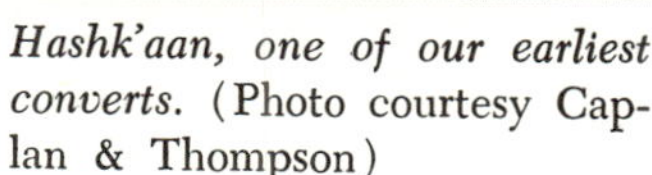

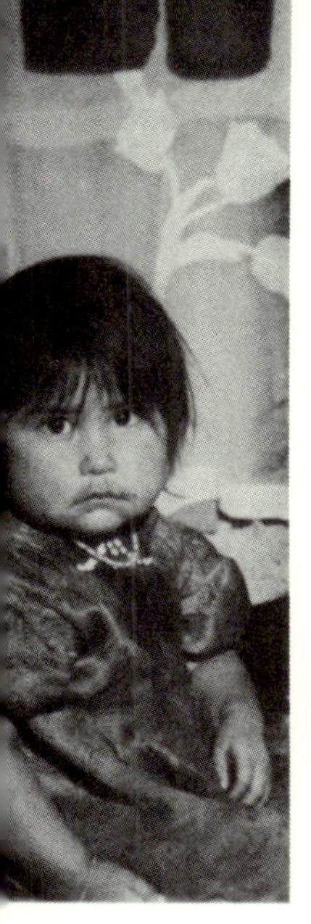

Daughter of the great Whitehorse and some of her children

An early visit to St. Mary of the Moonlight hogan church. Father Liebler, left front; Brother Juniper, standing, right rear

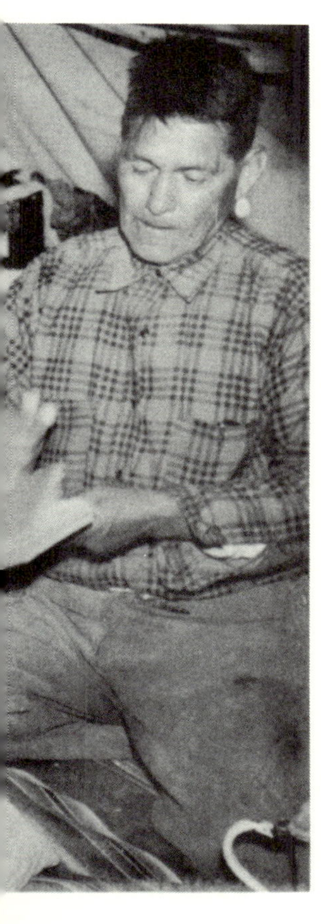

The preparation for a weaving operation. (Photo courtesy George W. Thompson)

Except for sheepherding, this means of transportation has nearly gone out. (Photo courtesy Clifford Gedekoh)

Toys are utilitarian

Jeannette gets a beauty treatment from Catherine Pickett

Shy damsels display family jewels

Every day is Mother's Day in Navajoland

At Bob Atene's camp, Oljeto, Utah, 1955. (Photo by Joan Liebler.)

Father Liebler demonstrating his expertise at a St. Christopher's Mission celebration. (Photo courtesy of Joan Liebler.)

The log church before it burned down in 1964.
(Photo courtesy of Joan Liebler.)

Harold Baxter Liebler, 1977.
(Photo courtesy of Joan Liebler.)

Harold and Joan Liebler, October 1978.
(Photo Courtesy of H. Jackson Clark.)

On the porch of the first building at Hat Rock Valley, near Oljeto, Utah.
(Photo courtesy of Joan Liebler.)

23

Among the prominent visitors of that summer was Senator Perry Jenkins, and he was particularly concerned over our lack of light. I had bought an old Army field dynamo with a capacity of something like five hundred watts, but the sandstorms of Navajoland were a bit too much for it and despite repeated overhauling and repairs, it proved to be just about worthless. Perry suddenly came out with, "D'yever go up into Wyoming?" We never had, but why should we? "I've got an old light plant up there at Big Piney and you can have it if you can get it. Ten thousand watts. Yours for the hauling!"

It seemed too good to be true. It was about time for Father Clement and the Brothers to get a bit of vacation, so we gathered all the gasoline ration stamps we could find, and they started off. Two weeks later they were back. The Ford pickup was just about scraping the ground under its load, but it hadn't broken down.

It seems that the driving force of the dynamo was an old Studebaker eight-cylinder gasoline engine, complete with clutch and drive shaft. It was something to hook this up to a system that had never given more than five hundred watts, but Brother Juniper was equal to the task and in a few days, or rather nights, we were ready to celebrate and run a movie for our people. We had taken pictures of various phases of our building projects, so here was a treat in store. Many of the Navajos had never seen a movie and certainly not one of them had ever seen himself on the screen. It went off well; as soon as the sun was down and darkness was sufficient to show up the images on the screen, we started, and it was another first, long to be remembered.

Bearing in mind the audiovisual trend that had recently taken over the church, I began to think of how we could use this little old silent movie projector, plus our now adequate source of power, to teach the Navajos. I got the address of a firm that advertised a series of films on the life of Christ, and I reasoned that the pantomime technique of the silent films, primitive as it might seem in contrast to the art of today's talkies, would be intelligible to the Navajo who knew no English, and I ordered the set. Of course, we spread the word, and the little schoolhouse was well filled. The picture was frightful. Wigs and false beards pasted on fourth-rate actors didn't really seem ideal for our purposes.

Jim Hatathley was in the audience, and he obviously had been patronizing a bootlegger, but as his chief interest was in going to sleep, I considered he would be quite harmless as long as he didn't snore. Toward the end of the first episode of the Gospel story he began to wake up and to comment unfavorably on the performance. In well-chosen if not elegant phrases of Navajo he left no doubt as to his evaluation. Unfortunately I agreed completely, but I had paid for the films, all five of them, and my New England training wouldn't let them go to waste. Yet if Jim started advertising "naálkid nchoigii," the program wasn't going to be a success. When the curtains were drawn from the windows to let the daylight in and the audience out, one of the younger Navajo men asked if we had any movies showing Navajos. Quickly I got out some of our own films, and in a few minutes we had the audience rolling in the aisles and roaring with laughter at their own or their neighbors' actions, and they went home overjoyed. Even Jim made it a point to stagger over to me, clasp my hand and say, "That was a good movie, really good movie," and the day was saved! Actually the next four in the "Life of Christ" series were a little better than the first—I doubt whether they could have been worse!

It was about this time that we began using the Mass of St. Isaac Jogues at our Sunday and festal eucharists. The idea of making use of Indian melodies for the chants of the liturgy was as old as the basic idea of presenting the Gospel in a "language understanded of the people," in my thoughts, but before beginning St. Christopher's Mission the only concrete application had been the arrangement of "Kyrie Eleison." I had come across a portion of the Hopi snake dance that fitted the liturgical words perfectly; not a note needed changing. Several years went by before there was leisure to work seriously with the project, but little by little there came the "Sanctus" and "Agnus Dei" to Omaha and Zuni melodies I had learned as a boy in school. All that remained was the "Gloria in Excelsis." The characteristic falsetto *e-d-c* found in so many Navajo songs gave the clue, and the descent from very high to very low that is characteristic of many Plains Indians melodies combined to inspire the "Gloria in Excelsis" that has aroused perhaps more comment than any other number in the Mass. When Mary Gail Evans, a medical technician in Dallas, began writing about coming to work with us, she mentioned, "I have encountered a number of theological students who know you as the composer of a Mass which incorporates an Indian war-whoop."

Brother Michael made copies of the score on a hectograph; later Helen's brother, Dr. William Sturges, made some photographic copies; but we never succeeded in convincing visitors that although we had a few more copies than we had staff members, the supply was not inexhaustible. Philip Berton finally was responsible for getting an offset printer to produce an adequate supply, and it was no longer necessary to frisk departing guests. We continued to use St. Isaac Jogues Mass at all our outstations and at the Mission church during festal seasons.

Is it necessary to explain that St. Isaac was among the first North American martyrs who gave their lives for the faith in Canada and northern New York State in Colonial days?

The question is often asked, "Why did you use melodies from other Indian tribes instead of Navajo melodies for the Mass?" The answer, not only because I couldn't find any Navajo melodies that would fit the words but because—far deeper than that—to the Navajo there is no separation of words from music. In fact, the language seems to have no word for "music." Ask a Navajo for such a word and he will say *hataal,* which means song, or a ceremonial involving songs. It is inconceivable that the words of a song be separated from the music or set to a different melody; consequently if a Navajo tune were used in the liturgy, the minds of all who heard it would run to the words and the underlying thoughts that they associated with it. We can sing "Danny Boy" or "My Gentle Harp" to "Londonderry Air" without being disturbed, but not so with Navajo music. Consequently the foreign melodies of Hopi, Zuni and Omaha do not convey any associated thoughts and can be identified with the liturgical words and ideas to which they have been set.

The Navajo attitude of perfection toward his songs, combined with a passionate dislike for the ridicule that is provoked by a less than perfect rendition, has somewhat retarded the oral participation we looked for when we began using this medium, but I still think the idea is sound and worthwhile.

Publicity came to the Mission, unsought, uninvited and in various unpredictable ways. Frank O'Brien wrote up a full page for a Sunday issue of one of the Salt Lake papers. The Denver *Post* produced another as a result of a broken spring in the Ford pickup; the lady who ran the garage couldn't understand why I didn't bite my nails or swear and curse because it took her three hours to get the spring. She *had* to find out how I could sit there quietly and read my breviary when I *had* to be back at the Mission with supplies to feed thirty visitors; so her friend, Marian Talmadge, a teacher at Denver University and a feature writer, came over to see us and explore this source of supernatural patience, and the *Post* article, later reprinted in their *Rocky Mountain Empire,* was the result. More recently the nationally circulated magazine *Coronet* ran a story full of old legends and myths about St. Christopher's Mission, plus some of the feature writer's own invention. Several church periodicals and even some trade journals, and *Columbia College Today,* have helped to perpetuate many items of misinformation, but always with kindly intent and, I think, harmless if not beneficial consequences.

24

Early in the spring of 1946 I was working in one of our gardens, when an elderly woman approached me with peremptory summons to church and prayers. I recognized her as one of a party of twenty-five or more who had ridden in from Montezuma Creek for the festivities connected with the wedding of one of their clan to one of our nearby people. All members of this party had been most regular in attending our morning and evening devotions, and for their benefit and instruction I had got out such of my barrel of sermons as seemed to be called for in these services. But right now it was early afternoon. I made an open ring with thumb and forefinger of my right hand, aimed at the sun and from there drew it down to about the area the sun would occupy at five-thirty, and explained in less successful words that evening prayers would be at that time. "No, no, that will not serve; right soon we are all going back to Montezuma Creek, but we don't want to go without prayers. Come *now!*" Who could refuse such a call! A few strokes of the bell gathered all the staff, and we had our devotions, made to order. When the entire party was mounted and ready to start off, the patriarch, known as Tsiithlagai ("White Hair," but in English called White Horse), made a speech, the gist of which was an invitation for us to come to his country and conduct prayers and give instructions there.

We knew that it was high time to start spreading over the vast territory assigned to us, and this seemed the opportune beginning. As soon as we could arrange matters Kenneth Thorpe, Helen and I took off. Kenneth had recently arrived from Chicago, having hitchhiked all the way, and as always, looking as if he had traveled by Pullman and limousine. He was unexpected, but welcome of course, as a man of his charm must always be in places where the ecclesiastical climate is congruent. Kenneth is not only a theologian of some merit, a poet and a philosopher but also an avid student of the American Indian and western lore, and he had at his fingertips just about all the data on the Navajo that had appeared up to that time in print.

One of our mares had a colt following, too small to pack and much too small to ride, but it provided amusement, if that were needed. We knew nothing about the land we were to travel except what one could guess from the inadequate maps available (which showed no road of any sort) and what we could get from the Navajos' descriptions. It seems that their camp was at the mouth of Montezuma Wash—a dry creek for 11¾ months of the year—and that an abandoned trading post would be an unfailing landmark. (The Navajo equivalent of "you can't miss it"—the cheering conclusion to every set of directions ever given west of the Alleghenies—is "just one road.") Well, we didn't see even one road, but we started out, frying pan ringing as it hit a canteen, cook pot and eating utensils rattling from our cantles and pommels. There was really no danger of getting lost as long as we kept the San Juan River in sight or didn't get too far away from it. By afternoon of the first day we decided to have one of us ride to the mouth of each wash we came to and report back. This slowed us down still more, of course. By sundown Kenneth reported that there was a beautiful camping place down by the river, just a half mile away. Fine. So we made camp. I picketed my mount and Helen's, but Kenneth was going to be really western. "Never picket your horse if you're riding all day. A horse has to eat, same as a human. *I'll* bring them in, in the morning." Well, I'm reasonably humane, but horses have to learn something about the hardships of missionary life, too, and I'd rather ride than walk. After Mass and breakfast next morning, he took my mount and hunted his. An hour or more later he came back, slightly discouraged. I let the mare rest a few minutes, Kenneth gathered fuel, and he and Helen boiled river water which we had allowed to settle overnight, as the supply of spring water we had brought from the Mission was nearly gone.

It was most likely that Kenneth's mount had headed for the corral at the Mission, and I started in that direction. I asked the first little sheepherder I met, "Where my horse?" and she pointed unhesitatingly to the west. In less than five miles I found her, placidly grazing, but when she saw me she set off at a good pace. This wasn't going to be an even race; my mount was weary, the runaway was fresh. But just as she started down a narrow, steep trail into a canyon I saw Eddie Nakai, who had a farm in the river-bottom land not far off, walking up the trail. A shout alerted him to the situation, and he held the mare at bay. I dismounted and walked down to her with the bridle in my hand. I had to lead her down some distance to find a place wide enough to turn her around, but this was nothing—if Eddie had not been there it would have meant chasing her all the way back to the Mission!

It was well after noon before our trek was resumed. The first catastrophe was Helen's announcement that her mount had the blind staggers or its equal. There could be no doubt that the animal was in a bad way and seemed to want to walk sideways rather than forward. Horseback riding had never been Helen's favorite mode of travel, although she took it up with zeal when necessary. I offered to trade mounts, thinking that I could perhaps leap to the ground more quickly if the horse should collapse. We traded and by chance I came in contact with a canteen slung at the saddle horn. My burned hand made clear the reason for the horse's sidestepping. There hadn't been time for the boiled river water to cool before putting it into the canteen, and there it was, searing the shoulder of the poor patient beast!

Wash after wash we crossed, after sending a scout down to the mouth of each, and toward evening we began to get a bit discouraged. A large mound of earth, or perhaps a little hill, was visible about a mile away. "We'll ride up to that," I said. "It should give a good view of the land ahead. If we don't see our goal from there, we'll make camp and then see how we feel in the morning."

There was a good view, and we saw the ruins of the abandoned trading post, the great peninsula at the confluence covered with a massive stand of cottonwoods, hogans, corrals, pelt racks and other indications of habitation showing that our goal wasn't far off. Our first visit was to two hogans toward the north. A clothesline gaily flaunted two or three towels with the familiar blue stripe and the inscription PULLMAN. This area was probably the farthest from a railroad of any in the continental United States; always a little slow on the uptake, I didn't think until later that many of these Navajos went out for months at a time in gangs to work on railroads to earn enough money to catch up on their delinquent accounts at the trading posts.

Montezuma Creek was quite dry, as usual. A vast expanse of level sand provided a fine meeting place. Most of the women brought parasols of vivid hue; and their best clothing, with the brightly colored shirts of men and boys, presented a picture fit for Hollywood. They must have numbered between sixty and seventy, and fewer than half of them had been at Bluff for the wedding, so that the whole basic instruction needed to be reviewed. The attention span of these people amazed me. Children of all ages and adults ranging in age from the early twenties to the eighties sat all but motionless for several hours as I went through the points of the faith—creation by the one true and living God, the disobedience of man, the sacrificial system of the Jews to keep alive the sense of sin and need of forgiveness, the fulfillment of it all in Christ by His birth, death, resurrection and ascension, and the descent of the Holy Ghost—and culminating in an all too feeble explanation of the Mystical Body, the redeemed people of God, sanctified by means of the sacraments. It was a heroic effort that reminded me of a story Bishop Manning of New York told of his own boyhood when he chose as a theme for a composition "The World and Its Contents." But to my amazement the Navajos seemed to grasp the gist of it and wanted to know when the baptism was to be. I sometimes wonder whether I didn't make a mistake in not taking advantage of the situation, but it seemed just too fantastically simple. The best I could do was to say that I would come as often as I could and that baptism would be open to all who sincerely believe and showed promise of perseverance. After all, had not St. Philip the Deacon baptized the Ethiopian eunuch with as little instruction? . . . But of course the Ethiopian had a background of messianic teaching.

One of White Horse's sons-in-law sought me out later when most of the congregation had started for their homes. He had many questions which I tried, with my still unfluent Navajo, to answer. Finally he took from his wallet a card which showed him to have been enrolled as a member of the Native American Church—a sect recently introduced from Mexico and embracing many Christian ideas both of belief and of behavior, and centering on the sacramental use of a certain type of cactus fruit known as peyote. He asked, "Is this good?"

To this day, after twenty years, it still tires me to talk for more than a few hours in Navajo; at that time I was nearly exhausted and I could see endless difficulties before me. I surrendered. "It is too hard for me to say in Navajo what I think about that." Without blinking an eye he replied in very tolerable English, "Then tell me in English!"

"Why, John, you old so-and-so—you just sit there and laugh at me for talking such poor Navajo when you can talk real good English!"

John looked solemn, in fact seemed really hurt, and I regretted speaking as I had. "No, Fodda. I don't laugh at nobody. I wouldn't do that." To the Navajo, ridicule is the worst possible insult. Then his face lightened with a smile. "I just like to hear you talk Navajo," he said.

It was the first of a number of such surprises. One day a typical old-time Navajo came in and began to complain that he needed medicine for his eyes. I called Helen and interpreted for her. There was some difficulty in our expressing the technical terms, and finally he got tired. In all but perfect English he came out with this story: "Well, you see, I had trachoma, and they gave me sulfanilamide at the hospital, and I just came around here to see if you got some sulfanilamide." Simple as that!

We hated to leave Montezuma Creek, but home we must go or risk having a rescue party sent after us. Kenneth explored the area enough to find the ruins of an old stone building which he designated the "future Church of Our Lady of the Desert." We found later that it was hot with litigation, and as at least three parties claimed ownership, we hardly felt we could afford to be embroiled. The ruin deteriorated more and more and was finally completely removed when an airstrip was leveled as a result of the discovery of oil a decade later.

25

Stephen Cutler Clark, D.D., was elected early in 1945 to be Bishop of Utah, succeeding Bishop Moulton, who had reached retiring age. I must confess that I had some uneasy moments. It was well known that Dr. Clark was an efficient, orderly business-like parish priest who had little time for emotional or sentimental exercises. Rumors even reached me that he had been chosen to "put down popery at St. Christopher's." In a missionary district the bishop is not elected, as in a diocese, by the clergy and representatives of the parishes but by the House of Bishops as a whole. As a result one would expect that the man selected would be a man of excellent judgment and executive ability, as well as full of evangelistic zeal. The "popery" practiced at St. Christopher's was a determined effort to restore, by God's help, all that the Anglican church had lost in the state-imposed Reformation. And while the bishops can lustily sing in the Litany hymn for the church ". . . all that she has lost, restore," most of them can be counted upon to set up formidable obstructions to every effort to make such restoration, or to limit such efforts to matters of superficial externals that, like sound and fury, signify nothing. This is not to criticize or belittle our bishops, who with few exceptions are of the cream of the clergy. The system of electing bishops by the clergy is ancient and Catholic and should work out ideally. But since the "Settlement" under Elizabeth I, it has been the policy to tolerate in the church wide differences of opinion even in matters of faith, despite our thoroughly Catholic official formularies, and the result is that not only laity but clergy can be found who are determined that what the church has lost shall *not* be restored. And consequently when an election comes up, each side, while it would like to see one of its own kind elected, realizes that this is impossible, and the result is almost always a compromise so far as churchmanship is concerned. And when you get a whole house of compromise men, only a miracle would bring about the election of a man with definite convictions in favor of restoring the Gospel "as this Church hath received the same" from St. Gregory in 597.

Only delusions of grandeur could have made me really concerned over these rumors that Dr. Clark was selected to "put down popery." I had no reason to think that he had ever heard of St. Christopher's or of me. But we had enjoyed such favor under Bishop Moulton, and I was so sure that we were now to have a very different sort of ordinary, that there were, I admit, some anxious moments.

After his election and before announcing his acceptance (for no man can be drafted into the episcopate), he asked all the Utah clergy to confer with him in Salt Lake City; and since I had come some three hundred miles further than any other priest, he kindly invited me to luncheon, along with some of the key men of the district. In the course of the meal he turned to me (I sat beside him) and asked, "What would you do, Father, if you were persecuted for your churchmanship?"

It was a quiet, personal question, and I doubt whether any one else heard it. I hesitated but a second.

"Why, I just don't know, Dr. Clark; it never occurred to me that I should be persecuted by the church for my loyalty to her faith and practice."

This was no time to defend, or even explain, my position. The retort was perhaps slightly mendacious, for I *had* given the matter thought, and while I had never suffered real persecution, I knew many who had. But it put the subject where it belonged, and in proper proportion: it pinpointed my conviction that any individual in the church who opposed her faith and practice was acting *ultra vires.*

I found Bishop Clark as fair a man as ever I want to meet. While he showed no immediate signs of intending to put down popery, he likewise showed no signs of going overboard to aid and abet us in our work. He was ready to be shown, and I made up my mind that St. Christopher's would show him.

Stephen Clark was consecrated in California, but his enthronement at St. Mark's Cathedral in Salt Lake City on January 26, 1947, gave an opportunity to his clergy and people to meet and greet him. I felt I ought to be there, but would not miss the regular Sunday Mass at the Mission; however, we set the Mass a half hour ahead, and I was on the road in the Dodge army truck by ten o'clock, a thermos of coffee and a sack of buns with me. It seemed a safe allowance of time for an evening function, even though there were reports of snow on the road. But on the road leading out of Price Valley there is a tunnel, and to my dismay I found that the truck's lights didn't work. It was still mid-afternoon, but darkness had set in before I got to a town. Fortunately I had a Navy surplus lantern with a powerful battery and so was able to continue with caution.

At the first gas station in Springville I was told, "They's a mechanic got a grodge cross the way; he just closed it up but he's gettin' a cuppa coffee at the caffay." I dashed across, found him just enjoying the last drop, and told my story. "Well, I was goin' to play some chess with a guy, but you just pull her up to that street light and we'll see what we can do." As he worked he asked questions about our work at the Mission, showing increasing interest. The "guy" came by to see what was holding up his chess partner, and although their passion for chess was obvious, it was also clear that here was a valid reason for postponing the game.

At last my mechanic found the ground–insulation inside the right headlight had eroded away–and from then on it was a matter of minutes to tape it up and reset the headlight. He told me that the Mormons (despite his addiction to coffee, he considered himself a loyal Mormon) were beginning to evangelize the Indians and were planning even then to go after the Ute tribe. As I got out my wallet to meet the bill, prepared for double pay for overtime, doubled again for Sunday, he smiled. "Pretty pore thing if one missionary can't help out another!" And he refused to take one cent.

This was only one of many manifestations of the generous attitude of the Mormons toward us. I should have liked to pay him, and did thank him profusely, but he urged me on. "Get goin' or you'll be late!" It was already time for the function to begin. Snow started to fall as I was leaving Provo, and I barely got to the cathedral in Salt Lake for the final blessing. The bishop realized that I had done my best, and seemed greatly pleased that the Mission was represented.

Three months later he made his first visit to us; he came, with appropriate humility, by public bus. Although he had not ridden a horse for nearly twenty years, he responded gladly to the proposal that we visit some of the Navajo hogans across the San Juan River. We saddled Beshlagai and Mogi, and the bishop showed by his easy seat that in twenty years he hadn't lost his technique. The river was fairly high—we had to lift our feet well up to keep the water out of our boots—but the wiry ponies were accustomed to leaning against the strong current and carried us safely across. The Navajo people on the other side were delighted to have the bishop visit them. Coffee and Navajo bread were brought out, and everyone, even the smallest children, shook hands with him. The bishop admired the well-irrigated hayfields and the cornfields being prepared for planting, and some of the Navajos understood what he said and smirked in a superior fashion when he remarked that the irrigation ditch on the north (white man's) side of the river hadn't even been cleaned for the spring water.

Both our ponies were thoroughly trained, and I regarded them safe for even a child to ride, so I wasn't prepared for what happened. As we approached Kathryn Mustache's hogan a gust of wind suddenly flapped a white sheet that hung on the line and so startled Beshlagai that she sank at least a foot downward and simultaneously leaped to one side, unseating our prelate and dropping him ignominiously onto the sandy ground. My book of etiquette had never told me what to do in such a case, but it didn't matter; by the time I had dismounted and extended a helping hand he was up, dusting himself off and laughing heartily with the Navajos, to whom the spectacle of someone falling from a horse is second in humor value only to that of someone falling from a burro.

On Sunday the bishop confirmed three Navajos. If further proof were needed of his sense of humor, please note: After the service he said, "Father, I am surprised that you don't know how to pronounce *Chicago*. It's not *Shikaygo*. You kept saying '*Shikaygo*' to the confirmands." So I had to tell him. Because of their shyness, Navajos are not good at picking up a cue, so that when it came to the renewing of baptismal promises that precede confirmation in our rite, I posed the questions in Navajo, and alerted them to make the response by telling them, "After me say . . ." This is "shik'ehgo." But I hoped the bishop wouldn't notice how poorly I had prepared the candidates in this detail!

If I was behind in my study of Emily Post, not so the bishop. No Anglo-Catholic could ask for a more complete manifestation of his approval of things as they were at St. Christopher's. Every genuflection and crossing, the use of miter and cope and chrism, the completely orthodox theology that underlay his admirably simple sermon—all spoke of his desire to be an essential part of the work of bringing the Gospel in its fullness to the Navajo people. Never again did I put any stock in the myth about his putting down popery. He did write me a letter asking that I make some very minor changes in the rite, and of course I immediately acceded to the request—and it was a request, not an order. He added a quite unsolicited approval of our practice of administering the Blessed Sacrament in one kind. I say unsolicited, because I would not think it necessary to have episcopal approval of a practice that has the tacit approval of the whole church both east and west, but Bishop Clark's spontaneous action in this matter showed not only that he knew his theology but that he was aware of the peculiar exigencies of pastoral work with the Navajos, suffering as they do from tuberculosis and many respiratory infections that are spread largely through the use of the common cup in the hogan. He saw at once that we could not fight the common cup in the hogan while administering it in church. That his enthusiasm had been aroused toward the Mission was shown by his return in six months—but first I must tell of a few other things.

Among those he confirmed was a lady named Stella. Her mother, Rose Holly, lived across the river and about twenty miles upstream. Rose was so badly crippled with arthritis that she couldn't walk but crawled on all fours like a six-month-old baby. Stella came to the mission (she lived only a few hundred feet away) and said that Rose had ridden her horse from her own home to Stella's in order to get instruction and baptism. Twice a day she came for an hour-long lesson, until I felt that she really understood the step she wanted to take; and on Christmas Day, after a month of accelerated instruction, she was baptized at the age of seventy-three. A few days later we helped raise her not inconsiderable bulk into the saddle, and waved a sad good-bye to this sweet old lady who had been won by her own daughter and the majesty of the liturgy to the obedience of the Gospel. The first fruits were the appearance of Rose's daughter, Grace, with her children, also seeking the source of the new strength that had come into their mother's life.

Here I may digress for a moment to extend the remark made above about the majesty of the liturgy. Remember that we had been in the area only two and a half years. None of us had mastered the Navajo language. I had my little barrel of stock sermons in Navajo and used to read one each Sunday; and I also read in Navajo the appointed Gospel for the day. We used the catechism in Navajo for instruction. All this was good as far as it went, and it helped the Navajo people to understand what it was we wanted to present to them. But I could do little counseling or answering of specific questions that were not "in the book." What won our converts was not simply the preaching of the Gospel, it was the New Testament in its most specific sense—as when Our Lord said, "This cup is the New Testament."

The following is not a quotation from any single Navajo, but it is a faithful symposium built out of the comments of dozens of individual commentators: "We know you have good, strong medicine. Some of us have seen the prayers of the short-coats. These men are good men. They help Navajos in many ways. Some few maybe are self-seekers, but we think they are mostly good men. They pray and they sing and they talk. Some talk crazy-like, some talk excitedly, some talk quiet like you. But it is just like going to a grazing meeting. The show-offs do the talking. We Navajos are mostly shy. Only a few of us are show-offs. In the short-coat meetings our show-offs like to talk, and pretty soon they get to be preachers, but we can see they don't know much more than we do. When we go to your church, we see things we never see any other place: candles and crosses and beautiful special prayer clothes of different colors. We know that these are just things that are *seen*, but the things that you *do* nobody else can do. We feel that the real Holy One is here in some way that he isn't any other place. This is what we call good, strong medicine. This is what we want."

I realize that this approach is directly counter to that used in the primitive church, when only the initiated were permitted to witness the divine mysteries. Father Staunton, who opened our church's work in the Philippines among the Igorot tribes shortly after the War with Spain, which brought the islands under American jurisdiction, used the primitive method with excellent success; he held his Mass privately and gave instruction publicly. To what extent curiosity stimulated conversion, who can at this late date say?—but the system worked. I seriously considered, before beginning the actual work of the Mission, reviving this ancient discipline. I am glad now that I didn't, although I could not at that time foresee the vast changes that would come over Navajoland. So the Mass was open to all who wished to attend, and in countless instances fulfilled the words of Christ, "I, if I be lifted up, will draw all men unto me." The most completely uninstructed Navajo, entering our church for the first time, knew at once that he was confronted by *worship*. This was no grazing meeting, no debate or gabfest; it was a group intent upon the Way that draws man to the Infinite.

Bishop Clark's second visit came only six months after his first. This time he drove his car, and Mrs. Clark came along. A gracious First Lady of the diocese she proved to be! Obviously unaccustomed to roughing it, she seemed to delight in making things do, getting along without necessities and having the time of her life. Rose Holly had been notified by special messenger, and both she and Grace were among those to be confirmed. Since Stella's hogan was only a few hundred feet from the church building, it was not worth while to hoist Rose up on her horse. We taxied her in the weapons carrier to the church door, and she crawled on hands and knees to her place. She called the bishop *shiyáázh*—"my son"—but I shall never forget the seraphic smile of peace that lit up her homely face as the apostolic hand was laid upon her and she received the "unction from the Holy One."

The bishop was keenly aware of something that many visitors and friends of the Mission forget or never learned: that our area is not simply in the vicinity of Bluff. The Utah strip of the Reservation extends from the Colorado line westward to the confluence of the San Juan and Colorado rivers and then to the point where the Colorado enters Arizona, and is bounded on the south by the Arizona line. It is only a small part of the Reservation, but it includes between twenty-five hundred and three thousand square miles, all very thinly populated.

The bishop wanted to see more of it. On Monday we took the jeep down to Monument Valley. On Tuesday the plan was to see the Montezuma Creek area, circling from Bluff to Hatch's Trading Post and down the wash to its mouth and then along the river back to the Mission. It would be a good day's run, and rather rough for city folk, so Mrs. Clark stayed home, and only Brother Juniper and I escorted the bishop. At that time none of the road was paved. Parts were graveled, but mostly there was just a dirt road designated on maps as "unimproved," if indeed the maps deigned to show them at all. We packed a lunch, stopped at all hogans within easy reach of the road and filled the bishop's kindly ears with plans for expansion. When we left the dirt road and started down the trackless wash, while he didn't show any clear sign of nervousness, he quite audibly voiced his thankfulness that Mrs. Clark hadn't come along. This jeep, which my son Bob had sent me from Germany, was a former Army vehicle and in many ways different from the station-wagon styles that appeared in later years. It had a vertical windshield which if not wanted could be laid flat on the hood, but it was the only protection against wind and weather.

We stopped at the ever-friendly Mark household—Laura Mark spoke better English than most Navajo adults—and at various other scattered habitations, each far enough removed from a neighbor to ensure an absence of quarrel over grazing rights. Here and there deep sand seemed to present a challenge, but the jeep sailed over it all quite undismayed. The bishop had read about these things, but this was his first encounter. Perhaps demonstrating a miraculous vehicle tends to make one a bit foolhardy; at any rate I saw some very wet sand ahead but assumed it would bear us up nicely. Not so. The jeep sank quickly until the body reached the level of the sand. Even the body went in an inch or so, but praise the Lord, it held. There was no traction whatever; the wheels spun like windmills. We got out, tried digging sumps to draw the water off, but it was useless; as quickly as we drew the water off, more came from an apparently inexhaustible source to take its place. After about an hour of futile labor, we saw a boy driving a small bunch of sheep, and I called him, asking about horses. No, he said, their work horses were all grazing far away. Day after tomorrow, maybe, but not now. He went on his way without, I am sure, any sense of having failed to be helpful. After all, what is a day, or two days? The bishop muttered that he *had* to be in Salt Lake the following evening for an important conference.

There was only one thing to do: hike to the White Horse camps at the mouth of Montezuma Creek and try to get a pair of saddle horses. Brother Juniper would make a camp by the jeep to watch it and its contents. The bishop was sportsmanship itself—"What are we waiting for?" He soon found that walking in deep sand, clad in city shoes, was quite an adventure. The distance could not have been more than six or seven miles, but it seemed a dozen. The creek near its confluence with the San Juan River makes a large gooseneck meander, so I led the way up the right bank and across the peninsula. We got to Slim White Horse's hogan just at sunset. Not a soul in sight. Worse still, no recent tracks. It is easy to get into a padlocked hogan through the smoke hole, but getting out again is another matter unless one knows that there are benches or tables inside to climb up on. A cool breeze had set in, and darkness was not far off. The only available shelter was a large *chaha'oh,* or shade; it had a covering only of brush, no windbreaks at the sides, and I knew that its floor would be thick with sheep dung. Hardly a place to invite a bishop to spent the night!

A desperate survey of the surroundings made me grateful for the darkness, which made it possible to see a glimmer of a fire in the east. It would have been impossible to guess how far away it was, and we were both pretty tired, but this represented our one chance of shelter and we made for it. Again and again as we came to lower altitudes the fire could not be seen, but I had taken bearings from the stars, and as we reached each ridge, it was always dead ahead. The barks of dogs told us we were getting nearer, and at last by the light of the fire I could see a woman squatting as if ready to sprint, and holding one of the dogs by the collar. Suddenly she stood up and started toward us.

"Oh, Fodda, I was so skett; I din know who it could be. Come, come, Fodda!" It was Wanda White Horse. She and her little children were alone, but now all fear had gone, and her heart was full of joy. She greeted the bishop hospitably and led us to the fireside. I posed our problem, although I realized that even if horses were available, to start out at night, with no moon, would be foolhardy.

"Got no horses here, Fodda. My Daidie and the others are all up in the hills. Tomorrow, soon as is see evvysing, my boy will go and my Daidie will bring horses." Most of the English-speaking Navajos called their fathers Daidie—a practice that struck us as a bit childish for an adult, but it probably derived chiefly from their difficulty with the sound represented by the letter *r*. *F* is just as hard, but they approximate it with a very windy *wh* sound. Wanda's expression "soon as is see evvysing" was her own rendition into English of a Navajo term for daylight.

Without waiting for us to approve her plan, she continued with more immediate concerns. "You eat aready?" and laughed at the absurdity of the question. "Sit by da fiah, I fix you some eat." ("Fix" is a widely used term for the preparation of a meal—one we from the East found no harder to learn than pack for carry, sack for bag and rock for stone. The English-speaking Navajos took these colloquial usages from the whites of the area.)

I don't recall saying it, but Bishop Clark in later years declared that I slipped a word of comfort to him: "I guess for tonight you and I better forget everything we ever learned about germs!"

Before many minutes had gone by, and certainly long before my aching legs were rested, Wanda had mutton, corn on the cob and coffee for us, and while we ate she spread a heavy quilt on the ground and brought out some woolen blankets. We were ready for them; the firelight allowed Vespers and Compline to be read, and we needed no rocking to get to sleep.

Wanda had breakfast ready soon after daylight, and we had hardly got to the last drop of morning coffee when her Daidie, White Horse, rode in with two spare mounts. He indicated that he felt honored that the bishop was to ride his horse and said he would be over later to bring them back. We took off with no unnecessary delay. Although he made no mention of it, I am sure the bishop was deeply concerned over Mrs. Clark, who must be really worrying about us, for we had planned to be back by nightfall at the latest. Neither of us counted on the type of worrying Helen would do—a worrying that expressed itself in direct action, as you will see.

There was a crude wagon road to the Mission, but it had many bends and turns and I was sure there must be a more direct horse trail. We found it, lost it in a sheep trail and found it again a dozen times. But always the bishop would fall behind, and I would have to rein in and wait for him.

At last he expressed his mind. "You have the better mount, I think. I could keep up with you on that horse." We exchanged horses. In three minutes I was a hundred feet ahead of him—and it was the same story.

"Let's face it, Bishop, you're just too good a Christian to make any speed on a Navajo range pony." I told him what the Tees Nas Bas trader had told me about there being no nice way to drive a burro, and he got a good laugh out of it. We pushed on. The Navajo way of riding is to keep your feet rhythmically swinging back and forth so that your heels kick the beast about once every three quarters of a second. Me, I prefer a switch; I find the Navajo style far more tiring than walking would be.

We must have reached the Mission early in the afternoon, and the first sight to greet us was Old Man White Horse, lying stretched out in the shade of an ironwood bush. I still don't know whether he deliberately sneaked past us as a lark or came by a trail so far from ours that we neither saw nor heard him. Of course, Mrs. Clark had been relieved to know that we were not far behind. But the second startling sight, hardly believable, was the jeep, peacefully parked; and soon Brother Juniper appeared with a pleased smile. Of course, I had hoped to see *him* again some time, but was reconciled to the complete loss of the jeep.

The bishop shaved, showered, drank a cup of coffee and was on the highway headed for that board meeting in Salt Lake City—and with a yarn that I am sure brought down the house, especially if he was a few minutes late, "for effect," as Mark Twain used to say.

It seems that Mrs. Clark had worried even more than I feared: doubtless her sleep was murdered by visions of scalping and torture rather than just getting bogged down or running out of gas. So Helen didn't wait for dawn but got the old weapons carrier and a tow chain, drove to Bluff and got Woody out of bed and took his chains along. By the time they left the well-traveled roads it was light enough to see our jeep tracks and to follow them to where Brother Juniper was standing guard. Threats of rain had inspired him to take everything out of the jeep, as he knew what a flash flood in one of those washes can do to a car or truck. When they started to snake the jeep out, the sandy bank on which the truck rode began to crumble, but by adding more chain they were able to get it on firm ground, and out came the jeep. Brother Juniper drove it home, as the engine had not been in the sand, and Helen and Woody brought in the weapons carrier, so they all got home long before the bishop and I did.

I heard later that the bishop got to Salt Lake City in time for the board meeting—and it's no credit to the vigilance of our Utah State Highway Patrol that he was able to do so.

In October and November of that year, 1947, I went east to give a number of talks, illustrated by movies, in parishes and to various groups interested in one or another phase of our work. I learned very quickly that in every place where Bishop Clark had spoken, the story of the jeep in the quicksands and his night in a Navajo *chaha'oh* was heard and enjoyed, losing nothing, I am sure, in the telling. In the course of this trip east I had dinner with Dr. and Mrs. Bertram Eskell. (This I mention for its connection with subsequent events; it would be impossible to mention all the kind people who extended their hospitality.) Mrs. Eskell—Joan—had arranged the meeting at the Church of St. Mary the Virgin on 46th Street in New York City, to be held that evening. Dr. Eskell asked many questions about the Mission, where Joan had worked for two or three months the year before. "Now I can see," he said to her, "why you love to visit the Mission." I doubt whether she told him she had handled one end of a two-man timber saw!

26

People often ask about this log church; most of our buildings are of native stone, and the church is the only structure of horizontally laid logs. We chose that medium because Norman Nevills, the nationally known "Riverman," was sure that a great dam was to be erected for power and for irrigation, and as Mexican Hat, his home, was at a narrow rock gorge of the river, he felt reasonably sure that that site would be elected, in which case all Bluff and the region for miles upstream would be flooded. It wasn't a happy thought for us, but if we built the church of logs at least we might float it off and set it down somewhere else. A stone church would be useful only to preach to the fish—and Navajo language is hard enough without trying fish talk!

So it was that the log church was undertaken. Father Clement designed it, in collaboration with the other staff members, but we never did work out all details—it rather grew up under our hands. Footings and a course of masonry outlined the floor plan so that the logs would not rot against the ground; even in this semi-arid country this is a necessary precaution. We got a sawmill operator to cut and deliver the logs, as we had no vehicle capable of hauling them over the sixty-mile trail. (Among the many myths circulated in regard to our work, perhaps the most preposterous was the statement that the log rafters were brought *by hand* from the sixty-mile-distant mountains.)

Clyde Sam, son of Hashk'aan, then our oldest and most regular communicant, undertook the task of removing the bark on contract. We supplied the drawknife and he was to do the rest. But by the time he was about one quarter through, he was offered a better job, and Hashk'aan himself took over. Only one minor difficulty arose. He pointed out that one log had been struck by lightning. He would not touch anything that had been claimed by lightning, not even to remove it so that he could get at the logs beneath. We performed this little act of kindness for him, and he went happily on. In a few weeks the cruciform nave began to take shape. Money gave out when the walls were up, and we had to get along with our east wing of the cloister chapel for something like two more years before we could complete the roof, windows and doors and the stone altar with its three steps and flagstone sanctuary floor. But it did get finished, and it served as our spiritual powerhouse for a good many years.

It was also a visible proclamation of our faith. Everything in it proclaimed the ancient and unchanging faith of Christendom, and at the same time our dedication to renewal, to the fervent desire to make the faith meaningful, realistic and relevant to the present age. The free-standing altar—the first to be built in Utah, or in any Indian mission or any church in the whole Southwest—was actually a return to primitive usage but at the same time a symbol of aliveness to current thought; the Mass was to remain a mystery as always but also a "show," as St. Paul called it—"ye do show the Lord's death till he come." Priests from many parts of the country, both Anglican and Roman Catholic, came to see how it was done. There were, of course, the modern imitators of Dean Swift's Big-endians and Little-endians, but animosities melted and the Presence was felt by many who came—and left in silence but later wrote to express their feelings in the experience of just being at this spiritual oasis in the desert.

Of course, this was too much for the Father of Lies. The story of his campaign will never, I hope, be told. He could not tolerate the dispensing to the Navajo of the means of grace in the sacraments or the cultivation of that devotion to the Mother of Our Lord which has done so much throughout the Christian centuries to keep alive the belief in the divinity of her Son. One match, applied on a Sunday afternoon in 1964, kindled a blaze that laid the whole structure in ashes by nightfall, building and contents a complete loss.

Apparently. But the God of Truth was not going to let the Father of Lies have his way without some witness to the truth. The statue of the Mother of the Saviour (often called "Madonna of the Navajo") remained standing triumphantly among the ruins. She seemed to declare to all who would listen, "Here I stand. Were I not Mother of God, you would have no Redeemer."

A few days later as Brother Juniper was raking over the ashes he recovered first a chalice, then a paten. They were the sacred vessels that had been delivered to me at my ordination to the priesthood in 1914. Black as your shoe but unharmed. A few hours' work by a competent goldsmith and they were good as new. We call them the miracle vessels, for they are together with the statue of Our Lady visible symbols of the faith that the arsonist's match tried to destroy. Two other chalices, a monstrance, a ciborium and other vessels of silver and gold were reduced to blobs. But I am ahead of my story.

Came the plague. Not being qualified to diagnose, I can't give it a proper medical name, but all the common symptoms of hepatitis were observed and whole families of Navajos came for medication. I did what I could, observing every possible precaution against contamination, but Helen and Brother Juniper both came down with it. Like true pioneer heroes they took turns getting up to attend to things that needed doing. School was closed, and from Monday after Mass to Saturday at Vespers all services were canceled. There was one casualty: a month-old baby who had not been brought in for treatment was buried on the Ides of March in native style in East Canyon. Five days later I came down with the illness. Helen was the only staff member able to get around and she did everything, just as anyone who knew her would expect. Two days after I collapsed Brother Juniper was again up and around. I got up (against medical advice) to offer the Mass on Sunday for a feeble but grateful congregation, and tumbled back into bed. Tuesday, Helen sneaked into Bluff and phoned Father Hawley in Durango. Father Hawley isn't the kind to waste time in emergencies and it wasn't for nothing that he was an active member as well as chaplain of the Civil Air Patrol. "I'll be there in half an hour with a doctor," he said, and hung up.

The plane circled the Mission and headed for Norman Nevills' crudely dozed landing strip. It was probably the only three-engine plane ever to make the landing. Dr. Clarke took one look at me and said, "Pack up, you're going to the hospital with me."

The landing strip ran north and south, and there was only the width of the river-bottom land between the take-off point and the south wall of the canyon. I shut my eyes, with perfect confidence in Horace Buchanan, the pilot, and could feel the plane banking to starboard, missing by a few hundred feet the sheer south wall. I had never seen the Ute mountain, Shiprock, or the intervening desert from the air, and my desire to sit up and look was the first indication that I was getting better. The day before I couldn't have cared less what was happening.

The sisters at Mercy Hospital in Durango were most kind as well as efficient. They put me in a semi-private room with a charming Baptist minister, who couldn't understand why I read the Bible so much—he "didn't think Episcopals or Catholics paid much attention to the Bible"—but felt better when he found it was a breviary, in a strange language, and only about 92 per cent Bible. All the routine tests were run, and Dr. Clarke was much pleased. "I guess you were on the road out when you were flown in, if I may mix a metaphor, and you can go home in a day or two. You need a little more rest and some special diet." Nine days after the flight Shirley Hawley and Betty Underhill drove me home, and that was well worth the whole incident, as anyone can appreciate who knows those charming ladies.

27

With Father Clement here to maintain daily services and stabilize the life of the Mission in my absence, it seemed high time to be reaching out more into the far parts of our territory. We made one more foray into the Montezuma Creek area before heading out to Navajo Mountain in the west.

A man named John Chapman had joined us with the idea of giving his life to God in an active way. He was gentle, patient and quite willing to set his hand to any task, yet he seemed less than radiantly happy. With perhaps somewhat inconclusive evidence, I assumed that the life was too refined, too elegant, for him. We now had running water in the kitchen, a stove in every bedroom and kerosene lamps, and it did seem to us pioneers that life was getting pretty sadly civilized. I felt sure that John missed roughing it, so I took him, with Brother Juniper and Helen, to Montezuma Creek. We packed the Army jeep and surplus trailer for our gear, and it looked as if we were once more to enjoy the good old days. By this time we knew the trails pretty well, and soon after noon got into the area where a number of hogans were to be found. We did not have to suggest prayers; the host invariably asked us to conduct a service. First his wife would spread one of the best blankets on the floor west of the fireplace, and if there were other families nearby a child would be sent with an invitation to come. It was at this time that I began to develop a sort of norm for informal "cottage meeting." A few moments of recollection would be followed by the "Kyrie," sung as we sang it at Mass, then the Our Father and other prayers in Navajo. Next would come a simple outline of the story of redemption and its application to individual souls through faith and the sacraments; more prayers, songs and a blessing.

At one place we were jeeping along the sandy bed of the dry wash, when a small boy in a red shirt came sliding down the steep bank and ran toward us. "My grandfather says come. He says come now for prayers." We didn't need a second invitation. Dan, as the small boy was called, ran ahead of us to herald our acceptance and by the time we got to the hogan the customary blanket had been spread and many small children had been dispatched to the nearby hogans of relatives. In a few minutes the hogan was well filled.

By this time I had sufficient familiarity with the language to make an impromptu sermon, based for the most part on the answers in the catechism, but I was less than adequately familiar with the informality of the people. In the middle of my sermon the sound of approaching hooves could be heard, and a moment later a man whom we later came to know well, Little Wagon, came in. At a glance he realized that this was a religious meeting; but instead of taking his place unostentatiously, he began greeting each member of the congregation with a handshake and a word of salutation as he circled the hogan. If I had thought about it at all, I would have expected him to postpone his greeting to me until after the devotions were over, but no such thought troubled Little Wagon. The dead-fish handclasp and the friendly "Yá'át'é" were for the preacher as well as for the others. I responded properly, and with difficulty resumed my train of thought. This charming informality, once one is prepared for it, may well be a symbol of the unity of believers engaged in worship; one is forced to think how often Christians worship together with little or no concern for worshipers at one's elbows. Would that the holy kiss to which St. Paul refers had not been reduced or even eliminated at the Reformation but had been extended to include all who join in the offering!

That night we camped by the river. Our water supply had completely run out, and we had to boil river water scooped up from a pond left by the receding flow of the river. In these ponds the sand had already settled. If we were to take the water from the river itself, we would have to wait overnight for the sand to settle and then wait hours for boiling and cooling.

John Chapman came up from one of these sumps with two small buckets which he had filled, and sat rather dejectedly on a sand bank. "Gee, I've been camping before—you know, with Boy Scouts. But golly, we always had at least running water and a Chinese cook."

Which shows how wrong I had been in sizing up the source of his unhappiness. He is now serving God in complete devotion, under monastic vows, with running water and electric lights. I'm not sure about the Chinese cook. And it also shows, if I may be forgiven a cliché, that it takes all kinds. . . .

28

Navajo Mountain gives its name to an area that has fascinated thousands who have heard of it and delighted hundreds who have made their way to it. I was first conscious of seeing the mountain when, with Norman Nevills and a group of thirteen, we went down the San Juan and Colorado rivers and stopped to hike up to Rainbow Bridge, said to be the largest natural arch in the world. The arch has charm and beauty of its own, but I think I was even more taken by the glimpse of that rounded, hazy promontory that is like no other mountain. Later I came to realize that it is actually visible from a number of points on the highway between Bluff and Mexican Hat, and between Mexican Hat and the state line, not to mention such sites as Muley Point on Cedar Mesa or the higher reaches of the Aneth Extension. It is the only Holy Mountain in our small area of about three thousand square miles, and only the pressure of work at home delayed my visiting it.

A group of us took the Dodge weapons carrier, laden with water, food and bedrolls. We knew nobody in that part of the country. We had heard something of Lisbeth Eubank, the teacher of the government school there, but to put it mildly we had no intimation of the powerfully dynamic personality that is Lisbeth! The road was not as bad as had been presented, but then few roads could be and we had had our initiation in other localities. Leaving Highway 47, or rather its extension in Arizona, unnumbered at that time, to head towards Shonto, we almost bogged down in blow sand, but the four-wheel drive was able to see us through. By taking it easy, making camp at dusk rather than risking unrepaired and of course unlighted washouts in the dark, we drew up at the school next day, only to find that the teacher was away. An intelligent-looking Navajo was in charge. He was polite but quite aloof, and we left our greetings for Lisbeth and moved on to the trading post.

The trader, Al Kerley, and his wife, Phyllis—fair and lovely as a mirage in the desert—and their two children were more than hospitable. Al wished that he could invite us to settle there, for his sympathies were more with "our kind" than with the "short-coats," but he rather sadly pointed out that in his opinion it would be useless. "The teacher is a Presbyterian, and the Presbyterian minister from Tuba comes up regular, and all the children in the school are signed Presbyterian, and it just wouldn't be any use. I sure wish we had a regular mission up here!" I couldn't help smiling at this familiar refrain. When I had first heard it, five years before, I marveled at the fervent religious spirit revealed in the traders as a class but was disillusioned. I winked at Al and said, "So you wouldn't have to close up shop and bury the dead, or take sick people to a hospital?"

He grinned knowingly. "Well, that, too. But these people need to be taught. They used to steal from me right and left, but I put a stop to that. I'd accuse just about anyone I thought might be guilty, and he would squeal on the one that really did it. I'd go to that one and demand my ax or shovel or whatever it was. He'd always bring it out. Then I'd tell him I was charging him for it on his bill, and if he stole anything more I'd get that back, too, and charge him for it. It sure worked. I never have to lock anything up now. But they need teaching in many things."

We arranged to have a Mass out of doors next morning. Every one who came to the store was told about it, and many agreed to come. All were most attentive, and I'm afraid they were less distracted than we by the multitudes of tent caterpillars that were letting themselves down from the cottonwood trees and gaily taking possession of whatever or whomever they landed on.

Coming home, I pondered a good deal on this whole subject. Here was a new situation. I had asked for the Utah strip, and in making the request had stated that as far as I knew, no Christian denomination was at work in that area. With our small staff and the enthusiastic reception of our Mission in the Montezuma Creek, Monument Valley and Mexican Hat areas, not to mention the constant beckoning of the people in the eastern part of the Aneth field, it seemed reasonable enough to confine our work, for the present, to parts where the Name of Christ was not being preached. However, these ruminations had not yet produced a decision on my part, when we were honored at St. Christopher's by a surprise visit from no less than the incomparable Lisbeth Eubank herself. She came in a battered Army jeep, accompanied by her son, Randy, a Navajo boy named Clem (he turned out to be the adopted son of Will Rogers, Jr., and was named Clem after the elder Will Rogers' late father), and a photographer named Cicero. The grand tour of the Mission in these days consisted of the Mission House, including the chapel in the east wing, and the old CCC shack that was serving as schoolhouse. Lisbeth had been, and still was, practicing the make-do methods, which for us has so many times spelled the difference between pushing on and giving up, and she squealed with delight over homemade refrigerators, pasteurizing facilities, school equipment (by this time we had benches and tables of pine boards), our walking plough attached to and drawn by the Ford pickup in "truck low gear," the homemade hay rake with teeth of cottonwood branches and the like.

The subject of our recent visit to the mountain came up, and I told her of the impression that Al Kerley had given and of my inward debate as to leaving that area to our Presbyterian brothers, since that, I had heard, was her denominational preference. The explosion could have been heard across the river.

"*Me* a Presbyterian? Hell, I'm just about as much a Calvinist as you are! Jesus God, I got off the heavenly bandwagon years ago; I'm an atheist. Or maybe you'd say an agnostic. No, I'm with those who would put all the goddam missionaries off the reservation. Much more harm than good they do. I must say that Mr. Binnit (the Presbyterian minister) is among the best. Yes, he comes up from Tuba on the opening day of school and sits there all day telling the parents where to sign and what to sign, so the Little People are all Presbyterians on the books. He usually gets up again just before Christmas vacation and totes his projector and screen along and gives them a show. Sometimes he works his way up once or twice after the snows have melted, or sometimes he gets the nurse or doctor to carry him up; otherwise we see him again the following September for opening."

Well, I've always said there's nothing like knowing where you stand, right from the start. At least there was not going to be any fencing; I could forget all I had learned about *dégager, coupé*, feint and thrust. We understood each other completely, it seemed. I knew almost at once that I could never beat an orderly retreat and leave the field to Mr. "Binnit"—much as I admired him and loved him. Once when a party of six or seven of us had been caught in Tuba City with no adequate camping equipment in the face of a fierce rainstorm, he opened his church basement to us, regretting only that he had no more luxurious quarters. Of him I had heard the story that he once taught our church catechism to a young man who wanted to be an Episcopalian, and so presented him, adequately prepared, to the Bishop of Arizona for Confirmation. And for this ecumenical action (long before Pope John XXIII had softened the hearts of almost all Christians) Mr. Bennet had been reproved by his superiors and perhaps relieved of his position (this last is an unconfirmed rumor which saddened me; anyway, he is no longer at Tuba City).

Mrs. Eubank didn't have to tell me that she was from Virginia, for although the southern drawl had been all but completely rubbed off through decades of Bureau of Indian Affairs educational work, the giveaway crept through again and again, and not least among the symptoms is the appearance of such names as Robert E. Lee Graymountain among the children she has helped deliver.

I found that she knew not only the heads of all families in the area but each child. There were then something like a hundred and thirty families; I'm not certain that she could recall the birthdate and census number of every one of them, but she knew most of them, and she knew how to find the rest of them quickly. She had probably saved the lives of half the then living population, often riding mule-back through heavy snow for miles, armed with a meager medical kit that always seemed to have what was most needed. I have seen her perform minor surgery at the kitchen table, with all the calm composure of a professor demonstrating technique to his students. But at the time of her visit to us, little of this came out.

"It seems to me," she said, finally coming to the point, "that you will just have to take our little 'communday' under your wing. How often do you think you could make the trip?"

"Well, now, you must pardon me for being a bit surprised. I don't often have atheists inviting me to preach the Gospel! But skip that—I could certainly get there more often than opening day and Christmas vacation. Possibly once a month, weather permitting? [Heavy snows often closed the road to all traffic from Christmas to some time in April.] But if the children are all signed Presbyterian, of course I couldn't give them instruction."

"The parents, my dear Father, are the only ones who have

authority to determine the religious preference of their offspring. I assure you they don't know the difference between Martin Luther, John Calvin, Henry VIII and Pope Gregory. If a priest offered to come and teach their children every month instead of once or twice a year, I have an idea that they would jump at the opportunity. Worth the chance?"

While we talked, Clem and Randy explored the area, Cicero snapped a few "terrific" exposures, then tea was served, and the party left in a cloud of dust such as only a jeep can stir up. It was a short visit, but results cannot be numbered. When opportunity presented itself, I drove up for a few days' visit. Clem and Randy, or both, guided me to the homes of all parents of children. The prospect of regular religious instruction appealed to many; the idea of a Christian missionary who not only did not want to destroy all that the Navajos held dear in their ceremonies but even participated on occasion, was a source of surprise and pleasure; and not a few expressed joy at meeting a missionary who at least took the trouble to try to talk and understand their language.

Only one family held out. Isabel Onesalt, although far from ready to accept Christianity, saw possible friction in a family that was divided, and as she had signed her older children Presbyterian, it didn't seem right to sign the younger ones for another kind of religion. It was a reasonable position, and one I could not help respecting, but it raised problems. Her children had to be extracted from classes when it was time for religious instruction, and a teacher or dormitory attendant had to keep them busy for the hour—an hour spent more than once in stemming bitter tears. The teacher could tap the refrigerator for the ice cream—which didn't appeal to me as a stimulant to orthodoxy, rewarding the recusants, but there wasn't much I could do about it. The new minister made one trip to find out what had happened, and the teacher excused his two students for religious instruction, even though it was not the assigned period. He kept them ten minutes and was off in a cloud of jeep dust.

Isabel later repented, so that the whole school was united, at least in religious instruction.

There was still Mr. Gray, the new Presbyterian minister, to placate. I made the trip to Tuba, and we smoked the pipe of peace. He proudly showed me the jeep in which he "made the trip to Navajo Mountain and back in one day!" I stifled the urge to ask him *why*. If I make a trip like this, I expect to do something more than that to make the trip worthwhile. I suspect that he was greatly relieved of the responsibility of making it even two or three times a year. With monthly visits of anywhere from two days to a week or more, we maintained the services and instructions, until the deluge of missionaries came following the discovery of uranium—of which more later.

On one occasion I heard that Raymond was ill at his mother's house. I always carried a bag of medical supplies with me on these trips, since it was only rarely that a nurse or doctor got up into the region. When I got to the house, I saw a number of saddled horses tied or hobbled and knew that a sing was in progress. Medicine men usually were cooperative, and appreciated my slipping them a few capsules of an antibiotic. I went in and took a vacant seat at the north side of the hogan. Some of the men glanced inquiringly at the singer, Long Salt, but he made it clear in a few well-chosen words that this "Bilagaana" was acceptable and a friend.

The sing proceeded. At the proper time Long Salt asked the hostess for a sack of corn pollen. She hunted in the orange crate that served as a cupboard and produced a Bull Durham tobacco sack, complete with tie string and circular tab, peeped into it to assure herself of the contents and passed it to the first man at the left of the door. He took the prescribed pinch, applied it to his forehead at the hairline, then to his lips, tossed a bit of it into the air and passed the sack to his neighbor at his left, who did the same. When it came to Long Salt, he did likewise, but when the powder touched his lips he uttered a grunt, poured some of the contents into the palm of his hand, threw it onto the ground and tossed the sack back to Raymond's mother. "That isn't pollen—it looks like it. Maybe it is just ground corn, but it's not pollen!" Covered with confusion, our hostess continued her search and came up with another, almost identical, sack. This she carefully took to Long Salt for his inspection, he approved it, and she gave it, as before, to the first man at the left of the door. Raymond recovered, without medication from me.

29

A few days after I got back from my first visit to Navajo Mountain rumors began to circulate in and around Bluff that the river was taking our whole village away. The spring floods were indeed formidable. Sand waves roared and turned white with rage, and standing near the shore one could hear and see huge chunks of earth plunge into the torrent that had undermined the land. I had never given this sort of thing serious thought; we were fifteen or more feet above the river level and I thought that we were perfectly safe, because the river would never rise to such a height. At any rate the river was cutting into the bank, and it might be only a matter of days before the Mission, the town and the farms in between would be on their way to the Gulf of Lower California.

Von Watkins and I were appointed a committee from the citizens of Bluff to seek help in Salt Lake City, and in a few days the Army Engineers had things under control. Truckloads of juniper trees and pine logs to make jacks for riprap were quickly put in strategic places, slowing down the silt-laden current so that the solid matter would drop and form new sandbars. With grateful hearts we watched the furious river subside.

A number of Navajos had been given employment as laborers in this project, and this was when we first saw at close range the results of bootleggers' activities. Knowing when payday was coming, an astute newcomer apparently brought in gallons of cheap wine, rebottled it in six- or eight-ounce pop bottles and sold these at prices of one to three dollars. Affluence went to the bootlegger's head, evidently, for just as we were about to close the net of evidence he made the fatal mistake of registering at a rooming house with a young girl. The sheriff was called and the community was relieved of one enterprising dealer.

30

Phyllis Johnson came to us out of a clear sky. A sophisticated young journalist who had been on some of the leading periodicals in the East, with beauty, and an intense interest in the Navajo, she was a valuable asset to our staff. Not content with just learning a few words of the language, she worked hard and in a few weeks was able to carry on a simple conversation. She learned not merely to weave but to go through all the preliminary processes that follow shearing—the cleaning of the wool by picking out burs and seeds, the washing in yucca root to get rid of the lanolin that would prevent dye from taking effect, the carding and the spinning and the setting up of the loom. The dyes she used were not bought from the trader; she gathered the herbs and stewed them according to the old people's directions, raising stinks that only dedication to an ideal would tolerate. Tall, and dark after a good suntan had settled, she loved being taken for a Navajo by visitors. Phyllis wanted to teach, and I wanted to see how the Montezuma Creek people would respond to a school, so I took her and Helen and Jimmy Jones (as guardian—he was about eleven then) in the Dodge.

The plan was to start school at about nine and close at noon. After all, this was but a test run, and I didn't want the teachers to wear themselves out. Furthermore, some of the children would be coming from some distance, and it would be impossible to send them home for lunch or to provide a lunch for them.

They came soon after dawn, not at nine. They waited with such patience as they could command for the teachers to get up and dress, prepare themselves a brief breakfast and gather the things needed for school. Needless to say, school didn't wait for any nine-o'clock bell. Nor did it close at noon. No, they were not tired. No, they were not hungry. No, they didn't feel it necessary to go home at all; they had come for school and that is what they wanted. They got it.

But let's let Helen tell about it, as she did in a letter to her brother. . . .

". . . Jimmy Jones, do you want to go with us to Doowozhi Bikoo [Montezuma Creek] for ten-day summer school? You could help us talk to those people because they do not know English and we know just a few words of Navajo."

"Yes, I go. I will get my blankets."

So the old Dodge weapons carrier piled high with a 55-gallon oil drum of drinking water, loaves of homemade rye bread, cans, garden stuff and food that could stand the burning August heat for a short time, bed rolls, books, crayons, charts, large pictures, cooking equipment—lurched and bumped over the narrow, rocky road. Somehow Phyllis Johnson and I shared one narrow bucket seat while Father Liebler drove, and Jimmie, nimble as a monkey, skipped about on top of the load, appearing first on one side and then on the other.

At the foot of the last steep hill, in a little grove of cottonwoods on the bank of the San Juan River, we unloaded the gear, and the Padre assured us that he would be back for us in about ten days.

There was not time to look up scattered families for school that first day, but there would be plenty of time next morning. As soon as supper was finished, Jimmie laid out his blankets very neatly, lay down on top until the air got cool and then crawled under.

Around 6:30 the next morning there were strange sounds added to the sounds of the grazing goats and sheep, and the teachers rolled over to find themselves surrounded by some twenty Navajos—from cradleboard babies to the Wise Ones in their 80's! Nothing like teachers smartly attired in sleeping bags! But somehow we wriggled out and led our flock a quarter of a mile up the hill to the ruined trading post where we held school. It had part of a roof against the burning sun, but the floor was large cobblestones over which we slithered and slipped, and upon which we sat for ten days. Our eager pupils stayed until six o'clock that evening. We urged them to take plenty of time at noon to go home for lunch but they just sat and waited, so *we* did not eat. Later in the week they got the idea that it was really *our* lunch we were concerned about so they tactfully withdrew and waited just outside the window. At ten minute intervals, big black eyes would peer over the sill to see whether we had yet succeeded in cracking our hard rye bread which grew more impossible each day. We barely had enough food for ten days, so lunch for twenty or twenty-five seemed impractical. Our water drum which was in the shade in the late afternoon was in hot sun all morning and as the water got very warm, more and more oil dissolved and mixed with the water so that it became rather tasty. We suggested that our pupils bring their own water, so they brought some open buckets of brown liquid, which we mistook for coffee, but which was the regular color of their water.

School was a gay affair, and with the aid of picture dictionaries we learned the Navajo and English words for many objects, and we learned handy phrases to use at the Trading Post and in dealing with whites. Many learned to write their names—perhaps "draw" them would be a better word. We were never so conscious of the strange idioms and inconsistencies of the English language. We told our pupils that it was too hot, and the next day they said, "Today is three hot." One shy girl held out her closed hand and said, "For you." I hesitated about holding out my hand and asked what she had. She struggled for words and finally answered, "Finger nails." Not too reassured, I held out my hand and got some thumb tacks.

A few children and older individuals knew a little English and we tried to tell them some very simple version of the Old Testament stories set in backgrounds so like the desert all around us, with scenes of pastoral life so like the Navajo way of living. The commandments we could read to them in Navajo, thanks to the Navajo language catechism given to us by our good friend, Father Haile Berard, O.F.M. of St. Michael's, but we tried with pictures, a few Navajo words and basic English to lead up to them. One eight-year-old lad, serious beyond his years, and guardian of several younger brothers and sisters, had spent weary hours in his father's broken-down jalopy. In fact, when the family named a baby Rex, the Padre said it seemed appropriate because they had more wrecks than any other family. When we told about the people of God struggling through the desert and coming to Mt. Sinai, we asked why they camped in that spot. Billie said wearily, "Oh dear, I suppose they broke down, couldn't get over the mountain and were stuck all night."

One evening after school a heavy, middle-aged Navajo, named Todichini Tso, stopped to talk with us. He knew only a few English words, but he spoke slowly in Navajo and used expressive gestures so that we could follow him easily. He told of the happy life of the Navajo when there had been good grazing, and the sheep had done well, and the children had grown big and strong. There had been peace. Then the white men began to come from a far-away land. They came across the wide waters in big ships with white wings, and with them came many troubles. Soon they came across the country on horses, and with big wagons, and they wanted gold and more gold. They dug great holes in our Mother, the earth, and this was not good. The Holy Ones were angry. The Navajos could not drive the white men away and there was more and more trouble. Then the white men began to promise to help, to make schools and hospitals, and "Washingdoan" began to write papers. The Navajos asked again and again for schools, and all "Washingdoan" did was to write more papers.

"Now you Eenishoodi have come and we are asking you for schools. We want school right here so our little children do not have to go hundreds of miles away and stay all year. Now maybe you will just write papers too? We think maybe the Eenishoodi really come to help us."

31

Land troubles came rather suddenly. I was never much of a businessman, and our relationship with the previous possessors of the land and with the community at Bluff and with the county officials had been so very friendly that I never felt any insecurity regarding the land, even though I knew that we had bought only the improvements upon it, together with the original squatter's rights—whatever these might be worth.

There came to Bluff a poverty-stricken man and wife with a bunch of undernourished children and some livestock and farm equipment. A kind citizen let them live in an abandoned log cabin. A neighbor asked me if there was anything we could do to help. Well, we had a stand of alfalfa and no mower; I said that if the newcomer would mow the hay and rake it into windrows, he could take half of it home for his livestock. He was most grateful and did a good job, stopping at the Mission House for a cooling drink and a friendly visit from time to time. The next thing I knew, he had filed on the land.

One reason I had not been concerned over our lack of title was that Dan Hayes, who knew the ropes as well as anybody, had tried in every way to get title, but the Powersight Reserve and other obstacles prevented him from doing so. He had been content, as I was, with his assertion, "There can't nobody put you off it." I was not astute enough to ask if I could put anybody off. Our nester's petition was denied by the Land Board on the basis of the land's not being suitable for homesteading. Instead of being content with that, the nester answered that there were people farming it and that he was "renting" part of the land. (The term *renting* seems less opprobrious than *sharecropping,* and is commonly used in these parts.) Of course, the Bureau of Land Management had to take official cognizance of such a trespass, and sent a field worker down with instructions to serve a trespass notice on us. As the good Lord would have it, he hit upon a field worker whose son had spent the previous summer with us. Upon relaying this information to the bureau, the field worker was told in effect, "Go down and see what you can do toward giving them a title."

The field worker, Douglas, came and spent a week or more studying the case. He served a number of trespass notices on farmers who had moved their fences out onto public domain, but he could do nothing more for us than appeal to the Color of Title Act of 1898. When our appeal was denied, as it was bound to be since we didn't even have a pastel tint, let alone a color, of title, I knew we must act, and act quickly.

At that time our mailing list consisted of only four or five hundred names. To each of these went an urgent appeal, setting forth the basic facts, and requesting that they communicate with their senators and congressmen as well as with the Federal Power Commission. Many of our friends mimeographed relays of our appeal to hundreds of their friends. Every member of Congress became so fed up with the plight of St. Christopher's Mission that the bills went through both houses without debate —and probably with sighs of relief! The Secretary of the Interior was empowered to sell the land to us; we paid for it; President Truman signed the patent; and our woes were at an end. We now felt not only that "can't nobody" put us off but that if we were so disposed we could put anybody else off. The nester who had tried to get the land from us protested that he had tried to file on some adjoining land and wouldn't for the life of him do anything to disturb his friends at the Mission. We let it go at that and were really grateful that I had been spurred on to do something that probably should have been done long before.

32

In the spring of 1947 the Provincial Synod met at Medford, Oregon. I had been elected one of the clerical delegates, and Archdeacon Bulkley told me gleefully that he would see to it that I got a chance to tell of our work. I knew the archdeacon well enough to trust him in this regard but wondered how he could manage it, not being on the program committee. "Simple. I happen to be chairman of the Indian Work Commission of the Province, and have to make my report: your talk will be a part of my report." It sounded all right, but neither of us had reckoned with the authorities who See To It that no propaganda inserts even a thin wedge. However, the gracious chairman, Bishop Gooden, said that I might have five minutes. I think it was this experience that first opened my eyes to the possibilities of presenting our project as a true romance. With one eye on my public and one on my watch, I packed the story into four minutes and fifty-five seconds, bowed to the chairman and sat down to an ovation that said in clear enough terms, "We want more!"

The ovation took nearly another five minutes—although the meeting was in the church building and Episcopalians rarely imitate the primitive church in this particular type of response to a speaker. As it died down the bishop smiled and said, "I think, in view of this, we might give Father Liebler another ten minutes." There were cries of "Fifteen," but I assured them that I could complete the story in ten more, and did so with, again, five seconds to spare.

There is one other mission of our church to Indians in Utah. It is to the Utes, on their large reservation several hundred miles east of Salt Lake City and probably about four hundred miles from us. When Father Hogben was the priest out there at Whiterocks, he invited me to bring a group to his place for "Bishop's Day"—an event he hoped would become an annual observance. It sounded like a good idea. The church has ministered to the Utes for many decades, and they have acquired a good church tradition. One of the things about mission work in virgin territory is that one has no obvious existing body into which new converts can be introduced; one has to build up the customary as one goes. I thought it would be good to show some of our converts the church in action.

We started off the day before in the old Dodge—five or six adults, several adolescents and a few children. Moab, a hundred miles from home, was the biggest city they had ever seen, with three- and four-story buildings and stores that sold different kinds of things, unlike the trading posts, which either did or didn't have anything you might want. There were traffic lights and overhead street lights; there were "rock shops" and a laundry and a bank. (Of all things—a store where they sell money! How silly can these white people get!)

Thirty-five miles farther I drew up so that they could see the railroad tracks. They had seen trains in pictures and in our movies, but this was a new idea—that trains have to have their own peculiar type of road to travel on. A few miles farther on the road turned westward and we saw a train in the distance. But a still greater thrill lay ahead: in Price Valley where we left the Salt Lake road to head northeast, we had to cross the tracks, but before crossing we had to wait for the train to pass. It passed slowly enough so that we could wave to the friendly passengers, who were probably just as thrilled as we, at the sight of this pickup-load of Indians in gala attire.

Father Hogben was the soul of hospitality and turned over the second story of Talbot House to us. Our womenfolk fixed some food, and we rolled out our blankets for the night. Clyde Sam served my Mass in the morning, and soon after our breakfast the Indian people started to arrive. Many came in wagons, but pickups or other motor vehicles were by now beginning to appear, and there must have been a hundred or more saddle horses at the hitching posts. The solemn Mass was somewhat delayed because the thurifer had been jailed the night before, but the sheriff released him for the function, and of course everybody had to wait until he had made his confession.

I was surprised to see several Navajos among them. One was an old woman who simply explained that she had lived with the Utes for many years. She hadn't forgotten her language, however, and I noticed that she and our people got together very quickly. The Utes are commonly spoken of as a people of a weak culture: the Navajos, on the contrary, have a strong culture. The tendency, then, is for a Navajo living among the Utes to retain his own tribal language, dress and other customs. But a Ute living among Navajos adopts the customs of his new neighbors. In the "Piute Strip," where many Piutes have remained since the land was purchased and turned over to the Navajo, virtually all the Piutes understand and speak Navajo (although with a patent Ute accent), but seldom does one find a Navajo who knows more than a few words of Piute. Superficial observers have sometimes jumped to the conclusion that the Utes are more intelligent, intelligence being measured by the degree to which an Indian adopts Anglo customs, but the inference is hardly justified by the facts. The languages, incidentally, are of completely different origin: Ute is Shoshonean, Navajo an Athabascan, language. They probably have no more in common than Hebrew and Mandarin.

The Bishop's Day ceremonies came off with great éclat; everything had been well planned. Mass was sung in a dignified and devotional manner, a barbecued roast fed everyone, a band supplied music, and an exhibition of horsemanship and other games closed the day.

33

One immediate result of the week-long school held at Montezuma Creek by Helen and Phyllis was the offer of two acres of land on which we might build a school. This offer came from the trader who was living not on Reservation land but on deeded land of his own. As previously mentioned, a trader with no missionary neighbors is expected, on the death of a customer, to bury him, and when a customer is sick the trader must close his shop and drive him to a hospital. After we had opened our school, we found out that it was the custom of the Navajos of that area to move to distant areas where fuel was more abundant as soon as cold weather came, and their trade would go to other trading posts. A school might keep them nearer home! Far be it from me to belittle the generosity of the trader's gift. It was a real gift, with no strings attached, and if motives were divided—well, whose are not?

We proceeded to stake out our land, and then to set batter boards to guide the laying of the foundations. Shoodi and his son-in-law, Sam, were engaged to lay up the walls. I had had my eye on a big outcropping of native stone not far from the trail.

It had a three-way cleavage and lay in pieces ideal for masonry, about the size and shape of the cobblestones that paved city streets when I was a boy. But the trader wouldn't hear of it. "Too soft, Father. Why, that stuff would crumble in your hands before you could lay it up. I can get you a good buy of cement and pumice blocks out of Cortez. You'll be real satisfied with that." Reluctantly I consented, hoping that the time saved in laying up the blocks would compensate for the additional cost. The truckdriver who delivered it got lost once and returned to Cortez, mission unaccomplished, tried it again and broke an axle. Whether or not the trader's cut on this deal amounted to anything at all, I am sure that the dealer did not make a big profit!

Bishop Clark, on his second visit, blessed the site, the walls being then a course or two high. When the walls were up, Brother Juniper took over, and with the help of Milton Darling, a volunteer, and two seminarian summer workers, Larry Lain and David Weden, completed the roof and set in windows and doors. Larry's work was chiefly the ferrying of the building materials from Bluff to the site over what is called a primitive road but hardly deserved the name of road at all. To save time, at many points where exposed surface rocks would reveal the "road" only to born pioneers, Brother Juniper painted marks to guide the drivers.

We had asked a good deal of advice from Phyllis Johnson, who we expected would teach the new school. But by this time Phyllis had got itchy feet. She was a career girl, who had already made a name for herself in journalism and who had a deep interest in Navajos, but she was in no sense committed to our religious viewpoint, and we shouldn't have hoped to keep her indefinitely.

But the Lord provides. He had sent us an accomplished priest, Father Botelho, who after some months of work at the Mission asked for the assignment to Montezuma Creek as teacher and priest. He worked hard at learning Navajo. With some gift for languages—he knew French, in addition to the languages of the Cross—he also had the asset of youth. He preached his first sermon in Navajo thirteen months after his arrival, and by that time he had gained an ease in communication, through informal conversation, that few have equaled.

We conveyed such household goods and school supplies as he thought he would need by truck, but he himself rode Beshlagai so that he could return to the Mission when necessary. Normally he came on week ends, except on the one Sunday of the month when Mass was to be offered at Montezuma Creek. (At such times the schoolhouse was turned into a church by the simple expedient of opening the triptych and revealing the crucifix.) Father Botelho had a charge account with the trader so he would not be short of supplies.

On his first return he reported, with a wry smile, "I have news for you—we have a boarding school! Not a day school but a boarding school! The children came, all right, the first day, but they brought their blankets. They said, 'It is too far for us to walk to school and back every day. We will stay here. Our families live far away and they will be there all winter, until it gets warm again in spring.'" So, by overwhelmingly popular demand, the school became a boarding school.

At the bishop's suggestion we called the school San Juan Bautista. Our river, the San Juan, had been named by the Spanish explorers in honor of St. John the Baptist, and as our church and school were within a stone's throw of the river, I thought it well to take on that dedication. But somehow "St. John Baptist Church" might create a difficulty in the minds of any who had heard of a Baptist church, and certainly we would not want to embarrass our denominational fellow Christians in any way. So the bishop's suggestion was followed—we used the Spanish translation—and church and school flourished for three full years.

When Father Botelho felt the need to move on, we took as boarders at St. Christopher's all the children whose parents wanted them to come, but about this time Uncle Sam had been aroused out of his torpor and had enlarged many of the reservation schools and established new ones—so that the need which had been so pressing (it was said in 1945 that there were schools available for less than 20 per cent of the Navajo children of school age) was no longer so. In fact, it was not long after this that we were amused at the sight of teachers beating the brush for pupils to fill their quotas! Since then there has been an almost predictable fluctuation; as population increase plus a growing enthusiasm for education results in insufficient available space in the schools, this is followed by further expansion of schools and consequent ardent recruiting on the part of school officials.

This may be as good a place as any for me to air my own ideas about Navajo education. We started our schools because none existed in our area. We closed the San Juan Bautista School, as I have said, and in 1961 we closed our school at St. Christopher's. This is not because we felt that the then suddenly available public school was sufficient but because we wished to put no obstacle in the way of desegregation. The school in Bluff had definitely been for whites. There was no legislation, no ruling, no test case—it was simply accepted. We had an Indian school, and the county had a white school. For a time the county reckoned our school as part of its system, paying a teacher's salary and providing all supplies, from pencils to coal. But when the United States Supreme Court began to get excited about segregation, it began to look bad to have an Indian school and a white school in Bluff.

The county greatly enlarged its school building to accommodate the number of Navajos, and at the same time "discontinued" the Bluff Indian school (St. Christopher's). But we continued on just the same, without county help, because the children refused to go to the public school and their parents asked us to carry on. In fact, a number of white children from Bluff came to our school, so that it was not segregated, either in fact or in theory. But in 1961 we decided in favor of helping desegregation to the extent of temporarily closing our school. We did agree to continue it if ten children absolutely could not be prevailed upon to go to the public school; there were only five, and they capitulated. I happen to be writing these lines on a day in 1963 when St. Christopher's School is being reopened, with Sally Frese as teacher.

The Church of the Living God cannot, save at her peril, refuse her divine commission to teach. "Go, teach all nations," was His command; and I am quite sure, as the church has always been, that this did not mean just the birds and bugs of the Holy Land, or even the catechism or the parables and the Sermon on the Mount. All knowledge and wisdom come from God and constitute, in a sense, a unit. Someone has said, with reason, that while an uneducated rascal will steal a ride on a railroad train, an educated rascal will steal the railroad. Shortly before typing this chapter, I read a very controversial book by one of the English bishops who constantly remind us that huge multitudes of people are finding that they can get along without religion. His particular solution of the problem does not now concern us, but what does concern us is the obvious fact that the world which thinks it is getting along just fine without religion is wrestling with juvenile delinquency, gang tyranny, dictatorship and who knows how many other problems to which it refuses the answer, having determined to get along just fine without it. With our American axiom regarding separation of church and state, of course the state cannot teach religion. The fault lies not with the public schools—they are powerless. The fault lies at our own door. Jesus told the church, "Go, teach," and the church has answered, "Let George [Washington] do it." Certainly we realized that St. Christopher's School was less than a drop in the bucket, but at least it told where we stood.

34

Newton Darling and I had just arrived at Oljeto early in the afternoon of the day before our regularly scheduled service, and at the trading post we were immediately besieged by several young men who had a problem. "You wanna hep dis man? Her wife gonna have baby, been tryin tree days, can't do it. You take him Kayenta, nuss down dere pitty good." I explained that we had a job to do—to visit all the hogans in the area and tell the people that tomorrow there would be prayers at the hogan that served as church; however, in view of this pressing problem, if the young men who were so eager to find help for their friend would do this for us, we would gladly take the woman to Kayenta, some thirty miles away. They agreed, and I drilled them carefully as to the time of day when the service was to be held, and the expectant father climbed in to guide.

Their camp was in the area northwest of Harry Goulding's Trading Post, and of course we had to take the short cut over sandy roads. Our vehicle was a suburban, sturdily built and roomy but not dependable in deep sand. Nine times we had to dig ourselves out and make a new start. As we approached the hogan a man came out, grinning from ear to ear, and without pausing for the conventional formalities declared, "Sitsói hazlíí, literally, "My grandchild has become." Of course, we went in, paid our respects to the mother and gave a blessing to her and the child.

She brought up the matter of a name for the child, a boy. The problem of naming children was then a comparatively new one to the Navajos of our area. The old tradition was to call a child Baby until the next one came along, a year or two later; then the first one would be called Boy or Girl until the Baby that followed had a successor, by which time Boy or Girl should have shown some personal propensity or feature that warranted a corresponding name—if only the adjective Fat, Thin, Tall or the like. But now "Washingdoan" through the Bureau of Indian Affairs required a stable name and assigned a number stamped on a metal disk that could be used for identification, and Washingdoan also looked with strong disfavor upon Navajo names that could not be spelled in English letters, or that could be written in a variety of spellings. For example, Smith, ("Hammerer") may be Etsitty, Atcidi, Otcidie, and the resultant filing problem would be exasperating. A left-handed man might be called Cly, Clay, Klaw, Claude or Clyde; the son of Harry might logically be called Harrison but is much more likely to be Harry's Boy and end up in school as Harris Boyd. One who as a small boy developed a mild passion for taking off his clothes was called Ha-dee-jay, and in a few years appeared on the trader's books as Hedges. All these, although far from perfect, are greatly preferable to the imaginative but highly undignified sort of name that is still found on the reservation: Pipeline, Sauerkraut, twins Pete and Repete, Whiskers, Manymules and so on.

But to go back to our newborn: The day was March 24, the Feast of St. Gabriel the Archangel, and the morrow would be the Feast of the Annunciation of the Blessed Virgin. What could be more natural than that the boy should bear through life the name of the angel who above all others was chosen to bring to Our Lady the great news of her election to be the mother of the Saviour? The parents liked the sound of the name, and found they could say it easily. And so the child was named Gabriel, a name of dignity, and acceptable to Washingdoan.

Since we were not in so great a hurry now, the proud father pointed out a better road for our return. Attendance at Mass the next day was very small. As far as we could find out, our messengers had not carried the news to a single family; their good deed for the day had been performed when they induced us to undertake the errand of mercy.

35

Convocation met in Salt Lake City in the summer of 1949. An important item on the agenda was the election of deputies to the General Convention, scheduled to be held in San Francisco in honor of the centennial. To my amazement I was not only nominated but elected, and the nominator, out of the goodness of his heart, volunteered to pay my expenses. This was important, for unless somebody had done so, I could not have gone; but far more important was this firm indication of the acceptance of our Mission. Utah churchmen had been uniformly kind, to be sure, but I had always had a feeling that they showed something that might best be called amused toleration. When it appeared that they really trusted me to represent them—and remember, we have but *one* clerical and one lay deputy—it was truly a heart-warming thing.

In our Mission economy a trip of a thousand miles is not to have but a single goal. Dozens of letters to people in the Bay area resulted in a dozen or more speaking engagements before various sorts of groups—church, DAR, civic and even one rather definitely leftist cell that probably had never been addressed by a Christian missionary or heard the story of the establishment of a mission to Indians. There was also an opportunity of visiting our seminary and the sister institution for the training of women workers in the church; here again it was good to feel accepted, even though the atmosphere was not exactly reminiscent of Thomas More, Becket or Aquinas. Perhaps the best way to tame a rebel is to love him, after all.

36

I was still at my devotions after Mass on the morning of July 27, 1950, when Newton Darling came running back into the church, picked up the two stirrup pumps and ran out again. We often use these to dampen down the sandy floor of church or common room, but his haste was a strange feature. I went out to see. The east wing of the Mission House was all but invisible for smoke, but there was no flame to be seen. I ripped off my cassock, grabbed a shovel and started to investigate. Years ago the home of the commissary of our Home Guard Unit had burned, and I recalled the stories about ammunition in all directions: all my .30-caliber shells were stored in my office at the south end of the wing. Unlocking the door, I was driven back by billows of thick smoke.

A couple from Martinez, California, had stopped in to visit. They were not dressed for fire fighting, so I asked them to rush to Bluff and get all the help possible. By this time Brother Juniper and Newton had located the flames in the north end of the wing, which adjoined but did not open into the main part of the Mission House. They were applying carbon dioxide and stirrup pumps and a hose of water to the affected parts. Our only source of water at that time was a 500-gallon tank fed by the the spring that had been the deciding factor in our choice of building site, and I had no idea how nearly full it might be. I got an idea, however, very soon as the pressure gradually dropped, but about this time Bluff appeared in full force. I doubt whether even a child remained in town to mind the store. They brought more shovels and tanks of water and apparently inexhaustible energy. When the roof cracked open and the fierce draft of this natural stove stimulated the flames, it became clear that we were not going to put the fire out; the most we could hope for was to prevent the rest of the Mission House from burning too. As the wing had been built some years after the main building, the masonry walls simply butted against each other and were not locked in. There was no opening, either door or window, and this was greatly in our favor. We had not yet put on the double roofs, but each roof was mud-covered, so that it was only necessary to keep the parts of the main house that butted against the burning wing saturated with water. Men took turns standing on the roof and sprinkling or dousing the threatened areas with bucketfuls of water.

Meantime the radiant heat from the fire had ignited the projecting *vigas,* or roof beams, of the west wing as well as of the main house, and I made this my stand. In the patio, where we still had a lot of sand, I could keep a vigilant eye on the two rows of *vigas,* and the instant one burst into flame I had a shovelful—or two or three as might be needed—to throw on it.

Women and children from the surrounding hogans and from Bluff carried everything out of the west wing and the main house, because we knew that if they caught fire, smoke would prevent such removal. The really inspiring thing was to see our neighbors showing their deep friendship in this unselfish labor of love. Mormons, Jehovah's Witnesses, deep-South Baptists, all were one in helping the Mission with all their might. As I leaned on my shovel for a moment between bursts of flame on the *vigas* it suddenly came upon me that everything I owned, except what I was wearing (a pair of Boy Scout shorts, moccasins and a thin shirt), had burned. Yes, my breviary, a few other books and my vestments were in the church, but all else was gone. It was a great sense of relief: it seemed that a load had been taken from my weary back—no more *things!* Foolishly I tried to tell George Brooks, a war veteran who stood beside me, how good it felt. That evening he returned with a pair of trousers, two shirts and a pair of shoes. There is no richness like poverty plus friends.

It must have been well into the afternoon when we all felt that the fire was completely under control. There remained only portions of the stud-and-wallboard partitions to burn out at their leisure; there was no further fear of conflagration. There had been no wind. Our good neighbors went home, and we went into the church to sing a Te Deum for God's mercy and the boon of neighbors who are friends.

Insurance took care of the rebuilding. The company made me their adjuster, which was hard on the Mission, as their own man might have been more generous than I could be under the circumstances. However, in several months we got our building back; but many priceless treasures were irretrievably lost. The diary of my exploration trip of 1941, which I had always resolved some day to type up, many valuable books, silver belts and other pawns—but the item that started the biggest legend of the year was the burning of that barrel of sermons that had been prepared in the Navajo language. As I have mentioned this was simply a collection of manuscript sermons, for the most part doctrinal and made up from the responses of the Franciscan Fathers' *Catechism.* Actually I was glad that they were gone. It was high time that I got away from relying on them and started making a real and new sermon for each Sunday. With so many other things demanding my time, and because it had been so easy with this collection on hand, I had come to depend on it. Well, within a few weeks the legend had grown to a translation of the Episcopal communion service into Navajo; not long after, they were saying that the whole Book of Common Prayer in Navajo had burned; and within six months it seemed that the fire had destroyed the first and only translation into Navajo of the entire Bible!

37

In a hospital in Norwood, Massachusetts, a young woman was experiencing a growing interest in St. Christopher's Mission. Norwood's Grace Church had organized a special guild to promote help for us, but this woman had bigger things in mind. Born with poor eyesight, she was denied her heart's ambition of becoming a nurse, but she made up for this by doing all kinds of work in the hospital, asking innumerable questions and remembering the answers, and reading everything she could find, and above all, "taking it to the Lord in prayer." Her letters began to arrive, one on the heels of another, and finally she asked definitely if we would accept her. The eye specialist who had been attending her wrote that the condition showed no indication of growing worse and that we need expect no serious deterioration in the years to come, so we welcomed her. Transportation was readily supplied by the Lains, who were driving from Cambridge.

This was Catherine Pickett. She threw herself wholeheartedly into the work, endearing herself to the Navajo people, and in a phenomenally short time getting to know not only their names but their relationship by family and by clan to one another. If because of distance or inadequate light she could not see a person, she would invariably recognize the voice. On one occasion, after she had been with us for several years, we had a visit from the state's top-ranking official in the Health Department's preventive branch. He asked if she would be willing when time allowed to give him a list of Navajos who had been diagnosed as having tuberculosis, and of their close contacts. "If you have a pencil and paper, I can give you the names now," she said, and kept him busy for several hours writing just what he wanted. She didn't have to refer to charts or other records but gave the heads of families, names and ages of children without hesitation.

As soon as the east wing was rebuilt we put up partitions,

and one cell was set aside as the "clinic." It had a hospital bed, a locking cupboard for medications and a few crude homemade bits of equipment, such as an oxygen tent and an incubator. The news of our expanding medical work spread, and a group of physicians in Salt Lake City arranged to come down and hold a clinic, with special attention to chest X-rays, eye examinations and general physical checkups. Nothing of the sort had been dreamed of before, and it wasn't easy, with no precedent to guide us, to make the arrangements. It was the Utah National Guard that flew the X-ray machine down as far as Blanding (our nearest landing field) in a bombing plane, and there was no trouble enlisting a local trucker to get it the rest of the way.

Drs. Davis, Muir and Muirhead were here in good time, and people turned out in droves. We set up an assembly line and herded the Navajos through from one doctor to another. At that time there were still very few Navajos who could speak enough English to act as interpreters, but we managed to teach the doctors or their helpers the essential phrases, such as "take off your shirt," "take a deep breath—hold it, breathe again." The Snellen chart was one made for illiterates and consisted of the letter *E* in all four directions; the person being examined simply indicated with three fingers extended the direction of the *E* when the doctor pointed at it. I don't remember how many tuberculosis cases were picked up at this time, but the greater number of them were shipped off to sanatoria and were later returned healed or arrested. A few cases of trachoma were discovered and treatment was begun, which for the most part we were able to continue, the greatest difficulty being that after a few days the patient felt better and failed to report for the remainder of the treatment. There were a few cases of pterygium and of course the customary impetigo, summer diarrhea, cuts and bruises—and the hypochondriacs who wanted "shots." Only one Navajo refused the routine chest X-ray. He protested that he was not sick and remained deaf to the idea that one can get tuberculosis and have it for some time before the discomfort or pain becomes noticeable. But he was adamant, and we could not force him. Some years later when we had our own X-ray machine, he came in, asked for "picture" and readily agreed to go to a hospital for treatment.

Catherine needed space for the many who came to her for care, and we set aside one cell in the east wing, after the log church had been put into use so that the east wing of the Mission House was no longer needed for this purpose. It was small, but much better than treating patients in the common room, or even outdoors. Catherine had been with us nearly three years when Jeannette came into our lives.

It happened like this: Early in Feburary, the worst time of the year for Navajo health, Cyrus Begay drove in with his pick-up and a number of sick children. "Lots of sick kids up my way," he said. "Why don't you take Catherine up there and take care of them?" We couldn't at that moment, but in a day or two we made an early start for the Hatch Trading Post area. Following Ira Hatch's directions, we came across dozens of hogans in which children were laid up with what lay folk used to call "this flu that's going around." The sun had set, and we really were tired as we passed the trading post on the way home, but Sherman Hatch came running out. "Did you go to Abraham's camp? He's got a sick kid." So we turned around and drove two miles up the wash. A lamp shining inside the tent guided us, and there was no difficulty finding the place. The sick kid proved to be the eighteen-month-old child whose fever had broken and who needed nothing so much as a bit of nourishing food. We left vitamins and baby food. But while Catherine was taking care of the details, I noticed a blanket spread on the floor, under which was a lump that moved now and again. I asked Abraham if there was a cat under there. He laughed.

"No. I don't know. My wife's sister's baby. Burned."

"Burned?" I cried in horror. "Really, badly burned?"

Again, "Hola—I don't know," he turned about as if to indicate that this was not his concern. Gently I lifted a corner of the blanket. It was a frightful sight. If you were to take a piece of raw beef, singe it, toss it into an autumn hayfield and then kick it around a bit, you would have a good picture of what Jeannette's thigh and buttocks looked like. Sticks and straws, gravel and sand, clotted blood—I have seen mayhem and death, but seldom have I been so moved. I estimated the child's age to be about the same as that of her cousin for whom we had come to give medication, but Abraham insisted that this one was three years old.

Catherine said in her most positive tone, "I can't do anything for the child here. We must take her home."

The foster parents consented readily. We wrapped the child in the softest blankets available, and Catherine carried her in prone position on her lap. Unwilling to delay our return unnecessarily, I was content with the briefest outline of the case. It seems that Jeannette really was three years old. Her mother had died four days after delivering her; her father was in a sanatorium for tuberculosis. The mother's sister, by Navajo custom, had the care of the child, but apparently such was the family's poverty that there wasn't enough food for anybody, and this little outsider got only the slimmest leavings. At three she had neither walked nor spoken, and when we weighed her the scales stood at sixteen pounds.

The burning had come about a day or two before our visit. Jeannette was crawling around in the tent alone. Apparently she got near the little camp stove on which a pot of coffee was boiling, and reached for it as a support to raise herself. The family responded to her cries and found her literally sitting in a pond of steaming coffee. The desolate thing about it was that we had been called in to minister not to this poor little sufferer but to Abraham's own child, who was really all but fully recovered from whatever had afflicted her. This whole incident is one of many which give the answer in readily understood language to people who ask us, "Why do you have to cram *our* religion down these people's throats when they have a perfectly good, beautiful and satisfactory religion of their own?"

At that time we had Mary Gail Evans with us, a medical technician, who helped Catherine with cleaning up Jeannette, packing her with pressure bandages over sulfa ointments and guarding against infection. It was a long, slow process. The child seemed more like a vegetable than like a sentient being. We had no way of knowing whether, once the burns were healed, we would find her a mute, an idiot or a normal human being. It was several months before Jeannette began to utter syllables that might convey some meaning. When at last we got a smile as a response, we felt amply repaid for our efforts. Of course, she won the hearts of us all, but Catherine truly became a mother to her. In time the father was discharged from the sanatorium and came to see his baby. He voiced the fear that Abraham's family might try to get Jeannette back when she was old enough to help herd sheep, and to avoid this we got a court to appoint Catherine as legal guardian.

At six Jeannette was ready for school, slightly undersized and of course retarded by the experience of malnutrition in the first three years of her life. Nevertheless, she still held her own with other children in her age group. Catherine's desire to make a nurse of her was readily understandable in view of her own disappointment. Whether or not these dreams see fulfillment no one can at this date tell. As I write Jeannette has had a year in the Shiprock School and more in the large Intermountain Indian School at Brigham City, Utah.

38

I do want to go on about Catherine and her important work but must not get too far from the chronological sequence of events.

Our good friend and religious superior, Bishop Clark, was seriously ill in the spring of 1950. Bishop William Lewis of Nevada was designated to take over as much as possible of his work, and happily for us this included an informal visitation. Characteristically he rolled up his sleeves, donned a coverall and repaired some plumbing that had defied our best efforts. He used to boast of being the only bishop in the hierarchy who held a plumber's union card! We took him on a little tour of inspection, including the fabulous Monument Valley area, which unfortunately was not at its best because of sandstorms that greatly reduced visibility. As if it were needed to impress him with the hardships of missionary life, we burst our gas tank with a stone tossed up by a tire. He in turn showed us how to mend the hole with yellow soap, and later how to build a baffle of sheet iron to take the shock of such blows and lengthen the life of this and future gas tanks. He blessed our altar in the log chapel and also some portable altar stones for use in outstation visits, and confirmed a class of Navajos who had been under instruction for some months. His sermon was a model of simplicity and spiritual power, easy to translate into Navajo. Unfortunately he could not stay over to grace our Corpus Christi celebration on the following day.

Bishop Clark died on St. Andrew's Day, 1950. For five months we were without episcopal leadership, except insofar as Bishop Lewis was able to spare time from his own responsibilities in Nevada. It was in January of 1951 that we heard in some roundabout way that our new bishop had been elected: he was the Very Reverend Richard Simpson Watson, Dean of St. Mark's Cathedral in Seattle, Washington. My life being among the lowly, I had never heard of him, but I wrote at once to a former classmate who lived in Seattle to get the lowdown. He defied all clerical tradition by answering promptly, and he gave the bishop-elect a very good press.

As his predecessor had done Dr. Watson came to look over the ground before making his decision. With proper humility he told us of the clergy that he had come to see if by chance it was "a job that Dick Watson could do." A discouraged and very tired handful of clergy, spreading themselves thinly over nearly ninety thousand square miles of Mormon territory, responded joyfully to his promised leadership, and he gave his *volo* to the presiding bishop. Jimmy Jones, who had helped us with the preliminary school at Montezuma Creek, and his brother, Jackie, represented the Navajo people at the solemn consecration on May 1. Jimmy had been confirmed by Bishop Lewis only ten months before, so the sight of a bishop was no novelty to him, but the sight of a large church full of people and of no fewer than twenty successors of the apostles laying hands simultaneously on one who was being made our bishop—*our* successor to the apostles—must have been an impressive one.

Bishop Watson left no doubt in anybody's mind about how he felt regarding St. Christopher's Mission by arranging a brief visitation within two months of his consecration. It was no doubt good for him to get a view of his new responsibilities by driving the three hundred and fifty miles on partly paved roads over mountains and vast reaches of desert. He left the last organized mission three hundred miles north of us, and it is not hard for us now to look back and think how he must have prayed that this great area could soon have an opportunity of hearing the fullness of the Gospel.

I had been doing a bit of pastoral visiting in the redlands country of Comb Wash and had come across an elderly couple who showed more than a passing interest in the story of the Redemption. The man was pretty obviously a terminal case of tuberculosis; he got about only with great difficulty. His wife, more limber and mobile, seemed able to care for him adequately. I used to bring a gallon or two of pure artesian water every time I came, and when it was clear that they really wanted all the graces of the Gospel, I baptized them, just eight days before the bishop's arrival. I resent the accusation that I wanted to "take the bishop over the bumps"! I was as eager to present this couple for the Confirmation as he was to administer the rite, and within an hour of his arrival at the Mission we were off for the Comb country.

The unimproved road through the pass presented as spectacular a view then as does the paved highway today of Utah's incomparable Painted Desert. Just west of the Wash we took off on a trail to the north, and then after a few miles on a completely uncharted path, which no one unfamiliar with the landmarks of the area could have followed. I appreciated the bishop's silent confidence in my driving but breathed an equally silent prayer of thanks when Blackhorse's *chaha'oh* burst into view as we crested a big sand dune.

The couple greeted us joyously, and in a few minutes the bishop had on his rochet, aliturgically decorated with red sand, and we were in the midst of what he must have considered the most informal service of his entire ministry. If there was a dry eye among us, mine were too blurred to see it.

The following day was Sunday and the Feast of St. John Baptist's Nativity. Word had got about that the new bishop was with us, and a large congregation turned out to greet him. He confirmed a number of adults and one child, Jackie Jones, who had gone to Salt Lake City for the consecration. By midafternoon the bishop was off in a cloud of dust.

Not long after, I took the necessary things along and offered Mass at Blackhorse's shade. He was failing rapidly, and his first Holy Communion was his Viaticum.

But to get on with the Catherine Pickett story. That one-room clinic was painfully inadequate, and we began to make plans for a building that would take care of present and some future needs. Visiting physicians, some of whom knew our problems well and others who did not, were uniformly sympathetic and understanding. They gave not only advice but encouragement. They agreed that we had to do what we could when professional services were not available. I think in all our dealings with the profession we encountered only one who was adamant in opposition. Helen and Catherine talked with him at one of the government hospitals. He warned Catherine that she hadn't the right "to give an aspirin pill" or any medical advice, and further threatened that "if you don't cease and desist I will personally see that your place is closed." Helen characteristically asked if we should leave a sick or injured person to die in a ditch, and she quotes him as replying, "Yes, such a person is not your responsibility."

But the majority ruled, and we went ahead with plans. Not least in importance is the fact that we would build with a view to future enlargement; for the present there would be eight rooms, each opening into a hall that was to run the full length of the building. But first we must have water. An artesian well took nearly two thousand dollars and left very little in the bank.

But by the time our plans were drawn we had accumulated enough to hire a gang of Navajo stonemasons to put up the walls. Unusually severe winter weather slowed the work down considerably; in fact, the masons took off for their distant homes, promising to come back when the snow should be gone. This gave us time to build up our bank account, but didn't help the sick and needy! Our quarterly newsletter carried stories of progress that must have sounded to our readers like admissions of lack of progress.

During that spring we had a visit from a group of boys studying at Verde Valley School in Arizona. One great ideal of that school has been to produce men and women on fire to eliminate racial prejudice and discrimination, and one means to this end is to send groups of students as project workers into areas where they will be able to get close contacts with those of other races. It happened that one of these boys, looking meditatively around the rustic common room of the Mission, remarked, "Gee, I've got an aunt out in California who'd just love to know about a place like this and help it along." The aunt started getting newsletters. Soon after, I had a letter from her attorneys stating that they had been instructed to send fifty dollars each month. Within a year we got a note from her saying that she was sick and tired of reading about the delays in getting that clinic done and for heaven's sake use this two-thousand-dollar check to get on with it! We did.

Using much volunteer labor and some paid labor, with Brother Juniper as chief full-time working foreman, we got the place ready to be dedicated and put into use by St. Mark's Day, 1956. At least that is what we thought. There were of course many last-minute things—putting in window screens, learning the ways of a temperamental oil-burning steam-heat furnace and radiators and adapting an antique thermostat contributed out of their museum by Minneapolis-Honeywell Company, for without reliable current we could not use a modern model—screwing in hardware fixtures, curtain rods, painting floors and re-enameling chipped items of medical and surgical equipment. It was Brother's idea to have a formal dedication and opening. I just thought we'd get the place ready and start to use it, but he was right in thinking that a lot of people would be interested, so we sent invitations to everybody we thought could possibly care about it.

Three weeks before the scheduled opening, when I went out to ring the Angelus, I was surprised to see a car parked in front of the clinic. I walked down and noted the caduceus symbol over the registration marker. Something was going on, evidently—or rather, had gone on. Dr. "Kind" (his middle name is Kind) had driven thirty miles or so in the wee small hours to deliver the first baby to be born in our not-yet-finished clinic. Catherine had hurriedly prepared a bed; complications were anticipated and she asked someone to drive to Bluff and telephone the doctor—and it was just as well, for the baby came with the cord about its neck ("better to be born that way than to die that way" was the comment of one who had lived in the days of short shrift for horse thieves!) and he had, of all things, six toes and six fingers where five ought to be. They were fleshy digits, boneless, and Dr. Kind snipped them off before the patient, Lucille, knew that this wasn't just normal routine at St. Christopher's.

We painted the floor under Lucille's bed and hung the curtain rods over the windows, and she took it all in good spirits. After all, it was something of an honor to be the first. She made another record by having her next three within three years, all in our clinic. Hardly had we tossed mother and baby out into the cold world when Nancy Yanito came in, bulging, and asking for the same bed. It looked to Catherine like a difficult delivery, but there wasn't time to call the doctor, so the customary relatives and neighbors came in and did everything in traditional Navajo way, complete with the woven "squaw belt." When we sent mother and baby away, Catherine announced in that firmest of all firm voices, "This is all, until the opening of our clinic. Anybody else comes, just send them to a hospital."

But the firmest of all firm voices must sometimes tremble, if ever so slightly. Ten days before the scheduled opening and dedication another pickup rolled to a stop in front of the Mission House. The young driver said, "My mudda piddy sick." I asked what the trouble was and prepared to put on my most authoritative tone announcing that we were in no position to take any patient in—they must go to a government hospital. Well, it seems he didn't know what the trouble was. So I asked the mother, who said, plaintively, "It's the baby."

I looked around, saw no baby, and prepared to tell her that we couldn't give absent treatment. By this time she had got out of the cab of the pickup and said, with a touch of impatience, "Right now! Right now I'm having the baby!" and a few drops of blood on her boot left no doubt as to the accuracy of the diagnosis. I bundled her back into the pickup; Catherine must have sensed the situation almost before we reached the clinic, for as the patient collapsed halfway to the maternity room she yanked a mattress from a stretcher and slipped it under the falling woman. Not exactly curb service, or drive-in, but as close as we want to get. So came the third baby before we were open for business.

As the scheduled day drew near it looked more and more as if we could never be ready on time. But we hadn't counted on Phyllis MacDonald. She it was who had secured for us a vanload of hospital equipment from Akron General, supplementing equipment previously sent from St. Luke's in Denver, Clarkson Memorial and University hospitals in Omaha, and several individuals. We should have known that when she wrote, "I'll be there in time to hang the drapes," she meant that she would See to Things. She did.

She and her husband, Clyde, and son, Bob, came bouncing in with sleeves rolled up for work. Once the curtains were up, adding a gay color to the scheme, and a dozen other minor details attended to, she dashed off to Blanding thirty miles away, to get flowers "from the florist." We could have set her straight, but she wouldn't have thought of asking, as who ever heard of a town of over a thousand inhabitants having no florist? She knows better now, but she also knows about the warm hearts of the Mormon neighbors who, learning of her need, loaded her down with forsythia and pear blossoms.

Finally came the day. The bishop and visiting priests said their Masses early; at seven-thirty we had High Mass for St. Mark's Day, with the bishop at his throne. At eleven we gathered at the church, formed a procession, and singing the Litany, walked in a body to the clinic. I had consented to the issuing of invitations, but I really didn't expect anybody to come any distance; picture my surprise when there came representatives not only of the tribe but of the Bureau of Indian Affairs, the Bureau of Public Health and medical centers as far off as Denver and Salt Lake City. The governor of Utah sent a personal representative when he found he could not come himself. Our project seemed so small in comparison with the need that we really felt humbled, but stimulated to make resolutions to utilize what we had to the full. The bishop blessed the whole building, outside and inside, going to all the rooms with holy-water sprinkler in hand. Later he addressed those present out of doors, and I did the best I could to interpret.

The speaker of the day was Mrs. Annie Wauneka, a member for several years of the Navajo tribe's Committee on Health. Her father, Chee Dodge, had been the first tribal chairman when the Navajo adopted the terms of the Indian Reorganization Act, and he made tremendous progress in leading the tribe from the conservative ways that centered on the sheep flocks, and that could not continue indefinitely because of range deterioration and population increase, toward a newer and more realistic culture. Annie had received sufficient schooling to enable her to read prodigiously. Navajos admire oratory, and they stood or sat for nearly two hours while she hammered away at the enemies of Navajo health—dirt, infection, ignorance. It might have been an ordeal for those of us who could not follow her thoughts, but the very enthusiasm and vitality she breathed forth were inspiring. What should have concerned us more was that the refreshment committee which had butchered six or seven sheep reported that virtually all the meat was stolen while Annie talked! However, a group of irate Navajo women don't sit around and bewail such a tragedy. In moments they formed themselves into a posse, and it wasn't long before they came back beaming, and laden down with the spoils of the counter attack. Everybody got fed, except the culprits, and I shudder to think of what happened to them.

From the day of the dedication to Catherine's departure from the Mission in 1961, I don't suppose there were more than two or three occasions when we didn't have patients in residence at the clinic. (I shall probably continue to use the word clinic, although it is not technically correct. Hospital is what it really was, but cannot be called because of arbitrary regulations. I tried to popularize the name nosocome, but for some reason it never caught on; I still think it is a fine name, if it does nothing more than send people scurrying to their dictionaries!) In addition to the things I have already told about Catherine, I must add that she had an uncanny insight into her own limitations. She knew what she could do and what she couldn't do, and when she came face to face with the latter, the patient had to be taken without delay to a hospital. I don't recall a single instance in which such a patient was not admitted. The hospital authorities seemed to have learned that if Catherine couldn't handle the job, it needed their full resources.

Of course, Catherine had to have help. Twenty-four hours of duty seven days a week is enough even for a missionary, without having the laundry and general cleaning to do, the sorting of medicine samples and the irrigating of shade trees that we hoped would give shelter against the hot sun of summer and the cold blasts of winter. We had to stretch the budget, but we made it work somehow. Some who tried for the job failed miserably, others did well but got itchy feet or the sound of ringing bells—wedding bells—in their ears. Perhaps the most interesting person to undertake this work was Leona. Leona has appeared in this chronicle before; she it was who asked if I wanted to "sell some rocks," who rode in and demanded a drink of water for herself and her daughter Dawcie (later found to be Dorothy) and who sent for me when her baby was dying. Leona had had some schooling, and understood much of what was said to her in

English. Catherine put a white gown on her and introduced her to the routine of the nosocome. She proved to be an excellent interpreter, and arrived on time in the morning so that Catherine could get to Mass. While Mary Gail Evans was with us, these two developed a splendid friendship, and each learned much about the other. We all learned more about the clan relationships of our people from Leona than we had done from all other sources combined. A traditionalist of the strictest school, she gained an insight into the white man's medicine that amazed us all. It was her experience at the Cortez hospital that made us realize the progress she had made. But that involves another story.

A sudden column of smoke rising in this dry country is a true smoke signal. It means, "Grab a shovel and run, not walk, to the fire." But before we at the Mission saw the smoke from Leona's brush-and-tarpaper shade, the five children who had been left there alone had begun the rescue work. Beth, the eldest of the five, had spent many months of her five years in Salt Lake City at the Shriners' Hospital, where she had been successfully treated for a severe congenital hip deformity. We often wondered whether first aid had been taught there to tiny tots; anyway, when we finally got the story put together, it seems that Beth got her baby sister out of the flames, clothing ablaze, and rolled her in the sand like an expert! She quickly marshaled the little group into formation and started for the Mission, where she knew they could get help. Meantime we had seen the fire and started with the jeep, which suddenly became an ambulance, and brought the five to the nosocome. The baby's burns obviously were critical, and a real ambulance was quickly put into commission. Leona was located in Bluff and went along to the Cortez hospital, some 110 miles away.

The doctor and nurses did everything possible, but it was decided that the baby must be transferred to a larger hospital by plane. It was while the arrangements were being made that Leona surprised the doctor as well as the nurses by her knowledge of such techniques as intravenous injections and pressure bandages and other therapeutic processes. Her ever-growing circle of admiring listeners were amazed at her relating "how we do it at the clinic at the Mission" and how the Navajos come from many miles around and how sometimes at special clinics, such as Dr. Bayer's baby clinics or Dr. Oaks' eye clinics, we have to feed as many as a hundred of them, as they come from so far away.

I wish I could put a happy ending to the story. The baby died at the Albuquerque (Bernalillo) hospital, not of burns but of pneumonia.

39

In our newsletter dated Midsummer, 1954, Catherine well sums up her work in the clinic, and I cannot do better than present it as she has written it.

JESUS SAID "HEAL THE SICK"

As we were coming out of Church one evening after Vespers a truck drove up; out of the back climbed a lady with a sick baby on a cradle board. It had been ill three days; lungs frightly congested; breathing could be heard in the adjoining room. We put it under oxygen at once. We had to use ice cubes to cool the improvised oxygen tent. The parents were apprehensive, having never seen such a device, but when the baby quieted down in about ten minutes they were greatly relieved, and even went to a relative's hogan for supper. When they returned the baby's condition was not greatly changed; however, under the oxygen it did not cry. Father asked if they would consent to the baby's being baptized, as prognosis was very poor; they did, and he did. The parents finally went off to sleep, but returned at 1 A.M. The baby had improved so much that he could be taken out of oxygen. At 3:00 the parents were amazed to see the baby sit up and smile at them! The mother nursed the baby, who showed voracious appetite. At dawn they took him home, and he has been well ever since.

I was busy caring for a sick baby and a convalescent just discharged from a sanatorium, when in came Suzie saying that her daughter Nancy would soon be having a baby. I offered the usual layette and medication, but Suzie shook her head. She took my hand in both of hers, and said, "Hago"—"Come." Reluctantly I consented: I felt the Navajo midwives were more fitted for the task.

At the hogan the expectant mother, a rare beauty, was just returning to her place after a bath and yucca shampoo. The family sat about, chatting by the fitful gleam of a single kerosene lamp. Children played about as usual; various relatives assembled. After a while, watermelon was served to all, including the expectant mother. After several hours, the ladies who knew about such things decided it was time for the patient to kneel on a sheepskin by the pole which had been erected with the "squaw belt" attached. As each pain came, she would pull on the squaw belt. I was assigned to a place on one side of the patient, an aunt to the other side. An uncle took his place behind the patient, putting his arms about her waist, and as each pain came he would squeeze downward, and the women on either side would press on her knees, and she would pull on the squaw belt. Between pains, everyone chatted. The hogan was well-filled, but only we four cared for the patient. As no one knew any English, I could get only snatches of the conversation.

At 11:06 the aunt said, "K'ad"—"Now!" reaching her hand under the patient's skirt and lo! the baby's head was resting in her hand. I handed her the sterile cord and knife; they handed me the baby, a pan of warm water and a bar of soap. By the time I had washed and wrapped the baby the mother was being tightly wrapped about the waist with the squaw belt. I showed her her baby, an exceptionally pretty one, and noted for the first time that it had two teeth! Penicillin for the mother, terramycin ointment for the baby's eyes, and I felt that my job was done; walked happily home under a starry sky.

Next morning, the mother was sitting up, beautifully dressed, the baby beside her. She thanked me and gave me a dollar, and indicated that the other three assistants had been similarly rewarded. Later, the baby was named Jane, after my sister and a nurse who had taught me what I knew about helping babies into the world.

A hogan in which a death occurs is abandoned, and sometimes burned. We had wondered how the Navajos would feel about the clinic if someone died in it. In November [1953] parents brought in a two-month-old baby with a very severe chest congestion, too weak to risk moving to a hospital. It was immediately put under oxygen, but that gave no relief. We feared tuberculosis, as the disease was prevalent in the family. We baptized the baby and did everything possible, but to no avail. The little life slipped away.

The body remained in the clinic till morning, when the burial took place. By late afternoon, several patients had come for treatment and only two of the local women appeared to have any hesitation. One of these, however, came with her father who wanted medicine for his new wife and baby—the father, a "longhair," entered boldly, and apparently his daughter did not dare show fear before him. She followed him, and has come in often since.

The Sunday afternoon before Christmas a man galloped in on a sweating, lathered horse; he said his brother had been stabbed with a knife by a white man the night before, and was still bleeding freely. Would Father come quick, take him to a doctor? Father and I set out in the jeep, with the messenger as guide. It was a fifty-mile trip by road and wagon trail. We arrived after dark; the man was in a serious condition. With great care we moved him onto a stretcher and into the jeep; the bleeding began again, and it was necessary to apply more bandages. Sixty miles over rough trails, unimproved roads, and the lights of Cortez appeared. We telephoned from the first house we came to; Dr. Speck met us at the hospital, took thirteen stitches, ordered penicillin. The poor victim was again loaded into the jeep; 110 miles by road back to the Mission; just before dawn we got the man to bed. Five days later he was well enough to attend the Christmas Eve party, and midnight Mass; three days later we took out the stitches and he rode home horseback.

Last summer some of us made a trip to Grand Canyon, and on the way back, as some of us had never seen Navajo Mountain, where Father goes every month, we decided to go there, too. On arrival we learned there was to be a Squaw Dance, to which we were invited. It was a colorful sight. Many women, in bright velvet blouses, were preparing meat, Navajo bread and coffee in a large brush shade over several fires. The dancing began late, under a full moon, around a bright fire. As we watched the dancing, the trader's wife told us that a man at a nearby hogan had a badly infected hand; we agreed to see him in the morning, and if necessary take him to the Tuba City Hospital. At Rex's place, one look was enough; he agreed to go but we must wait till a sing and a sand-painting were finished—a matter of an hour and a half. We retired to a hill nearby, under some piñon trees, till the ceremony was concluded; then began the 70-mile rough trip to Tuba. The bumping was painful, though we did what we could to pad his arm and hand with pillows: he was admitted, and we took off for the 150 miles home. Later we learned that Rex spent two months in the hospital, a thumb and finger were amputated, but he is otherwise well.

Word came in the dead of winter that many people were sick "on top" in the Montezuma Creek area. Helen and I made the trip, with Mr. Sleepy as guide. It was 41 miles, over rough terrain. There were seventeen people in the one hogan, all sick, some probably with pneumonia. The only water was a half-bucketful of melted dirty snow. We mixed some concentrated orange juice we had brought along—using a wash basin! There were only four cups and one spoon in the hogan. Helen used a nail to stir the terramycin into its diluent, on the fender of the jeep, while I gave shots of penicillin where needed. Mrs. Sleepy was the most seriously ill of all, and we brought her back to the Mission; after ten days she was taken home, well, and happy to find her family well too.

The above stories I have given to let you know something of the things we do—things nobody bothers about except ourselves, things we could not do but for your help. These instances are, of course, not routine. Many trips are made to nearby hogans, hardly does a day go by without some call for help. When the children had mumps they were visited daily. A local man, badly injured in a mine, discharged from hospital, had to be visited daily for dressings over a period of weeks. New babies and their mothers deserve, and get, daily visits.

40

To get the Pickett story into a unit I have purposely abandoned the choronological plan, and I must retrace my steps a bit.

On April 18, 1953, I was in the Navajo Mountain area, and that night, in anticipation of Mass at the school the following morning, I crawled into bed in the hogan used for examinations and treatments when the visiting nurse from Shonto made her periodic calls. Before dawn I was awakened by the sound of an automobile pulling up near the teacher's residence. Quickly slipping on my cassock and shoes, I went out to investigate; being the only man on the campus, I felt some responsibility in such a case. The vehicle proved to be our Mission pickup, and in it were Brother Joseph and Jim Floyd, with an emergency message for me. It seems the bishop had sent me a wire, ordering me to be at Parkville, Missouri, by Tuesday morning for a Conference.

I dismissed the message for the moment in my amazement that these two, who had never been in the Navajo Mountain area before, had found their way, and at night. They had left the Mission at nine in the evening, with nothing to guide them but a road map. The road to Navajo Mountain in those days was little more than a wagon trail that had been worn down by a few pickups and trucks, but it had numerous branches off to either side and no markings whatever except a lonely SLOW sign, which presumably some puckish highway worker had put up in one of the seventy-five or a hundred places where slow travel was recommended and where speedy travel would have meant insanity on the part of the driver. We used to use it as a landmark—"He lives about three miles beyond (or on this side of) the SLOW sign." Anyway, by sheer perseverance, good luck and the prayers of St. Christopher they had arrived. There was an old mattress in one corner of the "health hogan," and I invited them to come and rest till time for Mass and to tell me about the telegram. Where is Parkville, what's going on, and what has it to do with me? Well, it appeared that the National Council of the Episcopal Church had decided that all our missionaries to Indians—including many Indian priests—should get together to discuss ways and means and to learn from one another.

I didn't want to go. I had surveyed almost all our missions to Indians years before, and while I admired the fortitude and genuine religion that prevailed, I felt quite certain that their methods were inadequate, if not downright wrong and unfair to the Indians. I told the bishop by letter when I got home that I didn't think I could learn anything from a Conference, nor would they learn anything from me, but I said I would go because he wanted me to. I didn't want to go for another reason: It was Sunday evening when we got home, and air travel was the only possible way of getting to Kansas City in time. I had made up my mind that flying was strictly for the birds. Norman Nevills had taken me on my first flight: he cracked up a few years later. Buchanan had taken me to Durango Hospital, and he is no more. Ben Hershey took me on my third flight and that was the last I saw of this fine adventurer: he cracked up in Mexico. No, for the few years remaining to me on this earth my travels would be on this earth, thank you.

But so much for resolutions. There was a morning flight from Cortez to Albuquerque and a Santa Fe train from Albuquerque to Kansas City that would get me there in time, and I compromised. It was my first commercial flight, and I did feel a bit squeamish as the pilot revved up for the take-off, but the prayers of St. Christopher and the sight of an extraordinarily pulchritudinous stewardess combined to keep me right side up with care.

The courtesy and friendliness with which I was received at the Conference center took any remaining starch out of me. No one could have suspected that the creator of a hotbed of Romanism had appeared in their midst. We were not only comfortably housed and fed, as befits the clergy of an affluent and highly respectable church like ours, but there was a warmth of fellowship and a sense of unity of purpose that foreshadowed good things to come. At the initial meeting each of us was asked to speak for ten minutes, introducing himself by answering a list of questions, such as birthdate and place, schooling, previous work, present assignment, major satisfactions, major difficulties.

It will be recalled that in establishing St. Christopher's Mission, I had had some preconceived ideas that at that time received but little sympathy from official headquarters. These ideas had to do chiefly with a respect for native culture that would indicate a method of presentation of the Gospel, not as a contradiction but as a fulfillment of what the Indians, by their own and their ancestors' meditations and reasoning, had found to be a satisfactory way of life; and furthermore, a presenting of the Catholic religion as being the fullness of the Christian revelation, and as being the true religion of the Episcopal church, even though by the traditions of men much of it has been obscured and "made of none effect." Indians who had been untouched by the man-made traditions would, I thought, have no mental or spiritual block that would require us to "go slow" in our evangelistic work. It was for this reason that I had sought, and been given, a thitherto untouched area in Utah, that I might not be required to undermine another man's work, or even to build upon it. Now, imagine my amazement to find that by far the greater number of those missionaries at this Conference, judging from their self-introductions, were definitely on the St. Christopher road. Where twenty years before I had found Morning or Evening Prayer and sermon, with a monthly communion service, the normal spiritual fare in the Sioux country, now eucharistic worship with emphasis on both sacrifice and popular participation had come into its own. Absolution and other sacraments, long laid aside, were being revived; the clergy were acting and talking and being treated like the priests they really were. Similarly the old idea that Christianity must first make a clean sweep of what had gone before so that it could set itself down, as it were, in a vacuum had given place to the policy on which the English church had been built fourteen centuries before.*

I felt good. I was glad the bishop had told me to come.

---

* The following letter was sent by Pope Gregory to Abbot Mellitus on his departure for Britain (A.D. 601): "To our well loved son Abbot Mellitus: Gregory, servant of the servants of God. Since the departure of yourself

and your companions, we have been somewhat anxious, because we have received no news of the success of your journey. Therefore, when by God's help you reach our most reverend brother, Bishop Augustine, we wish you to inform him that we have been giving careful thought to the affairs of the English, and have come to the conclusion that the temples of the idols in that country should on no account be destroyed. He is to destroy the idols, but the temples themselves are to be aspersed with holy water, altars set up, and relics enclosed in them. For if these temples are well built, they are to be purified from devil-worship, and dedicated to the service of the true God. In this way, we hope that the people, seeing that its temples are not destroyed, may abandon idolatry and resort to these places as before, and may come to know and adore the true God. And since they have a custom of sacrificing many oxen to devils, let some other solemnity be substituted in its place, such as a day of Dedication or the Festivals of the holy martyrs whose relics are enshrined there. On such occasions they might well construct shelters of boughs for themselves around the churches that were once temples, and celebrate the solemnity with devout feasting. They are no longer to sacrifice beasts to the Devil, but they may kill them for food to the praise of God, and give thanks to the Giver of all gifts for His bounty. If the people are allowed some worldly pleasures in this way, they will more readily come to desire the joys of the spirit. For it is certainly impossible to eradicate all errors from obstinate minds at one stroke, and whoever wishes to climb to a mountain top climbs gradually step by step, and not in one leap. It was in this way that God revealed Himself to the Israelite people in Egypt, permitting the sacrifices formerly offered to the Devil to be offered thenceforward to Himself instead. So He bade them sacrifice beasts to Him, so that, once they became enlightened, they might abandon a wrong conception of sacrifice, and adopt the right. For, while they were to continue to offer beasts as before, they were to offer them to God instead of to idols, thus transforming the idea of sacrifice. Of your kindness, you are to inform our brother Augustine of this policy, so that he may consider how he may best implement it on the spot. God keep you safe, my very dear son. Dated the seventeenth of June, in the nineteenth year of the reign of our most devout Lord and Emperor Maurice Tiberius Augustus, and the eighteenth after his Consulship. The fourth indiction."—Bede, *A History of the English Church and People* (Penguin Books, 1955)

41

As the year 1953 rolled along, Brother Juniper reminded me that this was the tenth anniversary of our beginning. It seemed a time to slow down for a few minutes and take stock. With our noses so close to the grindstone, it wasn't easy to see what had been going on around us, to evaluate our own work or to take into consideration the changes in the life and culture of the Navajos. In the newsletter of that summer I summed up our findings, painting in words three pictures—the Navajo Before 1943, the Navajo Now (1953) and the Navajo in the Future.

When we first encountered the Navajo people, they were, to outward appearance at least, a happy, picturesque and contented people, living from day to day by herding their sheep and goats, with ample leisure to gamble, attend native ceremonials or perhaps put in a whole day riding by wagon to a trading post, bargaining and trading, perhaps staying overnight (every trading post had a hogan nearby), with a colorful religion full of charming ceremonies, songs and prayers quite adequate to all their needs. Actually they were deeply suspicious, undernourished, the most illiterate of all racial groups in the continental United States, with a high incidence of tuberculosis and other lethal diseases, as well as of such afflictions at trachoma, pterygium (almost unknown elsewhere on the continent) and with a religion which, for all its beauty, has no place for self-denial or for help to the needy outside of one's own clan.

These sad features were masked under genial smiles derived from a fatalistic outlook on life. One cannot fight "Washeendoan," and one must accept things as they are: be nice to the white man and get out of him what one can before he fleeces you. The stock-reduction program, wisely conceived as the only possible method of preserving the range for future generations of Navajos, had been ruthlessly forced upon the people without adequate explanation, and all they knew about it was that they could be put in jail for owning enough sheep to support their families. John Collier, one of our most enlightened and deeply concerned Commissioners of Indian Affairs, became a symbol of oppression, injustice and poverty. No one could in a few words, or in a few days, convince a Navajo who had for generations counted his wealth in the number of his livestock that he would be richer with fewer sheep. As well tell a housewife that she could run her kitchen better on half her allowance.

I have often wished that I had kept some record of the time when the people stopped asking us what we had come for. At first it was just routine, carrying a step further the introductory questions as to whence we came, whither going, with what purpose. Always there was a perceptible skepticism in their reaction to our statement that we had come to help them, to do them good, to give them something very important that we had to tell them. Both their religion and their experience made it hard for them to believe that anybody would help someone not of his own clan without an ulterior motive. They had in recent years been well enough treated by the whites and in some instances had developed real friendships, but sooner or later it came out that the white man wanted something. And so they tried again and again, hoping perhaps to catch us off our guard, to find out what it was we wanted. In time they gave up, but as I say I kept no record, and I can't even guess when that was. Certainly five years, possibly seven or eight, after our arrival.

However, long before our protestations of altruism were accepted at face value, we were put to the test. "Why you no teck me Blenny (Blanding)? Me go staw, you cah. Ha bout rah now?" In one of our earliest newsletters I wrote of the problem of where to draw the line between being "a good neighbor" and being "a good thing," and the problem is still with us. The idea dies hard, if at all, that the Navajo is doing the government a favor in letting his children go to the government schools; that he is doing the church a favor in allowing his children to attend classes in religion, or services of worship. Randolph vociferously criticized the Shiprock hospital as a place no one ought to be sent to; it was no good. Pressed for details, he submitted that the food was inadequate: "White man get sick, don't eat much; Navajo get sick, eat lots, get strong. Shi'rah hospital don't give nuff eat. No good."

I let my gaze wander along the sides of the canyon wall where small dwellings or perhaps granaries built many centuries ago by the prehistoric peoples nestled in crannies, and as if I were changing the subject, I asked: "Randolph, who made those little houses up there?"

"Ana'sazi, I guess."

"All right; long ago they lived there. You Navajos come along, fight with them and chase them out and take their land and their irrigation ditch. You make hospital for them? Even with just a little bit of food for them to eat, did you make hospital for them?"

Randolph looked rather crushed. To give him time for his rebuttal I admitted that we realized that there had been much injustice in our government's treatment of the Navajo, but the fact remained that *something* was being done—there *were* hospitals and schools, even though too little and too late—while the Navajos had done nothing for the people they drove out of the country.

By this time he had his answer:

"Can't do nossing for dem. Don't even know where dey are!"

42

Helen, driving a jeep in the Montezuma Creek area, picked up two women who were walking. Said one, "We was just a-wishing and a-wishing some missionary would come along!"

"Oh, are you interested in religion? You want a missionary to come see you?"

"No, just to ride. We got tired walking, and we was wishing a missionary would come along and give us a ride." It reminded me of the trader who wanted a mission in his area so that he would not have to close his shop for a hospital trip or perhaps a burial. A missionary outfit in Flagstaff issues phonograph records of handy phrases for missionaries in Navajo land, including the pointed declaration "We are not in the taxi business."

But life is not all like that. I have often told this seemingly insignificant incident to illustrate the undulation of the discouraging and the cheering phases of the life: I was in the Monument Valley area, looking for a family at whose home I had offered Mass some months before. They had moved, but I had a general idea where I might find them. At one point wagon tracks turned off from the trail, and I got out of the jeep to examine them. Children's voices could barely be heard and figures discerned on a ridge, perhaps a quarter mile away to the north. As I waited they ran toward me, shouting joyously. "Aha," the Tempter tempted me to say to myself, "Padre popular with the kiddies! See them come at the double!" Common sense made me answer myself, "You idiot, you know they just come because they want candy." The biggest boy, a lad of maybe twelve, won the 440-yard dash, and stood before me panting. I was waiting for him to hold out his hand and ask for *ak'estese,* but he only said, "When are you (puff, puff) coming to our house to make prayers?"

In those days one would seldom visit a hogan and not be asked to "make prayers." Of course, Mass can be offered only once a day, but we soon perfected a semi-liturgical cottage prayer-meeting procedure, beginning with "Kyrie Eleison" and the Lord's Prayer, a story-sermon, usually embracing virtually the whole Gospel from the fall of man through the incarnation and redemption of mankind, with the thought of justification through faith and incorporation into the mystical body of Christ. Even men who had heard the story from previous visits would listen spellbound to the story that tells itself. There may follow the "Agnus Dei" to the Hopi melody and an extempore prayer for all the family, present or absent, for the livestock and for rain in due season, concluding with an act of thanksgiving for God's bounty in the common things of life. Men are more outspoken in the appreciation of these informal services, as well as of the Mass when offered in their homes, but the women are more ready to offer themselves for the sacraments.

43

In the summer of 1954 the American Church Union—a voluntary group in the Episcopal church whose very existence is an implied indictment of our church, for it is dedicated to uphold her doctrines and practices—planned a Congress in Chicago. Although we could ill afford the time or the money, we agreed that I should go to it and set up a booth with pictures, newsletters, maps and a huge Navajo rug depicting our high altar. I maintained no record, but in all probability I spoke with more than a thousand people a day—bishops, priests, monks and nuns, layfolk of all ages and both sexes and of all degrees of interest in the work of the Mission. I returned home with a vague sense of its having been sort of worth while but quite unable to back this feeling up with any convincing data. One of the worst drunken brawls of the year took place the Sunday I was away; a gun was involved, but injuries were limited to cuts and bruises.

Not long after my return a letter from one Ruth Palmer of Evanston, Illinois, told of her interest in coming to the Mission, and outlined her qualifications (which included considerable hospital experience). Needless to say, she was accepted, and she arrived by bus a week or two later. At that time the northbound bus reached Monticello (fifty miles to the north of us) shortly before five in the morning, so that I could meet her and get back in time for Mass. I recall shooting two rabbits on that occasion, which Brother Juniper stewed for the evening meal. Ruth was pretty much of a wreck when she got here, being the world's worst traveler, but after a day or two of rest she turned out to be a delightful companion, a hard-working missionary and an accomplished singer, with a sweet, flutelike voice usually under perfect control but capable in a crisis of calling hogs from the next county. She had a memory second only to Catherine Pickett's and a knowledge of materia medica beyond any I had before encountered. Like Catherine, however, her weak point was vision, and after nine years she had to give up her work here to get training for what seemed inevitable blindness.

Soon after Ruth's first letter to me came another from a man who mentioned having met me at Chicago and declaring his desire to visit, with his wife, over the coming Thanksgiving holiday, and requesting at least an hour for conference on a subject dear to his heart. They flew to Cortez, rented a car and arrived Wednesday evening. On Thursday afternoon we had our talk, and it came to much more than an hour, for it had to do with his vocation to the priesthood and to the work of St. Christopher's, of which he heartily approved. My advice, of course, was that he persevere, consulting with his own pastor and with the Bishop of Chicago, both of whom knew him far better than I and who had the direct pastoral responsibility.

This visit of Wayne Pontious was only one, but by far the most promising, of many approaches to the Mission's problem of continued leadership. When I founded the mission in 1943, I was fifty-three years old. In fifteen years I would be ready for retirement under the canons and probably would be physically unable to carry on the constantly expanding work; yet those fifteen years had passed, we seemed no nearer to a solution than at the beginning. Not one of our lads had finished high school; in fact, very few had even started, and those few had dropped out. Frank Benally, after a rather sketchy attendance at our school, had taken a year or two at Chemawa Indian School in Oregon, and on the strength of that, plus the kindness of the headmaster of St. Peter's School in Peekskill, we got him out there. It was frightfully hard for him to keep abreast of lads who had been in first-rate preparatory schools, but he did well, considering the handicaps involved. A summer at home weakened his resolution to return to St. Peter's, and he ended up in the Marine Corps. Our hopes were not abandoned, however, and we looked forward to his taking up further studies after his discharge. A few other boys, among them Jimmy Jones and Clyde Sam, seemed to show promise.

The real solution seemed to come in sight with Philip Berton, of Lombard, Illinois, spending a few summer vacations with us. Philip had had all but his final year at Nashotah House when the great depression of the thirties put an end to his studies; he became a construction engineer and settled down to suburban life, but unlike most former seminarians he kept up his theological reading and his New Testament Greek and Old Testament Hebrew, as well as his Patristic Latin. Bishop Watson, after an interview with Philip and his wife, Kathryn, consented to his preparing himself under my "correspondence-school" directions for examination by the chaplains, and all seemed to be going well. The following winter we were all shocked to receive a telegram from the rector of Lombard telling us that Philip had died of a heart attack which struck him while shoveling snow.

There was nothing to do but offer a Requiem Mass and keep on working until God showed us the way.

Katie Berton led us toward a program of Daily Vacation Bible Schools in the summers. She ran two of them here; the following summer, with a few of our regular summer workers, we organized and carried out such projects in seven different parts of our area. The name might seem slightly mendacious, but only to persons who think that a Bible school is to teach the Twenty-third Psalm and the stories of Cain and Abel, of the child Samuel, of Daniel in the lions' den, and a few other select bits of ancient, if sacred, history. We aimed at giving even smallish children a basic idea of what the Old and New Testaments were intended to teach and how they actually worked out in practice—not as inspired books that miraculously appeared and that could be consulted and followed by the respective devotees of each but as books that grew out of actual practice and beliefs. Thus, as Abraham's faith in the one true living God precedes Moses' codification of the Law, so the life, death, resurrection and ascension of the Saviour and the recalling of these in the Eucharistic Sacrifice is actually the New Testament and precedes by many years the books called by that name. We were really amazed ourselves to find how much could be done in five all-too-brief days with a well-balanced program of song, instruction and recreation concluding with a simply sung Mass. Then, the inevitable coffee hour, which was really a quarter hour with Kool-Aid or Fizzies, and cookies.

These Bible schools could be held at Bluff in our school and church, at Oljeto and Montezuma Creek in our churches there or at Mexican Hat in the recreation hall, but in every instance there was a considerable amount of taxi work to get the children together; in the other areas we had to use hogans or shades made available by the residents, and in most cases the taxi work took hours. The programs were carefully planned out, but much ad-libbing needed to be done to adapt them to the different groups, taking into consideration the ages and education levels of the participating folk. At Mexican Hat, for instance, it could all be done in simple English; in other areas there might be few or no English-speaking Navajos, so that all had to be in the native idiom—except the games, which seem to have a sort of Esperanto all their own!

44

In the beginning of St. Christopher's Mission and the policies that governed it I was inspired in no small degree by the things I heard and saw in the Indian work governed by the National Council's Home Department. It was for this reason that I had sought diligently not only for a field that our church had as yet left untouched but for one where no mission of any denomination was to be found. Imagine my feelings when I got a letter from Bishop Watson telling me that on a given date I could look for the arrival of a "team" whose task was a re-evaluation of our church's work in the Indian field, and directing me in no uncertain terms to show them all courtesy and cooperation. The courtesy part hurt a bit, for I could not recall ever having been discourteous to a visitor no matter what his errand. The cooperation part caused me much concern, because I certainly had no intention of changing the methods and aims of the Mission to suit the ideas of some swivel-chair executives, nor of turning over our mailing list of benefactors, many of whom helped us just because our aims differed from those of the National Council. The whole thing put me to bed with a high fever, but in a few days I was again up and around, and when somebody knocked at my study door and said, "They're here!" I stepped out to welcome the Reverend Dr. Joseph Moore of the Research Institute in Evanston, and Dr. Reginald Fisher of the Museum of New Mexico in Santa Fe. They were still dazed at the sheer beauty of the place—"This is wonderful! This is simply, unbelievably exquisite!"

After the grand tour, which of course included some account of our methods and objectives, and some refreshment, they were almost speechless, and one of them, I forget which, admitted that he had hoped, somewhere, to find such aims and principles put into practice among our American Indians.

There were still the standard forms to be filled out, but Father Moore turned them over to me with an almost apologetic air. "Don't let these things worry you. Probably most of them just don't apply. They were prepared by people who had never seen a reservation, much less had any conception of this, the largest of them all. I saw enough on the way here, and you have confirmed my surmisings, to know that these forms are all but completely irrelevant; but, dear Father, just go through them, mark 'd.a.' to what doesn't apply and fill in as best you can, even with approximate figures and other data, what you think does apply. After all, I've got to use them, and I'll appreciate any help you can give."

The whole visit was a delightful surprise; and when their findings were finally issued, we were further surprised to learn that in their opinion St. Christopher's should be a sort of pattern on which Indian work might well be formed. I should have known that such a combination of names—Fisher and Moore (for the sainted martyr Thomas used both spellings, More and Moore)—would be found on the side of the angels! It seemed that we were no longer bucking the tide; the tide was definitely turning in our direction.

45

Among the pleasant surprises, I must mention one that came on a trip to Navajo Mountain. A number of summer workers went along on this trip, and when we heard that there was to be a squaw dance nearby, we stopped over so that they could see it, and perhaps take part in it. It proved to be unusually dull. The singers gathered around the drum, and produced song after song; someone tossed a log or two on the fire to keep it blazing; occasionally a girl would pluck a young man's sleeve and they would walk together around the fire in sun-wise direction, but quite independently of the drum rhythm. Observers, like ourselves, just sat and watched or chatted in subdued tones. Never, I think, were there more than two couples on the floor at one time. An hour of this and I was ready to get moving, but I still hoped, for the sake of the youngsters I had brought, that something a little more picturesque would happen. It did. A little girl, perhaps thirteen years of age, resplendent in velour blouse and satin skirt, necklaces, bracelets and rings, came up to me with little if any of the shyness that characterizes these people.

"Good evening, Father. Are you a priest?"

"Yes," I answered. "Why do you ask?"

"I go to Catholic instruction at school, and the sisters told me that we were now ready to be baptized and we should ask our priest in the place we live to baptize us. Will you baptize me?"

I asked a good many questions. Obviously she had received Roman Catholic instruction, as we had then no sisters at any of the Indian schools in Arizona, and this she unconsciously affirmed when I asked her to say the Creed and she said "Creator" where we usually say "Maker," "died and was buried" where we say "dead and buried." So I asked her how it had come about that her parents designated her religious preference as Catholic when they were not themselves Catholic. She smiled, with more of the native shyness, hesitated, then said: "They know you. They see you sometimes at 'Scription House store. They say they want you to teach their kids. Will you baptize me?"

Assured that I would not be poaching, I made further inquiries and found out that the family lived only a few miles from where we now stood, that she had eleven sisters and a brother (of course, more have come since then) and that, most important of all, she was well grounded in the faith. So we agreed to camp right near the squaw-dance grounds and be guided to her parents' home in the morning. One of the summer workers stood as sponsor, and Priscilla received her First Communion. Furthermore, with a simple booklet of instructions that she could translate into Navajo as she read it, she began teaching her mother the things she should know and believe to her soul's health, so that within a few months nearly the whole family was baptized, and they remain to this day among our most loyal communicants. The father and a daughter who had been kept out of school to herd sheep (most big families have at least one of these) held out, and in later years the father even signed some of his younger girls over to the Mormons, but the majority have remained steadfast in the faith.

46

One of our priests in a nearby diocese wrote to me that he had met a Roman Catholic priest in the course of his hospital visiting, one Father Flaherty (not his real name). Father Flaherty had sustained severe injuries but was making satisfactory recovery as far as the physical features were concerned; however, he chafed under the Hitler-like tyranny of his bishop and asked many questions about the Episcopal church. Would I (our priest wrote) let Father Flaherty come to visit for rest and recuperation? He had led him to understand that our Mission was not exactly a typical Episcopal outfit, nor were we equipped to handle semi-invalids, but he felt sure that Father would be no trouble whatever.

This was long before Pope John threw open that famous window, and the attitude of some Roman Catholics, particularly those of Irish descent, towards ourselves was not always completely friendly. My own experiences had been uniformly happy, however, and I had no fear of any misunderstanding. When Father Flaherty arrived, he made it quite clear that he was accepting us completely at face value—he loved the story about the late Bishop Manning's being introduced at a Knights of Columbus Communion breakfast as belonging "to the Republican branch of the Catholic church." The first few days he attended the community Mass, as well as Vespers; when he felt stronger, he offered his own Mass in the Lady Chapel, and on Corpus Christi Day he acted as master of ceremonies. That was the year Clarence was born in the clinic while the Mass was going on in the church.

Not many of us can boast of having taken part in a Corpus Christi Day procession on the very day of our birth, let alone within the hour! While we were at St. Christopher's arranging the altars, giving-last minute instructions to the flower girls and acolytes, an expectant mother sat anxiously in a pickup that was stuck in the swollen waters of McElmo Creek, thirty miles away. But her staunch escorts, with the skill characteristic of Navajos, shoveled and pushed and maneuvered and finally got under way again, arriving at the clinic as the last bells were ringing in the church belfry. The service was long, with its sublime sequence hymn, a sermon in English and a sermon in Navajo. We had already planned that the procession—an annual affair—would encircle the clinic building, as a sort of symbol of the integration of our spiritual and medical work. By the time the procession reached the clinic, there stood Catherine; in her arms was the baby—born, washed and wrapped since the service had begun. The parents selected the name Clarence. It was not our choice, but we wondered if perhaps the name might be a masculine form of Clara, the saint who is so often depicted bearing monstrance and Host? One can hardly imagine a more blessed way to begin life!

Father Flaherty had come planning to stay two weeks. After six weeks he didn't feel that he could delay surgery any longer, and took off; tears were in his eyes as he bade us good-bye—"the happiest six weeks of my whole life!" He died a few days later on the operating table, and we offered a High Requiem Mass for him the day after we got the news.

47

Because the passage of time dims the memory of even exciting or amusing incidents, I am going to select, almost at random, excerpts of a few of our quarterly newsletters, written when the events were still fresh in my mind. The first is from the first issue of 1956:

> One of the Christmas cards that gave us a good laugh was one done in doggerel verse, and concluding thus: "P.S. After all the riot Don't you love the peace and quiet?" because the riot of Chrristmas had hardly subsided before some real excitement came.
>
> It was a typical St. Christopher's Mission Christmas. We had movies the night before, while Fr. Liebler "sat," as is the duty of priests before the great festivals. In the morning there was an early Mass, well attended, followed later by the High Mass which taxed the capacity of the church—well over 200 by a conservative estimate. Many more would have come in, but also many more were on hand just for the fun and the food and the gifts (let the innocent cast stones if they will). The customary archery contest again showed the younger men as not lacking in skill and courage, although the prize went to a "Hosteen." Meantime Brother Juniper and his helpers were busily putting the final touches on a delicious dinner of elk meat (thanks to the Fish and Game Commission), beans and bread and cake (thanks to Vitakist). Well over 400 people were your guests and our, and at least 30 or 40 who came late were not sent away empty. There was candy for all,

and then gifts for the children—we had to draw the line at 14 years of age. It was a happy occasion, and only a few of the men feld it necessary to imitate their White brothers in celebrating with spirits; even these were less obnoxious than in previous years. All in all, it was a happy Christmas, with the emphasis placed where it should be—a joyous thanksgiving to God for the Gift of His Son. So, weary but glad, we settled down for the "peace and quiet."

Crack of dawn—nay earlier, three of us went to San Juan Bautista at Montezuma Creek, where "on the Feast of Stephen" we sang Mass for an unusually large congregation at about 9:30, baptized seven Navajos, and got back about dark. Early Tuesday morning the excitement began.

A young man who seldom visits the Mission rode in on his horse. In true Navajo style, he stood around; in answer to inquiries he "just happened in," but before long he broke down and said that Mrs. Constable's newborn baby was frightfully sick, and had been for four days; medicine men had sung over her to no effect, and if we would go to the river bank she would bring the baby over on a horse. We lost no time—turned on the red light of our "ambulance" and ignored speed limits. Met Mrs. Constable, riding towards the Mission, baby on cradleboard held before her on the saddle; the horse was quickly turned loose, and the baby was under oxygen in less time than it takes to tell it.

Obviously this was a case beyond our feeble facilities. Fortunately the telephone in Bluff was working: the cooperative sheriff in the County Seat called Fort Defiance, and in a few hours the hum of a plane was heard. Meantime our oxygen had given out, and a fresh tank had been flown in from nearby (75 miles by air) Cortez, Colorado. The Cortez plane landed on the gravel road above Cow Canyon; the Fort Defiance plane landed on the road west of Cottonwood Wash. (We had then no practical landing field at Bluff.) The baby was turned over to the Navajo nurse who came with the plane, and in minutes they were on their way to the Medical Center, 100 air miles to the south.

Next day Carolyn and Catherine took a full load of patients to the hospital at Fort Defiance—not emergency cases for the most part, just broken legs and things like that needing attention—by the old-fashioned, primitive medium of the automobile.

It doesn't seem possible that so many emergencies could be

crammed into a few days, nor can anybody tell how many lives were saved by promptly popping patients into the oxygen tent. Our future hospital, not yet formally opened for use, has actually been utilized more than it should. On New Year's Day two separate trips had to be made to Shiprock, and the following day another: 450 miles in all. We had to call on the local deputy sheriff for help at least once, and *his* car was broken down. Epiphany had come and gone before the pace slowed to normal. It all makes us realize that we are spending a great deal of time and money in travel. When our clinic gets really under way, we hope we can cut down a lot of this.

The great Chief White Horse has gone before us. Readers of our Newsletter back in the mimeograph days may recall how he rode in with twenty or more of his descendants for the marriage of a relative near here. Most of them attended our daily services. White Horse himself came and was deeply impressed. Mary Rose Allen styled him "handsomest man on the Reservation" and she was not far wrong. He asked us to come out to Montezuma Creek and hold services there. At that time we were just getting started here at Bluff, and it was not easy to get away, but before long three of us went, horseback, carrying all our camp equipment; we took two days finding the place from instructions. Had we been willing to let down our standards, we could have baptized fifty or more Navajos at that time—but we had determined to test and try all candidates and see to it that they were adequately instructed. After that, we made several trips, with equal enthusiasm on the part of the People, and when the trader gave us two acres of land we started to build our school and chapel, "San Juan Bautista," at Montezuma Creek, in the heart of the White Horse country. For three years Father Botelho taught school, and conducted services, tirelessly instructing the People in the Faith. Several of White Horse's great-grandchildren, who later came to our school here at St. Christopher's, were baptized, and only last spring and summer some others of his descendants. In October he announced himself ready, and on the 30th he was solemnly baptized, surrounded by numerous progeny.

It was his last visit to the church—he was then barely able to mount a burro, let along walk. A month later, at his home, he received his First Holy Communion; on St. Stephen's Day his Viaticum. His son-in-law brought the news of his imminent death.

"White Horse, he call all his belations and he told them 'I'm gonna die' he said, 'and so somebody go and tell Father come here and help me and put me under the ground, God's way,' he said. So, I'm here and now you come, please, now." Miners' bulldozers have widened and smoothed the old primitive road that used to take hours, and the jeep brought Father Liebler to Montezuma Creek in less than an hour. By sundown all was done as the Chief would have wanted it done. Here was a man of whom we can be certain that baptismal innocence carried him through his Christian life. May he rest in peace, and soon be admitted to the blessed company of those who like himself have washed their robes in the Blood of the Lamb, and at the Throne of Grace pray earnestly for the conversion of his People.

After the burial we gathered in the hogan. There was some talk among the unbaptized which implied the existence of a state of *ch'iindi*—the taboo that surrounds everything connected with a Navajo death. The widow spoke up briskly: "Didn't you hear what Father told us? When one is baptized, and the soul is in grace, there is no *ch'iindi,* There is no need to fear, all is peace." There was no contradiction; tentative assent was indicated by grunts of "aan, aan." Truly, "*perfect* love casteth out fear."

From the Easter, 1957, issue:

"New Year's Day brought us a signal honor. Radio Station KVFC—the only station we can usually hear in the daytime, and over which our weekly program is broadcast—had made announcement of prizes and gifts to be offered to the first baby born in the Monticello or Cortez hospital. Dr. Findley, now in residence at St. Christopher's, dashed to Bluff when he heard this and telephoned to KVFC, shouting, "How about us?"

They said, "Oh, dear, we forgot about your place, but we'll certainly do something about it if you get the first baby, even if we can't change the rules of the game at this late date."

Well, we certainly got the first baby! Lena Lansing had come in from the Montezuma Creek area, and by 8:05 A.M. she and her husband Tom were the proud parents of a fine baby girl, Grace. We were very happy to turn over to Lena gifts from KVFC—$10 in cash and a fine blanket and pillow; also a case of milk from Cow Canyon Trading Post in Bluff.

Dr. Findley's six months came to an end and we were all

desolated to bid him goodbye. Who is to take his place? We have a number of medical students who look forward to the joy of serving—in the years to come—but that doesn't help the Navajos right now. Our good friend Dr. Burnham has written to a prominent medical journal, appealing for some doctor who wants even a short taste of the joys of sacrificial life. Perhaps these lines will come to such a person. The need can hardly be overestimated. Our clinic, as you know, was planned for four adult and eight children's beds, yet we have had more than once a total of sixteen patients at a time. Catherine, with help from the rest of us, struggles manfully, but we do need a doctor, and soon!

By the time you read this, it will probably be a year after the formal dedication of our clinic by Bishop Watson—April 24, 1956. You'll be interested to know that we have had 54 deliveries in that time, and also have treated hundreds of patients. This does not include ministrations in hogan visits or roadside encounters—a not inconsiderable phase of our work.

On March 18 we had the unusual occurrence of two deliveries within five minutes of each other. One mamma came in about sundown on Sunday, and had her baby shortly after midnight; there wasn't time for Catherine to tie up and cut the cord before a pickup drew in at the clinic, and a frantic expectant father who had been violating all speed laws from Mexican Hat brought in his wife, set her on the examination table, and lo! a boy it was!

This story would be incomplete without a tribute to Alice June Clifton who, during her all-too-brief stay, put in heroic hours at the clinic under a maximum patient load while Catherine had to be away. We wish she would come back, but probably we scared her off!

Helen contributed this item for the pre-Christmas, 1957, issue:

One time when McElmo Creek was really rampant, the missionaries, after slithering over 50 miles of mud and clay, left the jeep and prepared to wade the icy stream, bucking the ice floes. The most essential medical supplies they had stuffed into inadequate pockets. Just then a little Navajo girl came on her horse, and signalled that she would take them over. Sister tried to mount behind the girl but in the middle of the attempt discovered that her habit skirt was less than adequately ample. 'Mid gales of laughter she admitted that she never had been so near to a horse before! The ferry functioned nevertheless. On the far bank sat a pretty Navajo woman in her full purple velvet skirt and scarlet blouse trimmed with fine silver buttons, obviously dressed for a holiday or a journey. Beaming, she said, "You take me back. I want to go to Mission hospital at Bluff. I will have baby today. People said to me, go to other hospital, but I say to them, no, only to Mission." We urged a safer road, but she sat. Two hours later, after our class and hasty ministrations to the sick of the neighborhood, she was still sitting, and no amount of persuasion could change her mind.

"We have no doctor now."

"I want Catherine; she knows."

"You cannot wade the wash—the horse is gone now."

"I can wade it."

"Maybe we will get stuck in the muddy trails; your baby might come before we can get to the Mission."

"I go with you. I had just a few pains, not very bad yet."

Who can stand out against such resolution? We had to carry spare gas as well as our medical kit, but together the three of us waded across to the jeep; over 60 miles we splashed and slid, racing against time but trying not to bump unnecessarily. Time and time again the mud made the headlight lenses opaque and we had to wipe them off and proceed. The moon was up when we got to the clinic, put the woman to bed just to get her up again to deliver a beautiful baby girl.

And the Easter issue of 1958 has these:

Routine evangelistic work goes on. But how can a beautiful experience be called "routine"? Only because it has to be done week after week on the same day—but it is never twice the same. Sunday means High Mass here at St. Christopher's, followed by Sunday School and Coffee Hour, but on the first and third Sunday of each month there is another Mass, in the afternoon, at Mexican Hat, where a number of Navajos are employed in the Uranium Mill. These are mostly schooled Navajos with an understanding of English, so that a priest with very little knowledge of the idiom of the country could still do much good work, although the families of some of the workers, in a few instances, know only Navajo. Comes Monday, and that means taking the whole day to go to Aneth, where one hour of school—3 to 4—is used to prepare these young ones for Baptism and the rest of the day is taken up in visiting the eastern part of our area. Comes Tuesday, and we are off to Kayenta where the children signed for us—mostly from Navajo Mountain region—are dealt with in the evening, after supper, as for technical reasons there can be no school time devoted to the things of God. These children are all communicants, and are being well grounded in the Faith. Comes Wednesday, and the Hatch Trailer School and area calls for an hour of instruction—again, 3 to 4, and the rest of the day in hogan visits. This all sounds very routine, but if so the picture is not truly painted. Who can describe the beauty of the landscape, the desert colors at sunset? Who can evaluate just stopping the jeep to talk to an old man or woman who in their mule-drawn wagon are taking a barrel of water or a load of fire-wood to their hogan. Who can tell what it means to pick up a hiking Navajo boy who has had a little schooling and is utterly muddled and confused to go back to the people he loves and who love him but who still live a life that his elegant school training has taught him to look down upon as ignorant and unsanitary and pagan!

One such boy said, "What that mean, 'Jesus loves me this I know'? We sing that in school but I don't understand it." There is no limit to what a Mission can do for these people—if we only had more workers and did not have to spread ourselves so thinly over the area!

Did we say something above about routine? In spite of jeeps and paved roads, electric light and radio, the pioneer life is not yet a thing of the past only. A few weeks ago Brother Juniper and Sister Mary Faith had to take an emergency patient to Shiprock Hospital, some 150 miles away by highway—and no highway! But let Brother tell it:

"It was mid-January, and close to midnight as well. A patient in our clinic had to have emergency hospital care far beyond what we could give him—severe cerebral injuries resulting from violent blows. Shiprock is only 60 miles as the crow flies, but the crow doesn't carry passengers, and experience has shown that the highway route, a little over 150 miles, is better. Thirty miles from home Sister and I ran into slick roads and heavy snowfall. Inquiring of a passing traveller we learned that the roads beyond were impassable; vehicles that were not stuck were turned back. So we did, too, but we knew of new access roads in the lower elevation that had been dozed by the oil and uranium workers. The new road was rough, but at first dry. Soon it began to snow and the temperature dropped sharply, and we were in slush and ice. A steep hill was too much for the ambulance, which started to slide into the ditch at the side of the road. We could go neither up nor down. Our patient was tossing wildly, groaning, ready to fight his assailant all over again—though he was as yet speechless and seemingly unconscious. Sister tried to quiet him, while I set out for help—a pretty hopeless gesture in that deserted area, but as luck or Providence would have it, a car came along, belonging to the Halliburton Oil Company, equipped with a telephone. The driver got in touch with one of the company's trucks and told the driver of that to come and pull out our ambulance. We kept our engine running for the sake of the heat, as the cold outside was intense; fortunately we had started with a full gas tank. Hardly was the telephone receiver hung up when along came a drilling rig truck. It was a matter of moments to hook on a tow-chain, pull the ambulance out of its ditch and for safety's sake up two more bad hills. Just as we thought all was well a rhythmical thump-thump told us of a flat tire. With all the help at hand it didn't take long to put on the spare. The only village, by this cross-country route, between us and Cortez was Towaoc, a Ute town and headquaters of the Southern Ute Agency in Colorado. Here the Ute police had been alerted, and were ready to give us escort, with sirens and red lights, all the way to the hospital at Shiprock. It was now daylight and the trip had taken eight hours—a little more than twice the usual time. The doctors examined our patient at once, but could give no prognosis. For days we telephoned them for news but could tell the anxious parents only that it was nip and tuck. Then we were able to tell them that if he pulled through another twenty-four hours, he would be out of danger. He did. And he was."

A cultural note from the Spring, 1962, issue:

The archery contest was again won by a young man, as in the last few years. This has sociological significance. Nineteen years ago, at our first Christmas, only old or elderly men participated; some brought their own home-made bows and arrows. No youth would touch a bow. Perhaps it was the fear of being laughed at; perhaps a sense that this was "oldtimers' stuff." Then archery had a renascence among Whites. There was even an archery club organized in the County. It became a symbol of advance in civilization. The full circle—and the young men not only participated but out-did their elders!

Dinner was served as usual—through a kitchen window as the line passed by. There was no warm place to sit, but some spread blankets on the snow and laughed joyously as they ate; others stood, but nobody complained. And, perhaps most remarkable of all, there was not a drunk in the crowd! In past years we have often had disturbances and sometimes violence, as the Navajos try to follow the example of the "superior" white race, but this year has broken that tradition and we devoutly hope that that time is done with forever. Certainly everybody had a good time. In future let us dream of a dry—and we mean *dry* Christmas!

48

With Wayne Pontious in seminary, pulling good grades and filled with enthusiasm for the work that lay ahead of him, we still had not given up the hope of native leadership, whether in priesthood or some other capacity. Frank Benally seemed the logical man, if ever he would get finished with the Marine Corps! He needed more schooling, of course, but he had a good head on his shoulders, and we felt sure we could get him into college, and later into seminary. In June of 1962, soon after Father Wayne had been ordained deacon, came a telegram: Frank had been killed by the explosion, virtually in his arms, of an aircraft tire.

At his mother's request interment was to be in Blanding Cemetery, and a group of our older staff members, who had known him from his early childhood, were on hand to greet the body and the escort squad of his peers and a commissioned officer. The grave was blessed, the committal and other prayers followed. A mournful staff drove back to the Mission.

In the twilight of that evening Father Wayne Pontious, the new vicar, arrived and took command.

Afterword

Joan Liebler

Presumably, readers will want to know what happened next. In what now seems a moment of mental abstraction, I agreed happily to write a postscript to the reissue of Boil My Heart for Me. What I didn't realize at the time was that while Father Liebler took almost two hundred pages to cover nineteen years of mission history, I am confined to a fraction of that to cover the thirty years that followed. A formidable task, but I shall do my best, and, as Father Liebler frequently said by way of encouragement, "Angels can do no more!"

Although Father Liebler finished writing the book in 1965, he felt that the appropriate cutoff time would be 1962, the end of his nineteen years as vicar at St. Christopher's Mission and the beginning of Father Wayne Pontious's vicariate. A New York agent sent the manuscript to a prestigious publishing house, where it remained for almost a year until it was returned with regrets. All who read it, in part or in whole, felt it was too good a story to remain unpublished, and Father spent several months working it over. In 1968, he sent it to Exposition Press, and it finally came out in 1969.

The book ends prophetically on both a sad note and a cheerful note: the death and interment of Franklin Benally occurred close to the arrival of the new vicar of St. Christopher's Mission, Deacon Wayne Pontious, along with his wife and their three charming little daughters. They were greeted with much joy and a sense of great relief that at last a younger man had arrived to relieve Father Liebler of the burden of responsibility and activity that had lasted several years beyond his age of retirement. Next to Father Liebler himself, Wayne Pontious was the most dedicated missionary priest St. Christopher's ever had. Early on he declared his intention to devote the rest of his life to the service of God and the Navajo people.

At the start, his principal objective was to build up the mission plant, which had deteriorated to some extent because of the increasing ages of Father Liebler, Helen Sturges, and Brother Juniper. Volunteer work groups from parishes all over the country had contributed much by way of extra buildings and had also been responsible for a great deal of the visiting to Navajo families living many miles from the mission. A number of volunteers had stayed for varying periods of time over the years. But the number of resident staff was variable, which meant that in order to sustain our connection with outlying areas, mission maintenance was not a high priority.

After newsletters announcing Father Wayne's arrival had gone out, it was not long before a group of young people arrived to form the volunteer mission staff, and in due course the buildings took on a brighter look. The all-important ministry in the outstations went on successfully. Mass was celebrated in the little chapel at Montezuma Creek, in Navajo houses and hogans in areas north of the mission, and as far away as Navajo Mountain and Oljeto. Thanks to the years of work Helen Sturges and other workers had put in, the new Indian boarding school at Aneth had around two hundred children registered "Episcopal," but it needed eight of the staff to go there every week to conduct religious education. The mission school and the clinic flourished, and church services were well attended. The People were in and out constantly, some with needs to be met, some just to visit, and kept the kitchen staff busy preparing and serving communal meals. In addition, the new vicar devoted much time and effort to studying the very difficult Navajo language.

But trouble was brewing in the form of growing hostility by the new staff members toward Father Liebler and his conduct of the church services, principally the Mass. Ultimately, the beautiful little log church was burned to the ground.

In writing this, I debated for some time whether to dismiss the whole tragic episode with one sentence: A mentally disturbed staff member burned the church down. But when I considered that the causes lay far back in the very purpose of the mission, and that the hearts and minds and loyalties of everyone ever connected with the mission are involved, I felt that both historical truth and responsibility to readers must be respected.

Harold Baxter Liebler was indeed a priest with a vision, but to clarify the mind-set of the newcomers, as well as Father Liebler's, a few details are in order. In many conversations with Episcopalians, I have found an almost total lack of knowledge regarding the origin of their church and their Book of Common Prayer—a book that defines the theology of the church. There seems to be a somewhat vague notion that church and prayerbook "jest growed" like Topsy on American soil, whereas it derives from the English Book of Common Prayer, which in turn derives from the church of Rome. Few Episcopalians have ever really studied their Book of Common Prayer. But Father Liebler, as a liturgical scholar, had studied it from cover to cover.

Nothing if not logical, Father Liebler did just what he promised at his ordination: to "give (his) faithful diligence always so to minister the Doctrine and Sacraments, and the Discipline of Christ, as the Lord hath commanded, and as this Church hath received the same. . . ." To fulfil this promise throughout his ministry he not only taught his people the Catholic faith but exposed them to the beauty of Catholic ceremonies.

Navajos are very appreciative of ritual, but, once started it must be maintained with precision. It is so important to them that, for example, should a medicine man make a mistake in even a nine-day sing he must start all over again. The objective in Navajo ritual is to create or restore harmony between the person for whom a chant or ceremony is performed and all the forces and objects of nature. (Anyone interested in this subject would be rewarded by reading *Navaho Religion* by the late Gladys Reichard.) Father Liebler was also careful at all times to observe taboos. For example, he never touched both sides of a house or hogan door simultaneously, as by so doing any evil spirits in the place would be trapped, a contingency that would in no way contribute to the popularity of the visitor! On one occasion a woman came to Father in great distress because a "skinwalker" had been peering down the smokehole of her hogan. Father gave her a small jar of holy water and told her to throw the water in the skinwalker's face saying, "Go away in the Name of Jesus Christ." Which she did, and later reported that she had had no further trouble. At any rate, given the great care and precision in Navajo ritual, Father Liebler was determined to do no less in exhibiting the beauty of the Christian Mass.

Since the separation of the Anglican and Roman churches, there has been "warfare" between the Catholic and Protestant factions in the Anglican church. The situation at St. Christopher's Mission demonstrated in microcosm just how drastic this warfare can be. The group of young staff members who came as volunteers after Father Wayne arrived at the mission were mainly Episcopalians. However, their church backgrounds had been mostly in what would be called "low-church" parishes, and they could neither understand nor accept the Catholic rituals and ceremonies used by Father Liebler. Any attempt at explanation proved futile.

The fact that he was still a deacon when he arrived at St. Christopher's put Father Wayne in a difficult position, since Father Liebler still performed all the priestly functions. Father Wayne's ordination six months later did not make it any easier. The staff members continually bombarded him with requests to be more assertive. Father Wayne, whose love and admiration for Father Liebler was unbounded, adopted a wait-and-see attitude, intending that if changes were made they should come over a period of several years.

Space does not permit a detailed discussion of the nature and reasons for all the desired changes, except to note that two major causes of hostility were, first, Father Liebler's use of the American Missal when celebrating the Holy Eucharist. This was an English translation of most of the Roman Missal, used in a number of "high-church" parishes. Second, he insisted on giving communion in one kind, the consecrated wafer. The newcomers were particularly incensed at not being permitted to receive consecrated wine from the chalice, but as Father Liebler pointed out, he had spent nearly twenty years trying to explain to the Navajo that they were endangering their health by using a common cup in their homes.

Father Wayne himself made it clear that he was in favor of a return to the more simplified services of the standard Book of Common Prayer but refrained from exercising his authority in the hope that compromises could ultimately be made on both sides. Yet the anger and hostility toward Father Liebler reached a point where he himself became deeply hurt and even angry. It seemed that none of his explanations was ever heard with any degree of sympathy or understanding, only an increase of hostility. Being only human, he reacted by a complete refusal to compromise in any particular.

The climax came in 1964, a few months after a new staff member arrived on the scene. Let us call him Harold. He was in sympathy with Father Liebler's churchmanship but was quickly told that if he was "for" Father Liebler, he was "against" Father Wayne. He was a mentally disturbed young man in that he was, as we later found out to our cost, an arsonist. The truly ungodly atmosphere of anger and hostility working on his own mental problems finally resulted in his setting fire to the church and an attempt to burn several other buildings. This occurred on a day when both Father Wayne and Father Liebler, along with several other members of the staff, were away celebrating Mass at two different outstations. Only two or three people remained at the mission. The best efforts of the Bluff fire department could not prevent the church from being reduced to ashes. It was some comfort that even those most hostile to Father Liebler were warm in their expressions of sympathy to him. And Harold, after he had been arrested and was in the Monticello jail awaiting trial, wrote a letter to Father expressing his sorrow and contrition.

This has been mentioned in the book, but it will bear repetition: A day or two after the insurance investigators had left, Brother Juniper was sifting through some ashes in the former sacristy when his eye was caught by a gleam of silver. He pulled out two fire-blackened but intact objects: the little silver chalice and paten given Father at his ordination. They were sent to an authorized jeweller in Phoenix and in due course returned in perfect shape, shining brightly. Those precious objects are now in the possession of Father's grandson, the Reverend John Liebler, pastor of the Church of St. Peter the Fisherman in New Smyrna Beach, Florida.

The saddest part of the whole matter was that with a little more love, a little more compassion, a little more understanding on all sides, and a little more patience for a year or two, the tragedy might well have been averted.

While it would not be quite true to say that all hostility toward Father Liebler and the "old-timers" ceased, attention was diverted to the building of a new church. Eventually an architect came on the scene and produced a sketch and ground plan of a church, which sent the newer staff happily into orbit and the oldsters into near cardiac arrest! A huge building with three triangular-shaped sides, it was thoroughly impractical for the area—as time has proven. It has now deteriorated badly and is no longer used as a church. "Looked like an Inca temple," one Navajo youth observed.

Nevertheless, the mission work progressed well and the Navajo people came to like and respect Father Wayne. By 1966 he had acquired sufficient knowledge of the language to preach his sermons in Navajo. Father Liebler kept his resolution that when that happened he would retire to Oljeto, in the Monument Valley area of the reservation. Many years before, he had bought from the state of Utah a quarter of a quarter of a "school section" on which there was a hogan church that had not been turned over to the Diocese of Utah.

When Father announced his intention of retiring to Oljeto and "building myself a little shack," Helen, Brother Juniper, and I were struck with the same thought: "At seventy-seven he's going to build himself a shack in the middle of the desert? Who's going to bring him water, firewood, and all the other necessities of life?" So in 1966 we all went along to help Father "retire." One tent, one small shack, one trailer, and a camper were our luxurious accommodations. In addition, no running water, no indoor plumbing, and no electricity made us feel we were right back on square one, starting a new mission. We weren't far wrong. But, as was frequently the case with any of Father Liebler's enterprises, our situation soon improved. Well driller George Petty of Blanding, who felt he owed Father for a past kindness, brought his rig to our camp. After some mysterious calculations known only to experienced well drillers, he decided that a spot marked "X" in the desert sand was the exact place in which to drill for water. So he drilled. And he found water at 80 feet, but he drilled deeper, to 120 feet. "An underground river, I think," he told us. Thereafter a pump and a generator to run it were installed, and we were spared the task of hauling water from the trading post or the Seventh-Day Adventist hospital, both several miles away. A few years later electrical and telephone lines were brought in and everything was up to date in Hat Rock Valley.

We had a house built, or rather, two houses connected by a passageway, so our more primitive life-style was somewhat alleviated. Once the local People realized that we were there to stay, we found an increasing number attending the hogan church on Sundays. Then the great project was begun: we planned to build a real church. We drew up a floor plan, and I wrote to an old friend back east, a draftsman, who sent us a splendid set of architectural plans. He later came himself to see how everything was getting on. We decided that listening to him and Brother Juniper arguing over some building technicality was as entertaining as a Three Stooges movie! We were fortunate in finding Henry Phillips, a Navajo stonemason, to do the actual building, and in 1971 the church of St. Mary of the Moonlight was completed. We thought it was the most beautiful church in the Diocese of Utah. Henry and his men had laid up a double wall of flat rocks in the style of flagstones, with stunning effect.

In order to pay for the church, and in view of the fact that we were once again operating as a mission, we incorporated as Hat Rock Valley Retreat Center, a nonprofit organization, and appealed to all our old friends to help us with mission expenses. They responded generously. All of this involved maintaining a mailing list, sending out newsletters, and keeping financial records. I told Father I would be obliged if he would refrain from retiring again.

It is good to be able to relate that in the intervening years much of the hurt and bitterness caused by the events at St. Christopher's had been healed. Father Wayne and Father Liebler found time to go off together to a retreat at the beautiful Catholic Charismatic monastery in Pecos, New Mexico, and several of the mission staff expressed their regrets for their earlier attitude. Technically Father Wayne was vicar in charge of all ministry to the Navajo members of the church in the Utah strip of the reservation, but he asked Father Liebler to be the official priest-in-charge and administer St. Mary of the Moonlight as an outstation of St. Christopher's. Which Father Liebler was only too happy to do.

Since their arrival Father Wayne and his wife had been blessed with the birth of two sons, but they had to cope with the tragic illness of one of their daughters, Mary Jane. Around 1969 she started suffering from tumors in various parts of her body. They were found to be benign, but the effect was as devastating as if they were cancerous growths. This necessitated many periods of hospitalization in Salt Lake City and, though her mother was with her, Mary Jane frequently asked for her daddy. This meant many trips in great anguish of mind for Father Wayne as well as the curtailment of his ability to function effectively at St. Christopher's. Mary Jane died in 1971 and was buried in the cemetery at St. Christopher's.

In that same year the Reverend Otis Charles was elected and then consecrated bishop of the Missionary Diocese of Utah following the resignation of Bishop Watson. He came to St. Christopher's on an official visit and showed great interest in the welfare of the Navajo people in his jurisdiction. But it was not until 1973 that he made certain demands concerning the organization, which changed its policy and direction forever.

Bishop Charles believed strongly in self-determination for minority groups, a laudable ideal but one that in this case failed to consider the reality of the situation. He informed Father Wayne that from then on the mission work must be conducted exclusively by Navajos. All Anglo staff were to be dismissed; Navajos were to take their place and were to run the mission themselves. Father Wayne did his best to explain conditions on the Utah strip to the bishop. Father Liebler's arrival almost thirty years before had helped to improve the educational and medical standards of the local Navajos, but they were still far behind the Navajos of Arizona and New Mexico. Father Wayne told the bishop that while he was all in favor of training Navajos to take more responsibility for the operation of the mission he could only do it by gradually phasing out the Anglo workers and substituting Navajos whenever appropriate. This Bishop Charles refused to accept, and Father Wayne subsequently resigned to return to his hometown in Kansas. The volunteer Anglo workers also left. Which meant that there was no one to visit the People, to help them when they needed help, or to visit and instruct the two hundred children registered as Episcopalians at the Aneth boarding school. Inevitably, many of the adults and children eventually joined other denominations.

Until a priest could be found for St. Christopher's, the bishop requested Father Liebler to say Mass on Sunday afternoons at the Bluff mission, fifty miles north of St. Mary of the Moonlight. Seven months later, the Reverend W. Herbert Scott arrived to take charge of the mission, then with a considerably reduced staff of only three or four people. As a result, his initial activities were circumscribed by the amount of time required to train and oversee his staff.

Before Father Wayne left he had enclosed the area of the old cruciform-shaped log church with fencing, seeded it with grass, and planted a few trees. The altar, which Father Liebler built with his own hands, was stabilized and still stands. The Navajo madonna and child, made many years before, was restored with a glass dome placed over it for protection against the weather.

Regular Sunday and Holy Day services were conducted in our mission at Hat Rock, as well as the beautiful but somewhat complicated services of the last three days of Holy Week (the Triduum). Our little group was also fortunate in having the privilege of daily services in the chapel in our doublewide mobile home, as Father had been given a faculty to have what is called an oratory (private) chapel.

In 1974 Father was honored by the state of Utah with its Award of Merit "for long, dedicated service devoted to providing health services to the Navajo Indian community of Utah." A great day for us in Salt Lake City. In that same year, at eighty-nine years of age, he celebrated the sixtieth anniversary of his ordination to the priesthood. Bishop Charles and six other priests of the diocese concelebrated the Mass, and Navajo and Anglo friends provided us with a splendid feast afterwards.

In the following year St. Mary of the Moonlight became an independent mission of the Diocese of Utah. Father, feeling his years, asked the bishop if he could provide a younger man as vicar of St. Mary's. In October the Reverend Roland Kawano, a Japanese from Hawaii, was installed as vicar but left the following year to accept a call to a parish in Los Angeles.

Due principally to the efforts of Bishop Charles and the Good Shepherd mission in Fort Defiance, Arizona, members of the Episcopal missions in Utah, Arizona, and Rio Grande (a portion of New Mexico), had been meeting frequently with a view to uniting all three mission areas under one bishop. In 1977 the merger was approved by the House of Bishops. The new entity was known as the Navajo Area Mission, or the Episcopal Church in Navajoland.

In the same year Father Liebler received an honorary doctorate from the seminary where he had received his priestly training, Nashotah House in Nashotah, Wisconsin. From there two of his sons, Dr. John Liebler (M.D.) and Dr. Robert Liebler (D.D.S.) escorted him to Miami for a visit with all the members of his family, including his wife, Frances, who had been in very poor health for some years and was then living with their oldest son, George. While there, John gave his father a thorough medical checkup and found that Father Liebler had an enlarged prostate. It was benign, but after its removal the urologist required Father to remain in his care for several months. He was removed to the house of his youngest son, Bob, and it was arrranged that I should go to Miami to keep house for both of them and chauffeur Father. In three months Father was declared fit to return home. His family had long urged him to retire in Florida, but Father insisted that he would live and die among his beloved Navajo people. Which indeed he did.

His wife, Frances, died at the end of the year. A few months later a telephone call from Bob Liebler revealed the fact that Father's family, anxious to ensure that someone would care for him in his declining years, urged him to ask me to marry him. We were both happy to oblige and were married in October 1978.

At St. Christopher's, priests came and went. (One of them, learning of the unhappy events of the past few years, took it upon himself to conduct an exorcism of the entire plant—a procedure we all approved.) They had various reasons for leaving, but all suffered from a lack of adequate staff to serve the mission and its outstations. At St. Mary of the Moonlight, Father's health began to fail noticeably. He was also heartsick over what seemed to be the collapse of his dearest dream: to see the Episcopal church come closer to reunion with the church of Rome. In November of 1982 Father entered the hospital in Cortez for tests. Since none produced sufficient evidence for a definitive diagnosis, I was able to bring him home to Hat Rock. But, much to my distress, I found that none of us could take care of him adequately, as he had become completely bedridden. We had no choice but to move him to the Seventh-Day Adventist hospital where doctors, nurses, and aides gave him what was truly tender, loving care. I was able to be with him the greater part of every day and sometimes well into the night. For many years there had been friendship and esteem between Father Liebler and the Franciscan Fathers headquartered at St. Michael, Arizona. It was a great blessing to Father Liebler that Father Valentine Young, pastor of the Catholic mission in Kayenta, came to give Father the Sacrament of Anointing of the Sick and visited him several times to bring him the Holy Communion.

By what seemed to us God's loving providence, George and his wife had visited us only two months previously, and John and Bob arrived while Father was in the hospital. So he had the happiness, while nearing his end, of seeing his three much-loved sons. Two days after John and Bob came to see Father Liebler, Father Valentine brought him what proved to be his last Holy Communion. Half an hour later, having fought the good fight and kept the faith, Father Liebler entered into the joy of his Lord.

The funeral service was conducted by the first bishop of the Episcopal Church in Navajoland, the Right Reverend Frederick Putnam. The church was crowded, and some thirty cars followed the hearse on the fifty-mile journey to Father's final resting place at St. Christopher's Mission. His mortal remains, clad in the alb his mother made for him when he was a young priest and a blue-and-white chasuble, with a rosary and the Bible given him by his ordaining bishop in his hands, lie in the north arm of the fenced area of the old log church. When I asked one of the Franciscan priests present to pray for the repose of Father's soul, he responded, "I'll not only pray *for* him, I'll pray *to* him!"

You may want to know what happened to those of us who followed Father to the Hat Rock mission. Helen Sturges had bought a house in Sun City, Arizona, where she retired after Father's death and where she died in 1985. Brother Juniper, on a visit to his home in Wisconsin, renewed acquaintance with an old sweetheart, a lady who had been widowed twice. They decided to make up for the lost years by getting married and lived happily until his death in 1990. Me? In March of 1983, I was received by Father Valentine into the Roman Catholic church, and in November of that year I came to live in Moab, a lovely, friendly little town bounded by mesas, mountains, and the Colorado River, some ninety-five miles north of the mission in Bluff. It is still possible for me to visit the places and people I love, if only once a year. And some of the People visit and occasionally stay.

In 1983 Father Steven Plummer became vicar of St. Christopher's Mission and is there still. He is now the first Navajo bishop of the Episcopal Church in Navajoland. He is a dedicated man, and is doing his best with the help of his wife and a very limited staff, to continue the work begun many years ago by the priest-with-the-long-hair. Angels can do no more!

At this writing, the mission of St. Mary of the Moonlight has been closed for lack of staff. Its future disposition is not yet known.